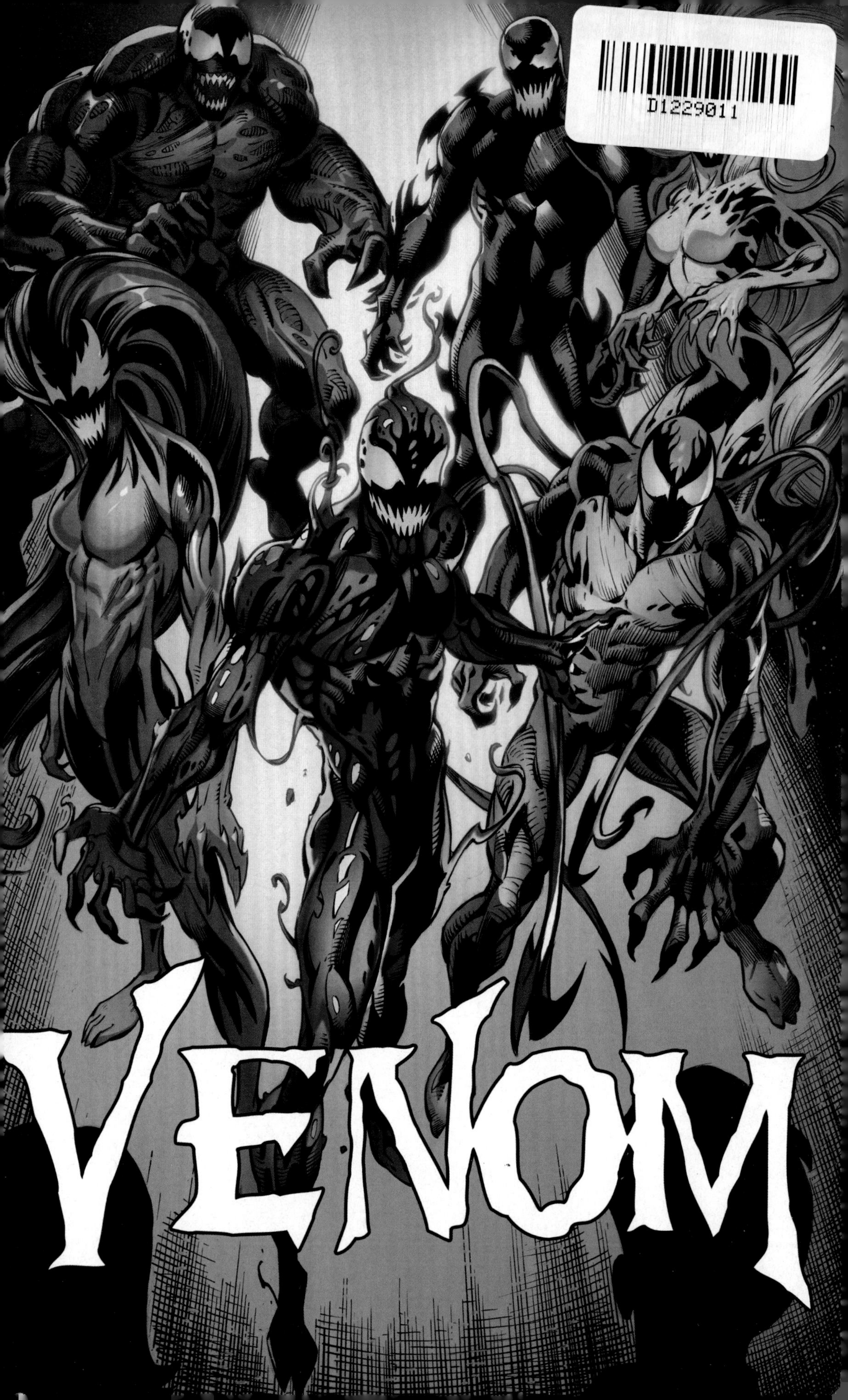
VENOM

YEARS AGO, PETER PARKER (A.K.A. THE AMAZING SPIDER-MAN) ACCIDENTALLY BONDED WITH AN ALIEN BEING CALLED A SYMBIOTE. WHEN PETER REALIZED THE COSTUME WAS ACTUALLY AN AGGRESSIVE LIVING ORGANISM, HE REJECTED IT. BUT DURING THEIR TIME TOGETHER, THE SYMBIOTE HAD ACCESS TO SPIDER-MAN'S GENETIC CODE AND NOW GRANTS WHOMEVER IT BONDS WITH SKILLS SIMILAR TO HIS: WALL-CRAWLING, THE POWER TO GENERATE BIO-ORGANIC WEBBING AND UNIQUE ABILITIES TO SHAPE SHIFT AND BECOME INVISIBLE, TURNING THEM INTO...VENOM.

ALTHOUGH EDDIE BROCK AND THE VENOM SYMBIOTE HAVE BEEN REUNITED, THE SYMBIOTE'S PREVIOUS BOND WITH A DANGEROUS CRIMINAL NAMED LEE PRICE HAS LEFT IT EMOTIONALLY UNSTABLE. WHILE THE SYMBIOTE STILL DESIRES TO BE A HERO, ITS UNPREDICTABILITY HAS MADE LIFE VERY DIFFICULT FOR EDDIE, WHO HAS STRUGGLED TO FIND WORK AS A REPORTER FOR THE *FACT SHEET* AND FOR THE OPPORTUNITY TO PROVE VENOM'S RENEWED HEROISM TO THE PUBLIC.

WITH NOWHERE ELSE TO GO, EDDIE'S BEEN FORCED TO TURN TO LIZ ALLAN AND ALCHEMAX FOR A SPECIAL SERUM TO KEEP THE SYMBIOTE'S MORE VIOLENT TENDENCIES AT BAY....

COLLECTION EDITOR **MARK D. BEAZLEY** :: ASSISTANT EDITOR **CAITLIN O'CONNELL**
ASSOCIATE MANAGING EDITOR **KATERI WOODY** :: SENIOR EDITOR, SPECIAL PROJECTS **JENNIFER GRÜNWALD**
VP PRODUCTION & SPECIAL PROJECTS **JEFF YOUNGQUIST** :: SVP PRINT, SALES & MARKETING **DAVID GABRIEL**
BOOK DESIGNER **JAY BOWEN**

EDITOR IN CHIEF **C.B. CEBULSKI** :: CHIEF CREATIVE OFFICER **JOE QUESADA**
PRESIDENT **DAN BUCKLEY** :: EXECUTIVE PRODUCER **ALAN FINE**

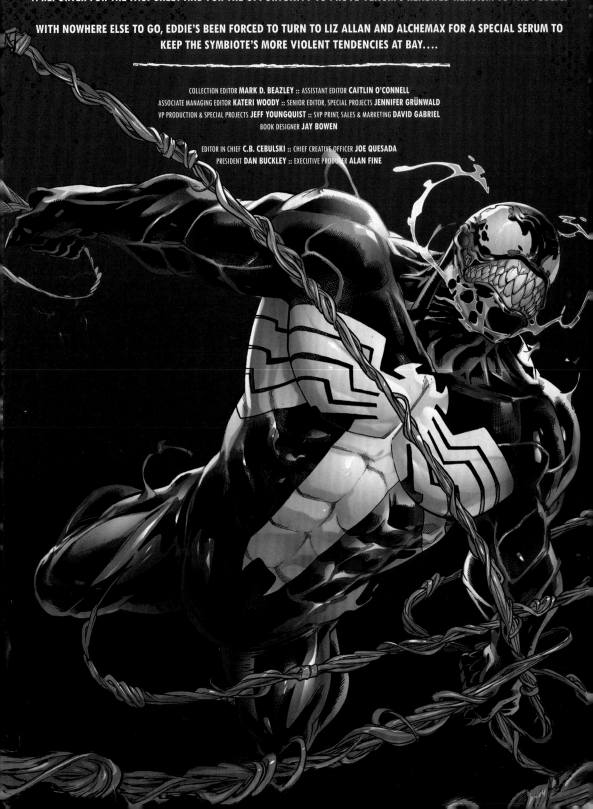

MIKE COSTA
WRITER

#161 "TANGLED WEBS"

JAVIER GARRÓN
ARTIST

**DONO SÁNCHEZ-ALMARA
& ERICK ARCINIEGA**
COLOR ARTISTS

#164-165 "THE NATIVITY"

MARK BAGLEY
PENCILER

SCOTT HANNA
INKER

DONO SÁNCHEZ-ALMARA
COLOR ARTIST

VC'S CLAYTON COWLES
LETTERER

JAVIER RODRÍGUEZ & ÁLVARO LÓPEZ (#161)
AND RYAN STEGMAN & MORRY HOLLOWELL (#164-165)
COVER ART

TOM GRONEMAN
ASSISTANT EDITOR

DEVIN LEWIS
EDITOR

NICK LOWE
EXECUTIVE EDITOR

VENOM VOL. 4: THE NATIVITY. Contains material originally published in magazine form as VENOM #161 and #164-165, and AMAZING SPIDER-MAN #362-363. First printing 2018. ISBN 978-1-302-90983-3. Published by MARVEL WORLDWIDE, INC., a subsidiary of MARVEL ENTERTAINMENT, LLC. OFFICE OF PUBLICATION: 135 West 50th Street, New York, NY 10020. Copyright © 2018 MARVEL No similarity between any of the names, characters, persons, and/ or institutions in this magazine with those of any living or dead person or institution is intended, and any such similarity which may exist is purely coincidental. **Printed in Canada.** DAN BUCKLEY, President, Marvel Entertainment; JOHN NEE, Publisher; JOE QUESADA, Chief Creative Officer; TOM BREVOORT, SVP of Publishing; DAVID BOGART, SVP of Business Affairs & Operations, Publishing & Partnership; DAVID GABRIEL, SVP of Sales & Marketing, Publishing; JEFF YOUNGQUIST, VP of Production & Special Projects; DAN CARR, Executive Director of Publishing Technology; ALEX MORALES, Director of Publishing Operations; DAN EDINGTON, Managing Editor; SUSAN CRESPI, Production Manager; STAN LEE, Chairman Emeritus. For information regarding advertising in Marvel Comics or on Marvel.com, please contact Vit DeBellis, Custom Solutions & Integrated Advertising Manager, at vdebellis@marvel.com. For Marvel subscription inquiries, please call 888-511-5480. **Manufactured between 7/20/2018 and 8/21/2018 by SOLISCO PRINTERS, SCOTT, QC, CANADA.**

10 9 8 7 6 5 4 3 2 1

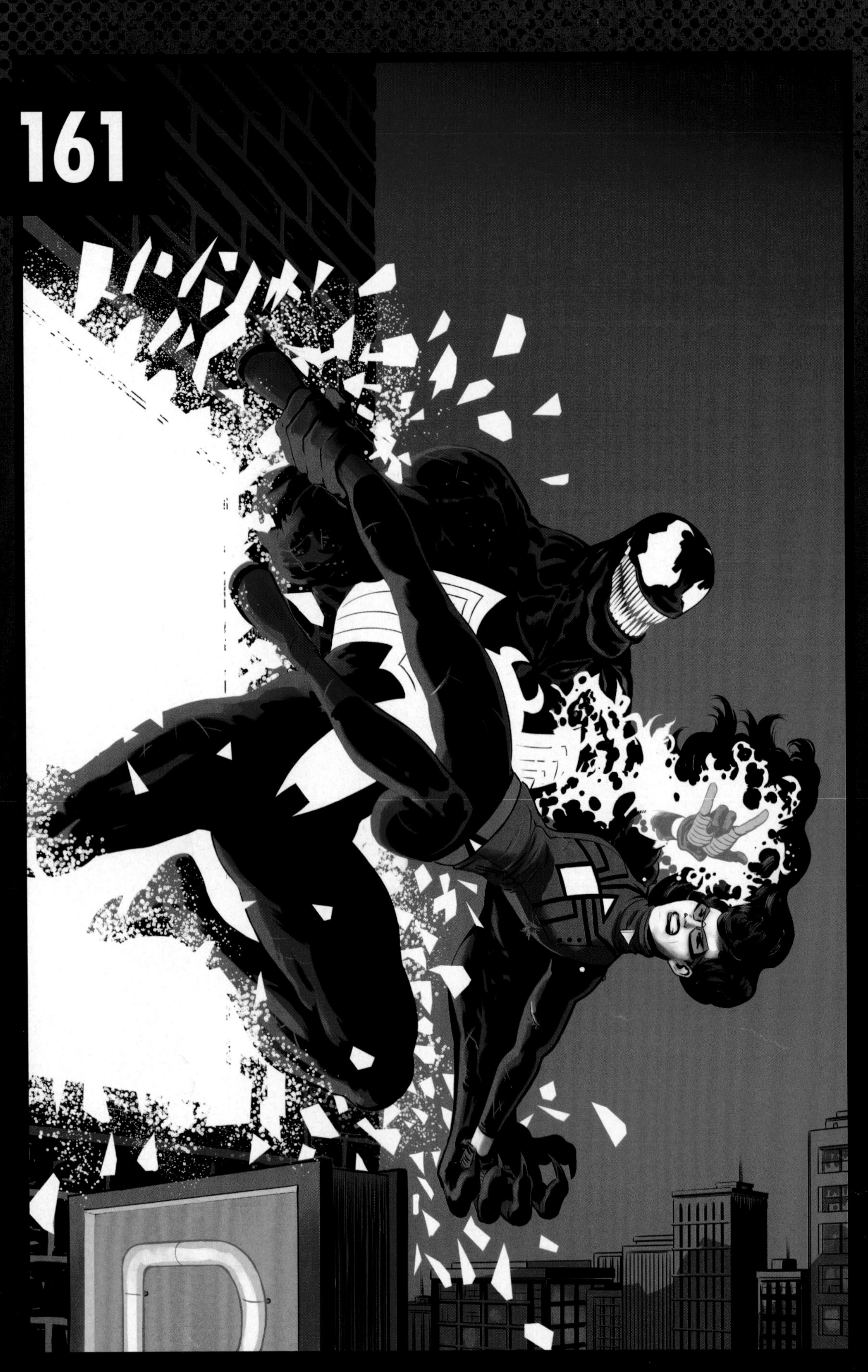
161

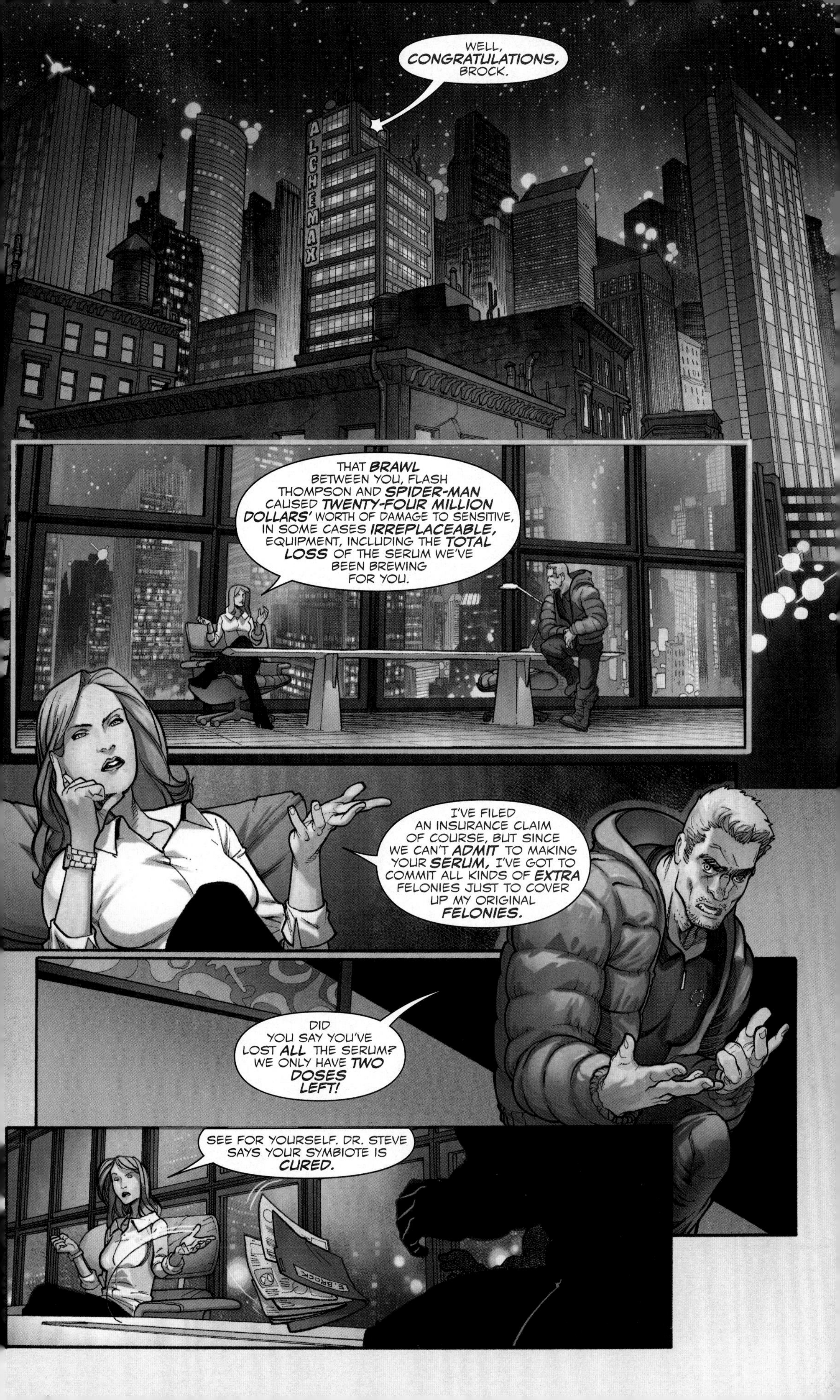
WELL, CONGRATULATIONS, BROCK.
ALCHEMAX
THAT BRAWL BETWEEN YOU, FLASH THOMPSON AND SPIDER-MAN CAUSED TWENTY-FOUR MILLION DOLLARS' WORTH OF DAMAGE TO SENSITIVE, IN SOME CASES IRREPLACEABLE, EQUIPMENT, INCLUDING THE TOTAL LOSS OF THE SERUM WE'VE BEEN BREWING FOR YOU.
I'VE FILED AN INSURANCE CLAIM OF COURSE, BUT SINCE WE CAN'T ADMIT TO MAKING YOUR SERUM, I'VE GOT TO COMMIT ALL KINDS OF EXTRA FELONIES JUST TO COVER UP MY ORIGINAL FELONIES.
DID YOU SAY YOU'VE LOST ALL THE SERUM? WE ONLY HAVE TWO DOSES LEFT!
SEE FOR YOURSELF. DR. STEVE SAYS YOUR SYMBIOTE IS CURED.
E. BROCK

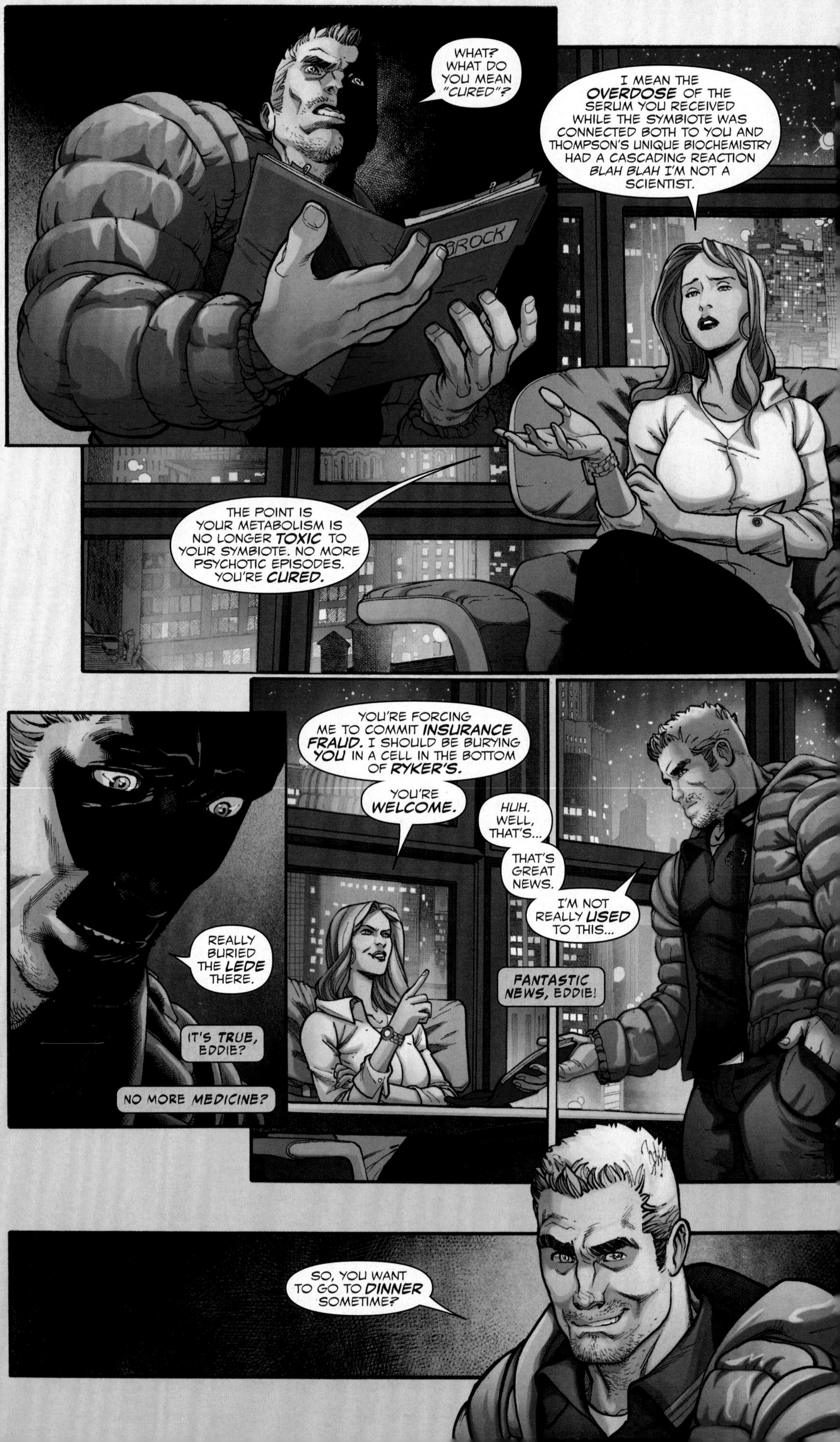

WHAT? WHAT DO YOU MEAN "CURED"?
I MEAN THE OVERDOSE OF THE SERUM YOU RECEIVED WHILE THE SYMBIOTE WAS CONNECTED BOTH TO YOU AND THOMPSON'S UNIQUE BIOCHEMISTRY HAD A CASCADING REACTION BLAH BLAH I'M NOT A SCIENTIST.
BROCK
THE POINT IS YOUR METABOLISM IS NO LONGER TOXIC TO YOUR SYMBIOTE. NO MORE PSYCHOTIC EPISODES. YOU'RE CURED.
REALLY BURIED THE LEDE THERE.
IT'S TRUE, EDDIE?
NO MORE MEDICINE?
YOU'RE FORCING ME TO COMMIT INSURANCE FRAUD. I SHOULD BE BURYING YOU IN A CELL IN THE BOTTOM OF RYKER'S.
YOU'RE WELCOME.
HUH. WELL, THAT'S...
THAT'S GREAT NEWS.
I'M NOT REALLY USED TO THIS...
FANTASTIC NEWS, EDDIE!
SO, YOU WANT TO GO TO DINNER SOMETIME?

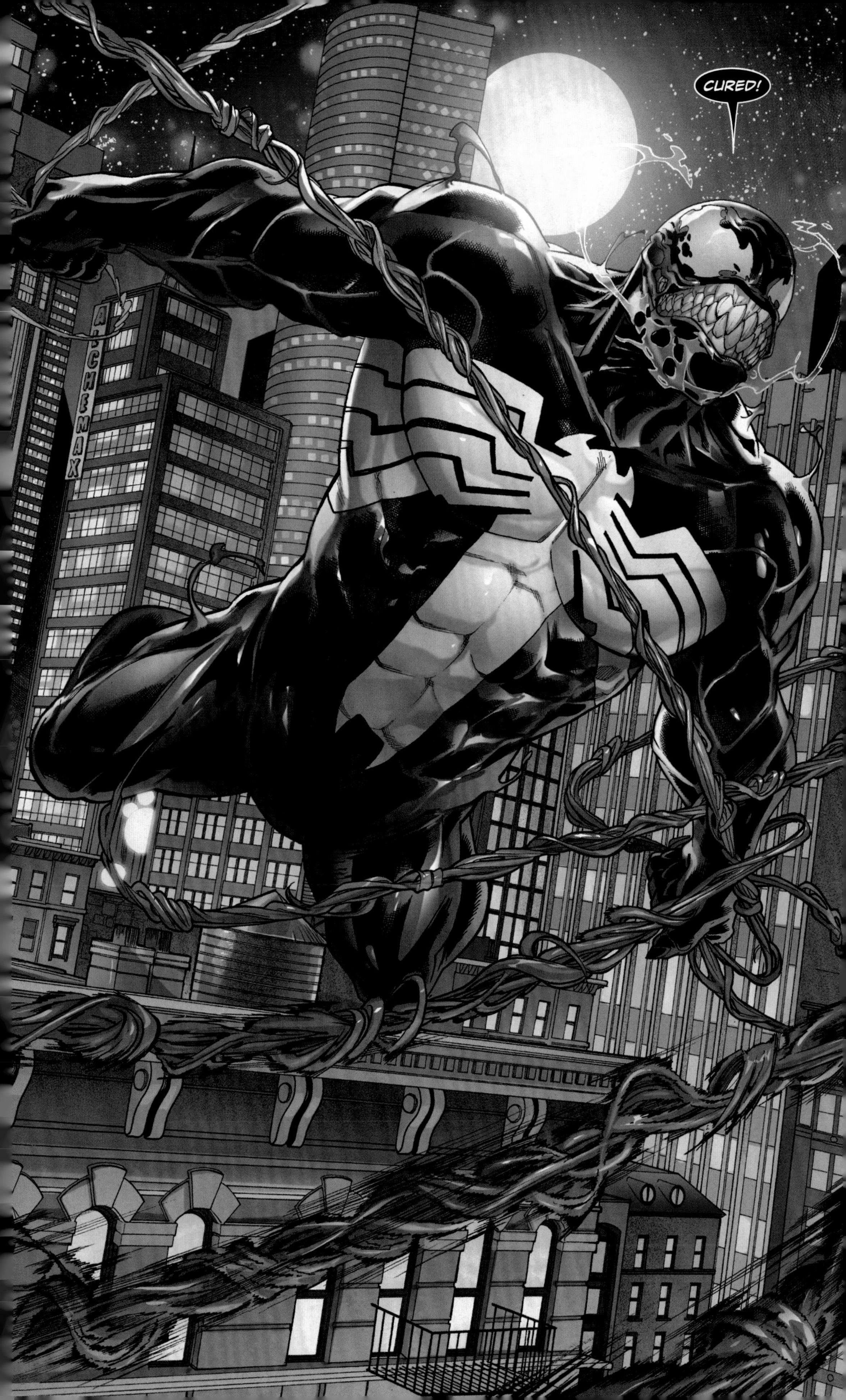
CURED!
ALCHEMAX

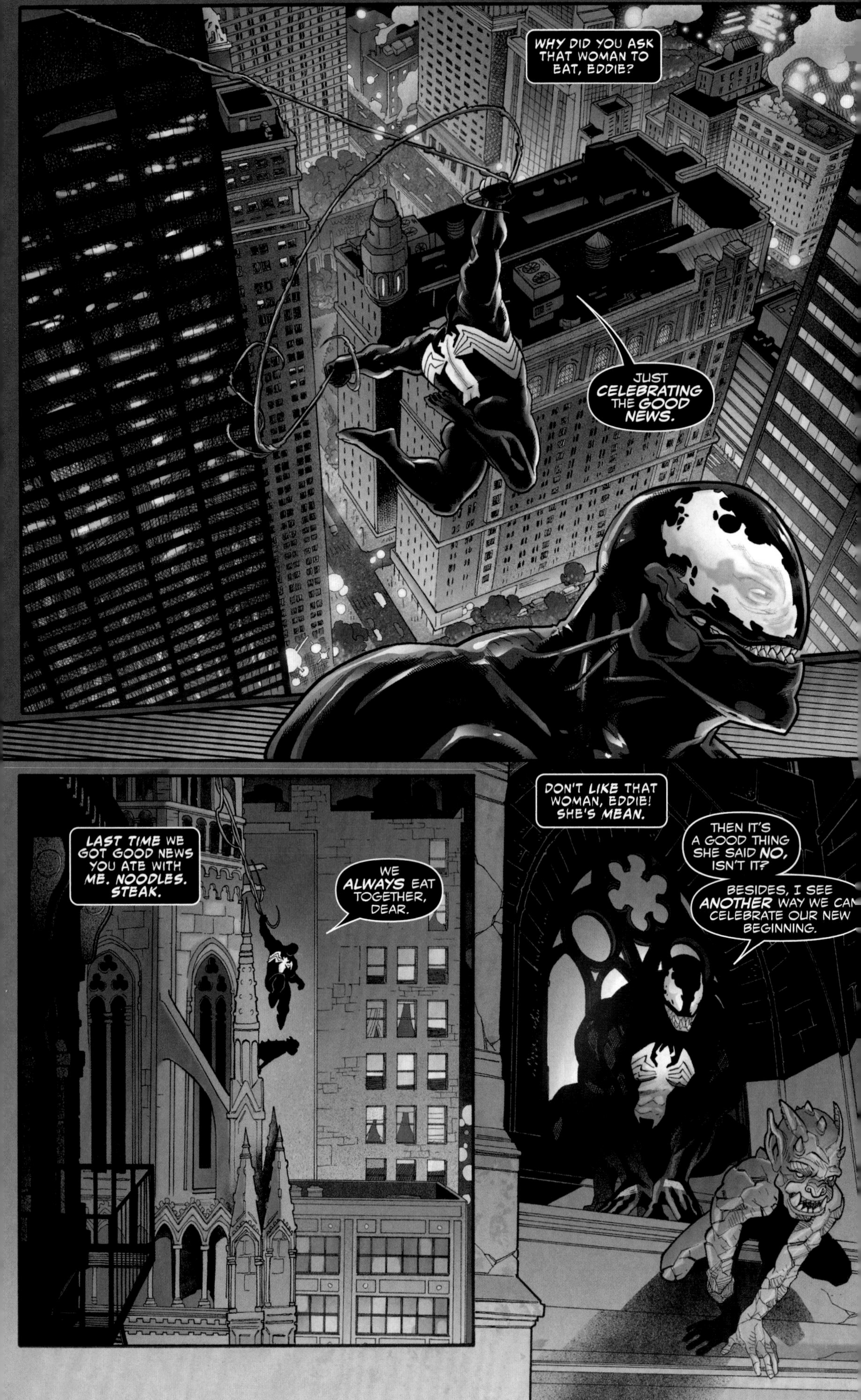
WHY DID YOU ASK THAT WOMAN TO EAT, EDDIE?
JUST CELEBRATING THE GOOD NEWS.
LAST TIME WE GOT GOOD NEWS YOU ATE WITH ME. NOODLES. STEAK.
WE ALWAYS EAT TOGETHER, DEAR.
DON'T LIKE THAT WOMAN, EDDIE! SHE'S MEAN.
THEN IT'S A GOOD THING SHE SAID NO, ISN'T IT?
BESIDES, I SEE ANOTHER WAY WE CAN CELEBRATE OUR NEW BEGINNING.

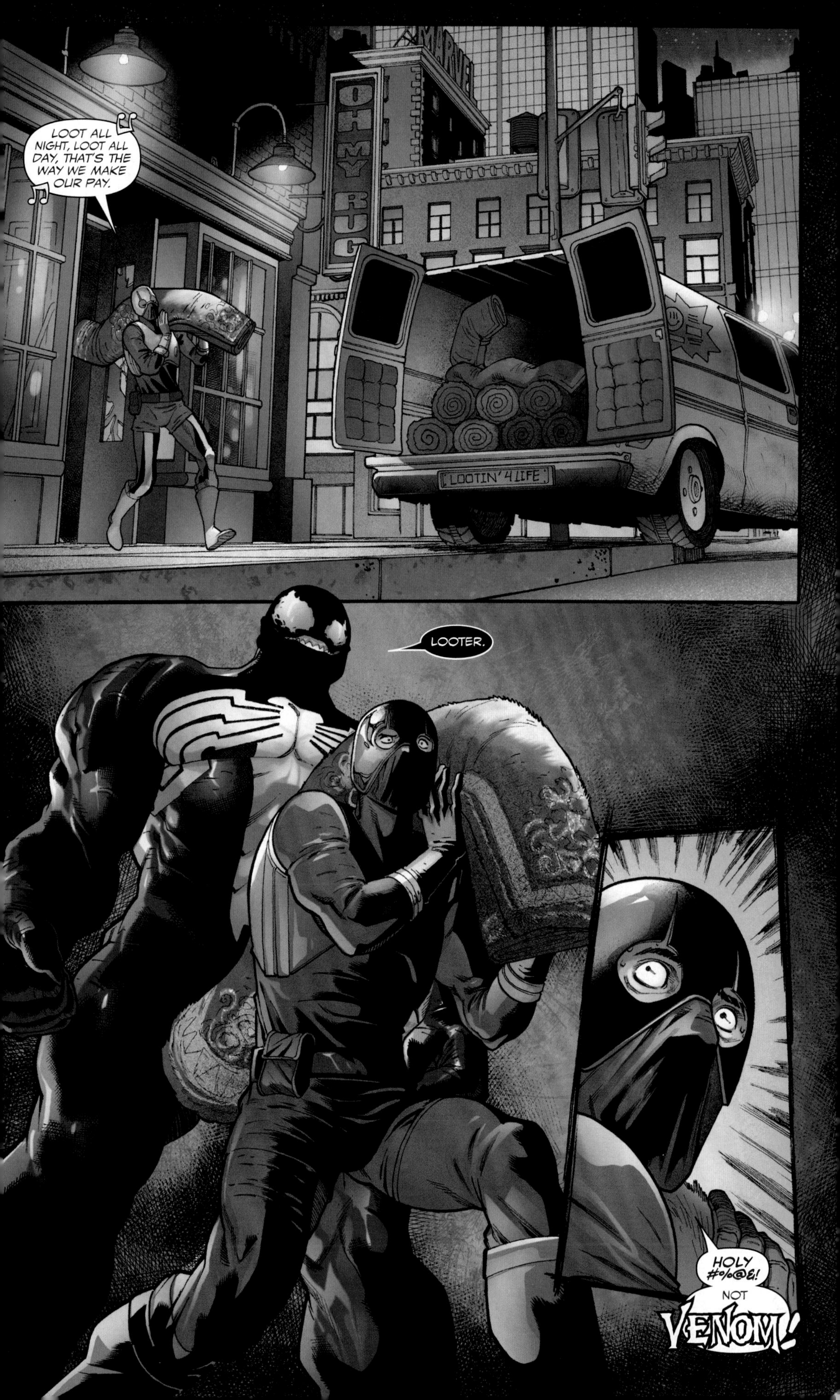

MARVEL
OH MY RUG
LOOT ALL NIGHT, LOOT ALL DAY, THAT'S THE WAY WE MAKE OUR PAY.
LOOTIN' 4 LIFE
LOOTER.
HOLY #%@&!
NOT VENOM!

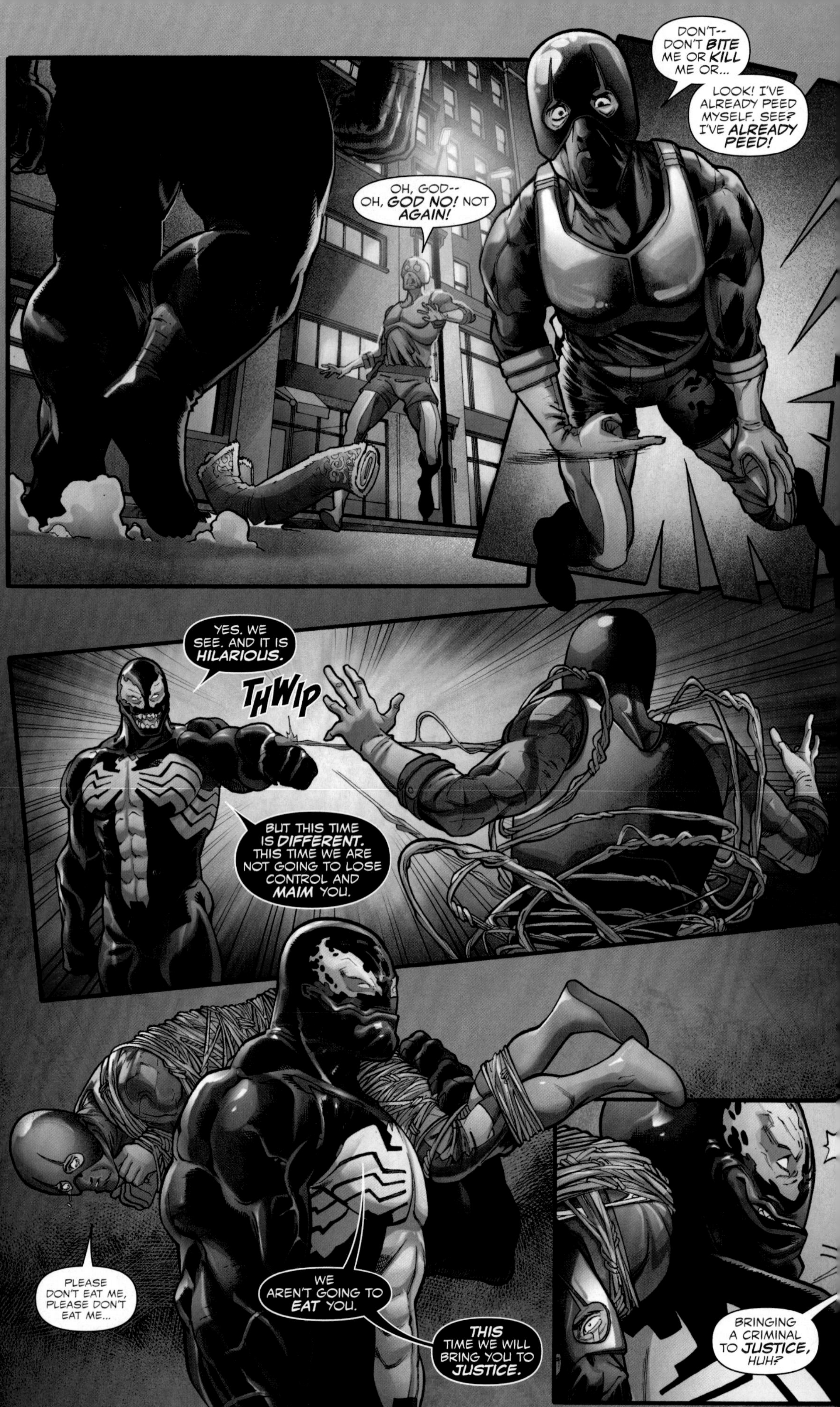

DON'T-- DON'T BITE ME OR KILL ME OR...
LOOK! I'VE ALREADY PEED MYSELF. SEE? I'VE ALREADY PEED!
OH, GOD-- OH, GOD NO! NOT AGAIN!
YES. WE SEE. AND IT IS HILARIOUS.
THWIP
BUT THIS TIME IS DIFFERENT. THIS TIME WE ARE NOT GOING TO LOSE CONTROL AND MAIM YOU.
PLEASE DON'T EAT ME, PLEASE DON'T EAT ME...
WE AREN'T GOING TO EAT YOU.
THIS TIME WE WILL BRING YOU TO JUSTICE.
BRINGING A CRIMINAL TO JUSTICE, HUH?

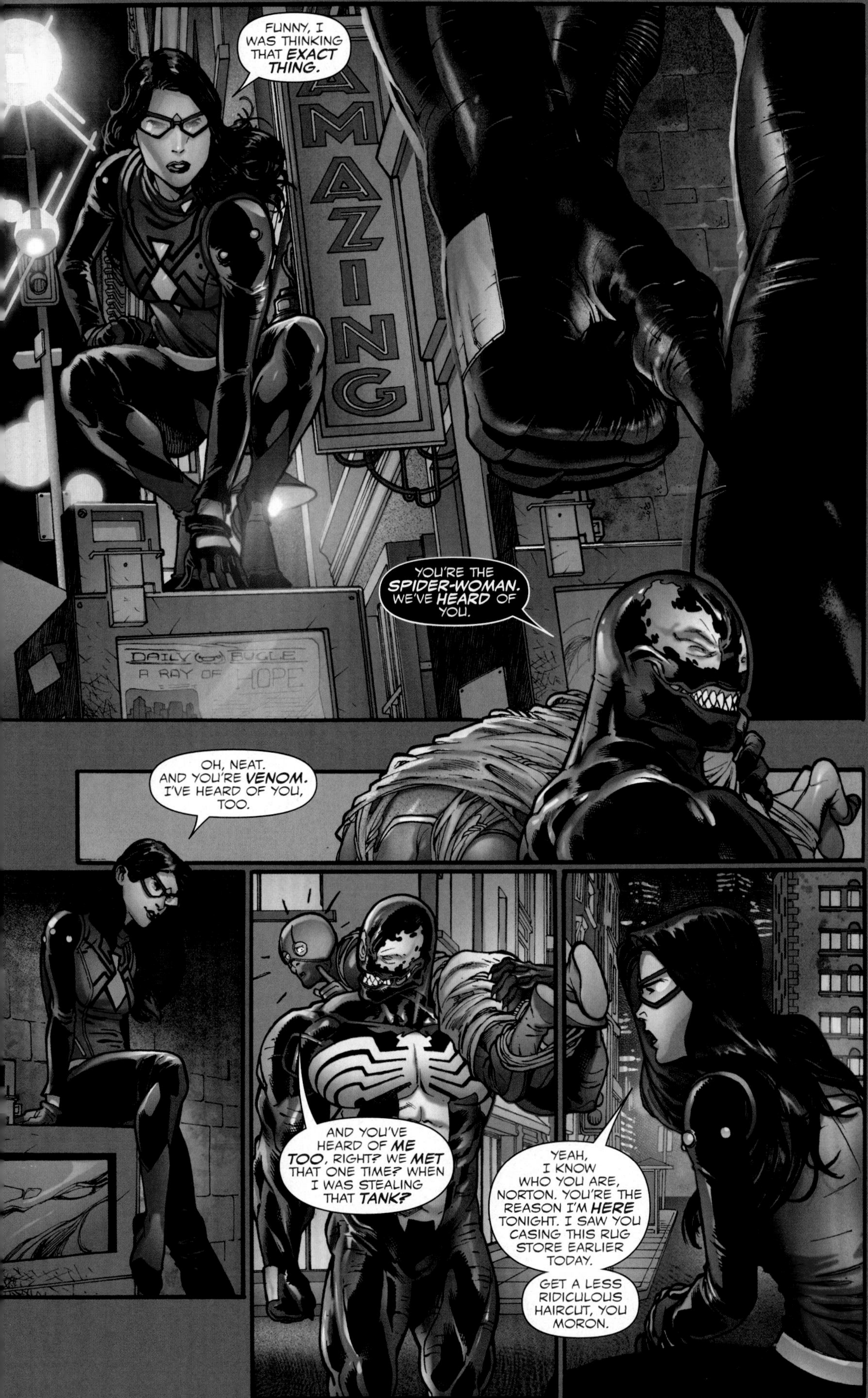
FUNNY, I WAS THINKING THAT EXACT THING.
DAILY BUGLE
A RAY OF HOPE
YOU'RE THE SPIDER-WOMAN. WE'VE HEARD OF YOU.
OH, NEAT. AND YOU'RE VENOM. I'VE HEARD OF YOU, TOO.
AND YOU'VE HEARD OF ME TOO, RIGHT? WE MET THAT ONE TIME? WHEN I WAS STEALING THAT TANK?
YEAH, I KNOW WHO YOU ARE, NORTON. YOU'RE THE REASON I'M HERE TONIGHT. I SAW YOU CASING THIS RUG STORE EARLIER TODAY.
GET A LESS RIDICULOUS HAIRCUT, YOU MORON.

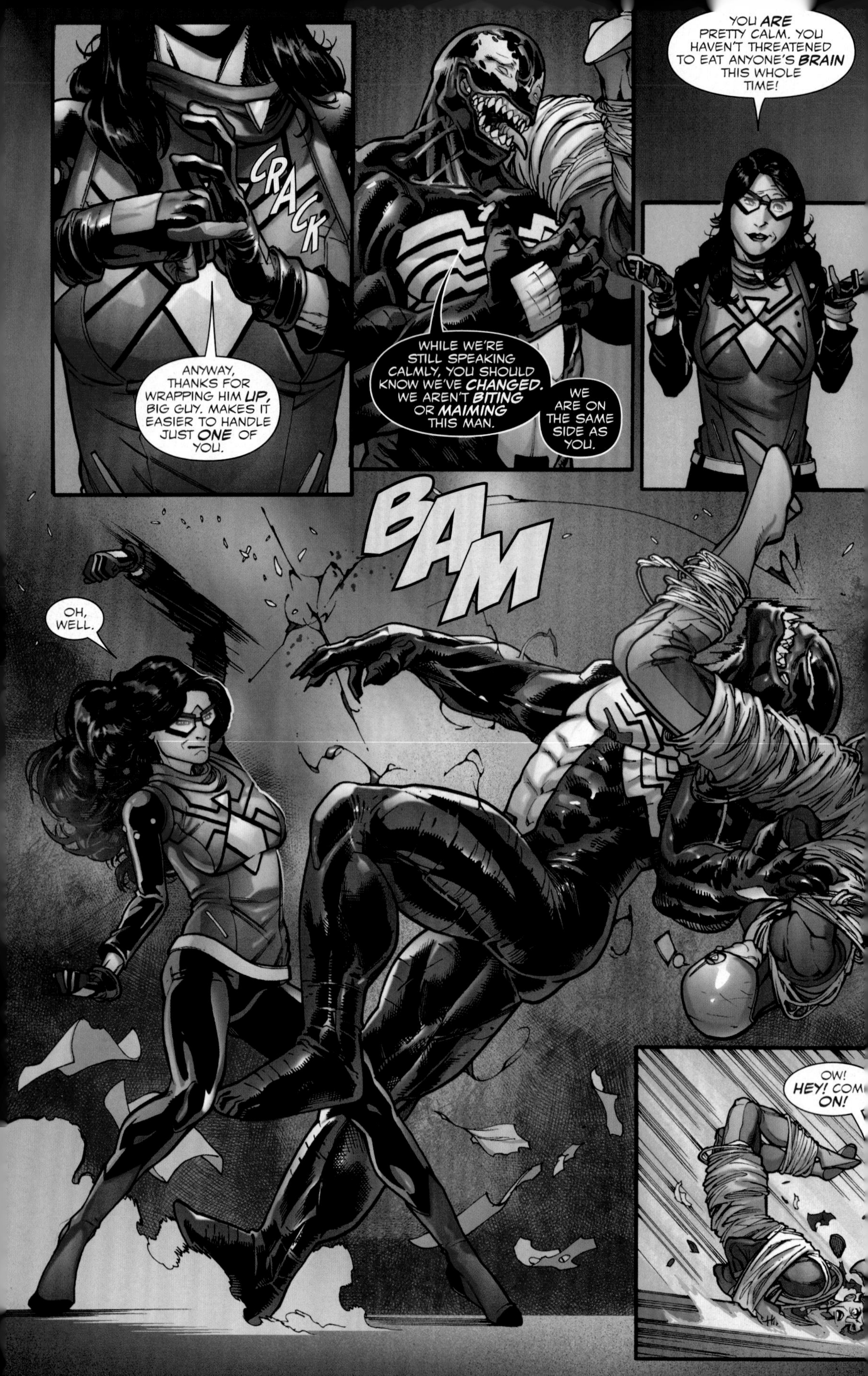
CRACK
ANYWAY, THANKS FOR WRAPPING HIM UP, BIG GUY. MAKES IT EASIER TO HANDLE JUST ONE OF YOU.
WHILE WE'RE STILL SPEAKING CALMLY, YOU SHOULD KNOW WE'VE CHANGED. WE AREN'T BITING OR MAIMING THIS MAN.
WE ARE ON THE SAME SIDE AS YOU.
YOU ARE PRETTY CALM. YOU HAVEN'T THREATENED TO EAT ANYONE'S BRAIN THIS WHOLE TIME!
BAM
OH, WELL.
OW! HEY! COME ON!

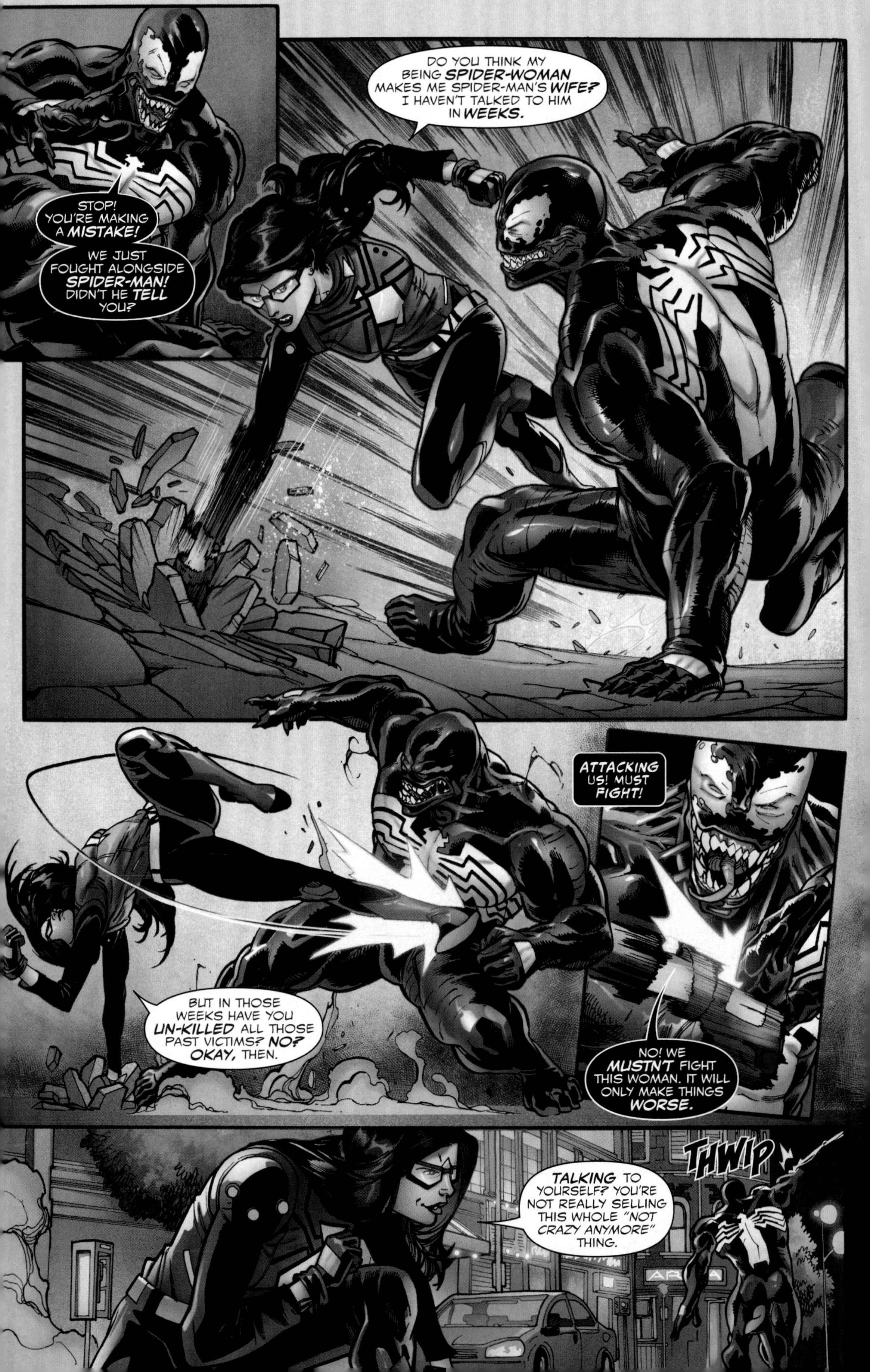

STOP! YOU'RE MAKING A MISTAKE!
WE JUST FOUGHT ALONGSIDE SPIDER-MAN! DIDN'T HE TELL YOU?
DO YOU THINK MY BEING SPIDER-WOMAN MAKES ME SPIDER-MAN'S WIFE? I HAVEN'T TALKED TO HIM IN WEEKS.
BUT IN THOSE WEEKS HAVE YOU UN-KILLED ALL THOSE PAST VICTIMS? NO? OKAY, THEN.
ATTACKING US! MUST FIGHT!
NO! WE MUSTN'T FIGHT THIS WOMAN. IT WILL ONLY MAKE THINGS WORSE.
THWIP
TALKING TO YOURSELF? YOU'RE NOT REALLY SELLING THIS WHOLE "NOT CRAZY ANYMORE" THING.

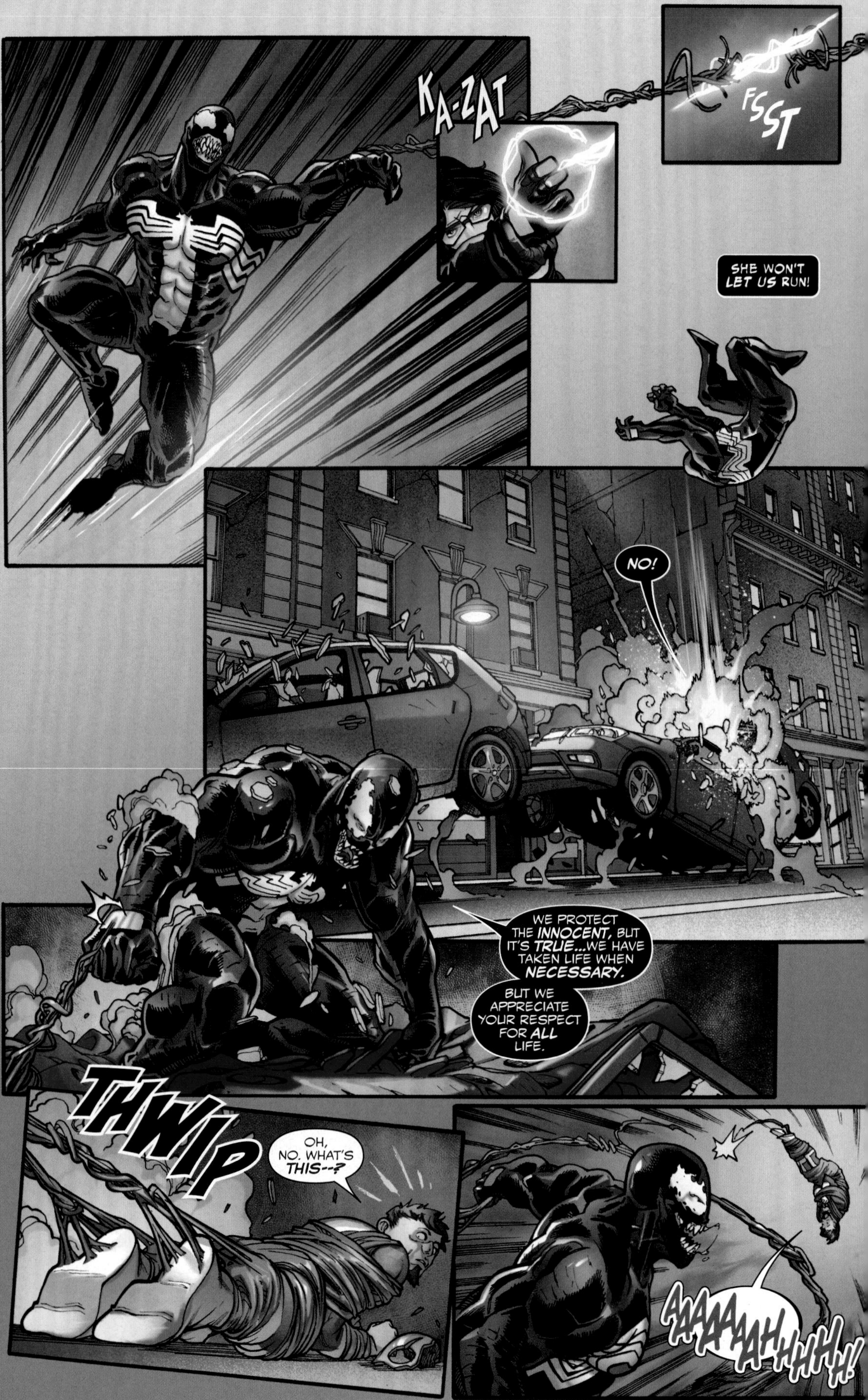

KA-ZAT
FSST
SHE WON'T LET US RUN!
NO!
WE PROTECT THE INNOCENT, BUT IT'S TRUE...WE HAVE TAKEN LIFE WHEN NECESSARY.
BUT WE APPRECIATE YOUR RESPECT FOR ALL LIFE.
THWIP
OH, NO. WHAT'S THIS--?
AAAAAAAHHHHH!

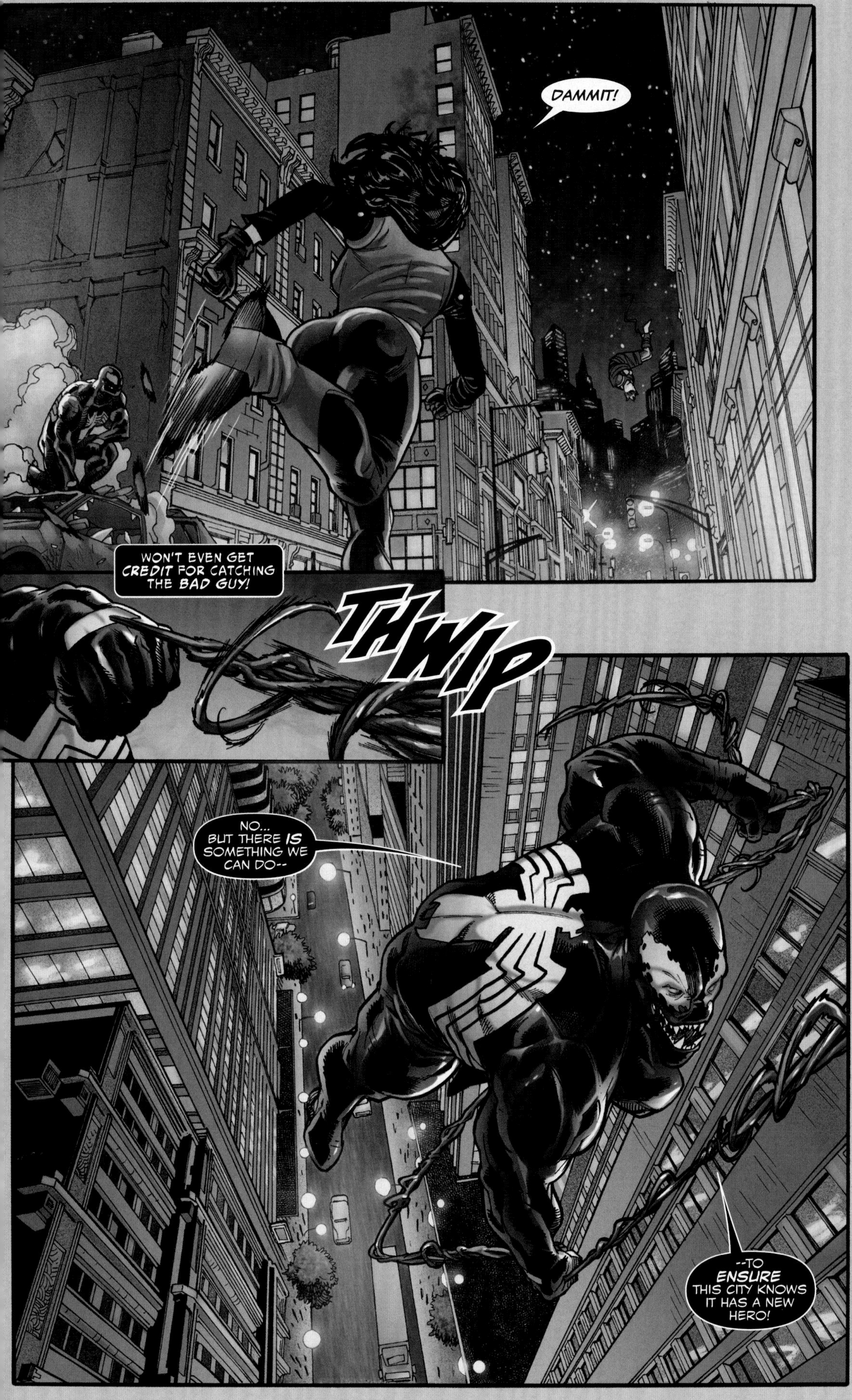
DAMMIT!
WON'T EVEN GET CREDIT FOR CATCHING THE BAD GUY!
THWIP
NO... BUT THERE IS SOMETHING WE CAN DO--
--TO ENSURE THIS CITY KNOWS IT HAS A NEW HERO!

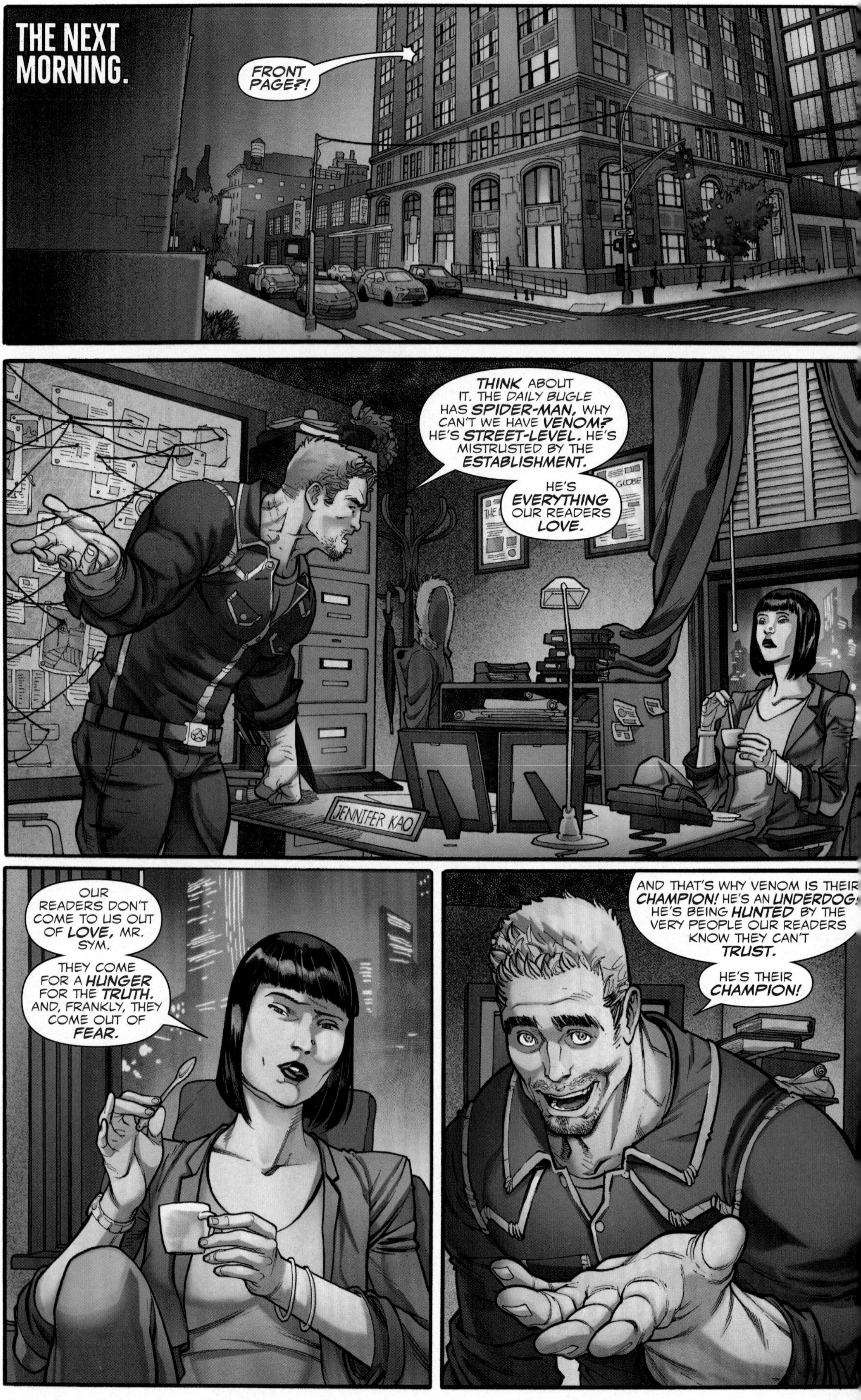
THE NEXT MORNING.
FRONT PAGE?!
PARK
THINK ABOUT IT. THE DAILY BUGLE HAS SPIDER-MAN, WHY CAN'T WE HAVE VENOM? HE'S STREET-LEVEL. HE'S MISTRUSTED BY THE ESTABLISHMENT.
HE'S EVERYTHING OUR READERS LOVE.
GLOBE
JENNIFER KAO
OUR READERS DON'T COME TO US OUT OF LOVE, MR. SYM.
THEY COME FOR A HUNGER FOR THE TRUTH. AND, FRANKLY, THEY COME OUT OF FEAR.
AND THAT'S WHY VENOM IS THEIR CHAMPION! HE'S AN UNDERDOG! HE'S BEING HUNTED BY THE VERY PEOPLE OUR READERS KNOW THEY CAN'T TRUST.
HE'S THEIR CHAMPION!

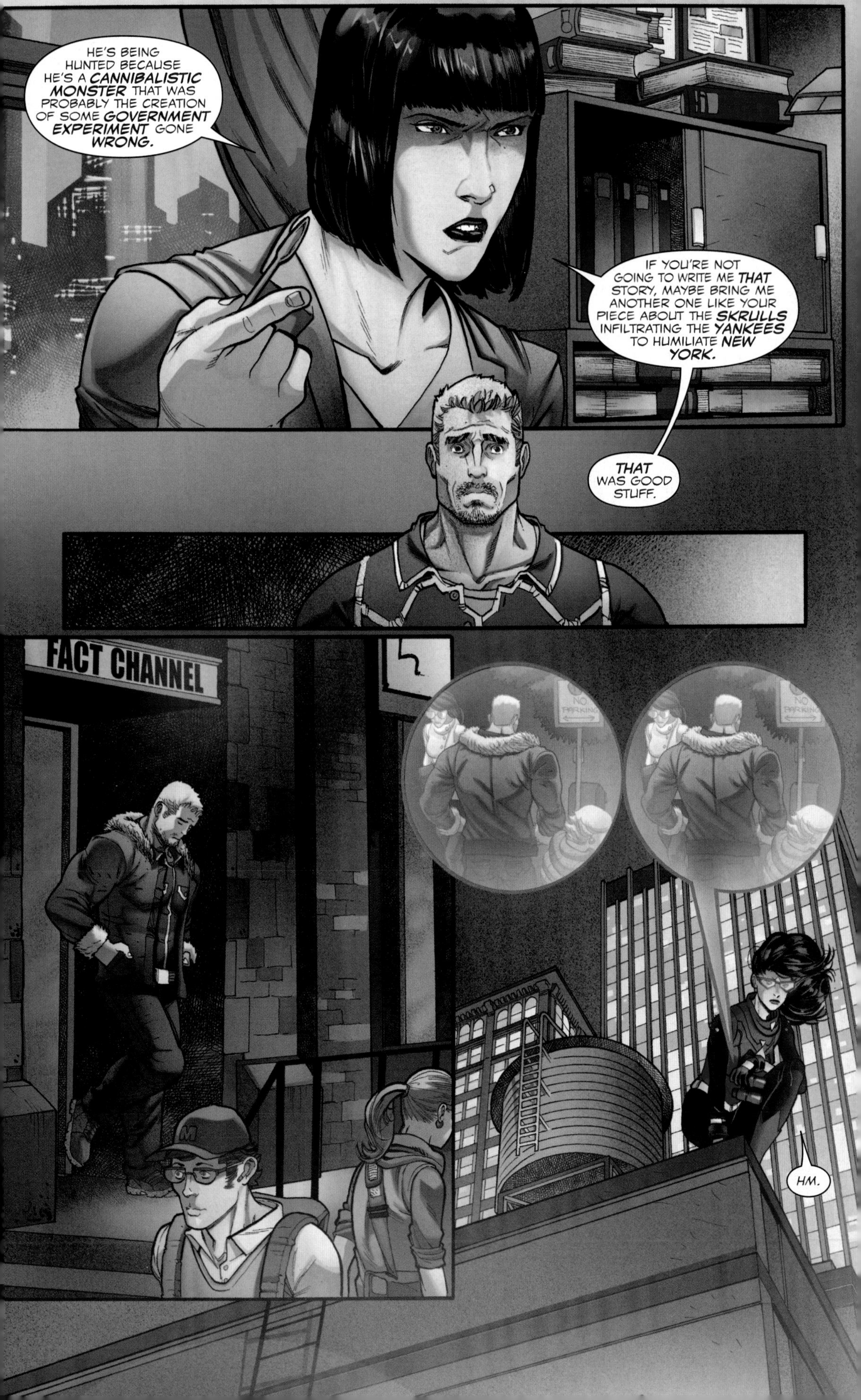
HE'S BEING HUNTED BECAUSE HE'S A CANNIBALISTIC MONSTER THAT WAS PROBABLY THE CREATION OF SOME GOVERNMENT EXPERIMENT GONE WRONG.
IF YOU'RE NOT GOING TO WRITE ME THAT STORY, MAYBE BRING ME ANOTHER ONE LIKE YOUR PIECE ABOUT THE SKRULLS INFILTRATING THE YANKEES TO HUMILIATE NEW YORK.
THAT WAS GOOD STUFF.
FACT CHANNEL
NO PARKING
NO PARKING
HM.

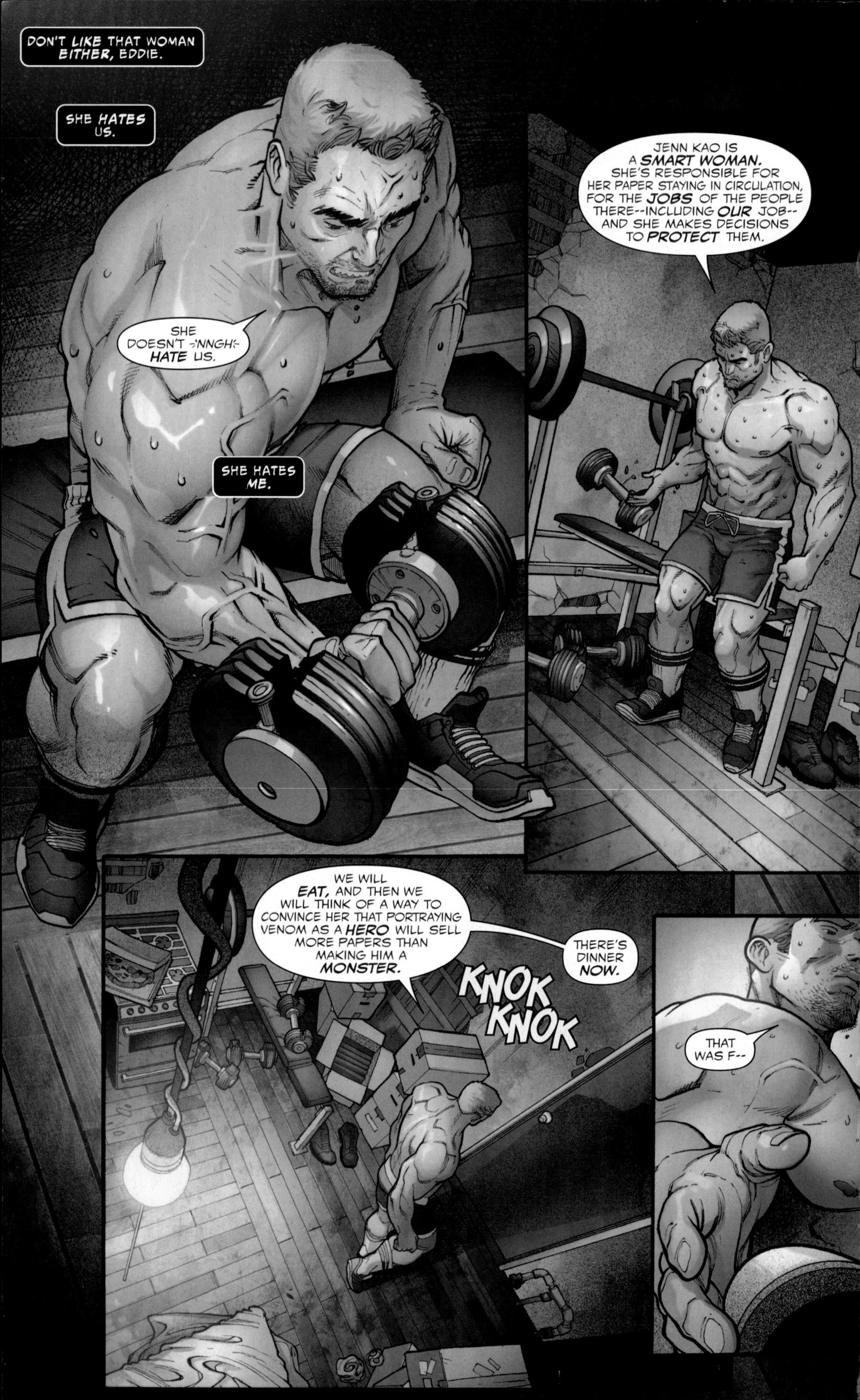
DON'T LIKE THAT WOMAN EITHER, EDDIE.
SHE HATES US.
SHE DOESN'T -NNGH- HATE US.
SHE HATES ME.
JENN KAO IS A SMART WOMAN. SHE'S RESPONSIBLE FOR HER PAPER STAYING IN CIRCULATION, FOR THE JOBS OF THE PEOPLE THERE--INCLUDING OUR JOB--AND SHE MAKES DECISIONS TO PROTECT THEM.
WE WILL EAT, AND THEN WE WILL THINK OF A WAY TO CONVINCE HER THAT PORTRAYING VENOM AS A HERO WILL SELL MORE PAPERS THAN MAKING HIM A MONSTER.
THERE'S DINNER NOW.
KNOK KNOK
THAT WAS F--

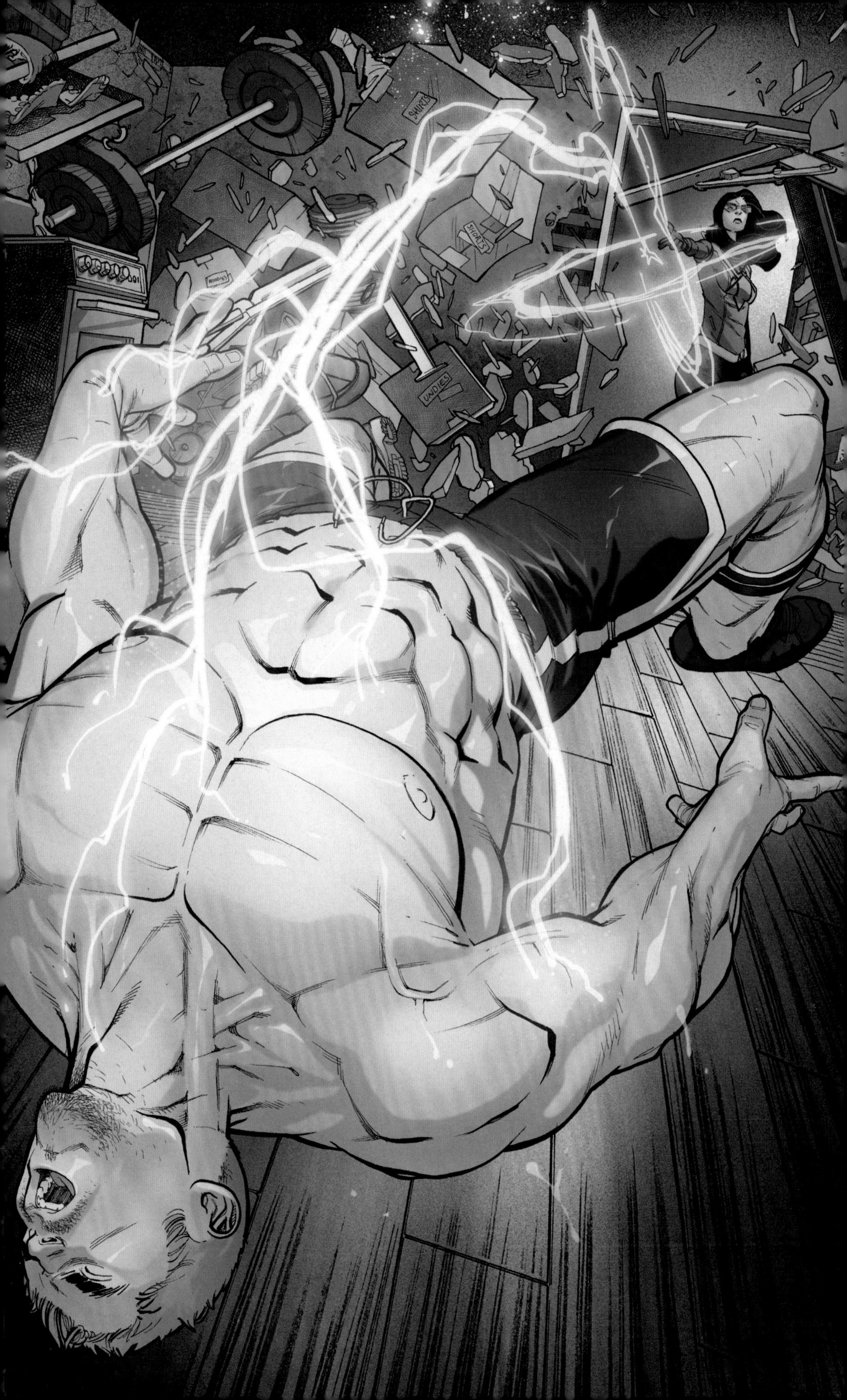
SHIRTS
SHORTS
UNDIES

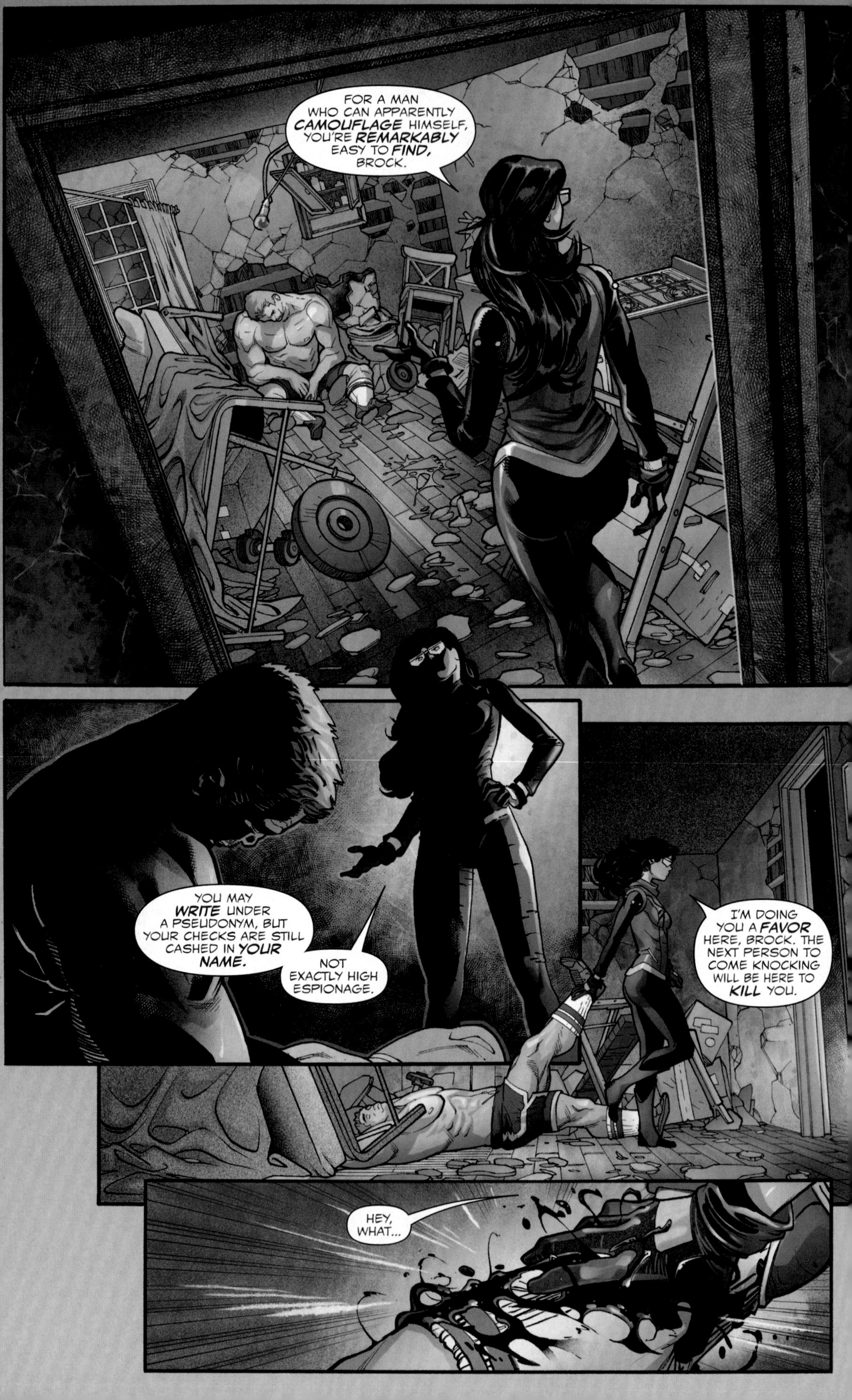
FOR A MAN WHO CAN APPARENTLY CAMOUFLAGE HIMSELF, YOU'RE REMARKABLY EASY TO FIND, BROCK.
YOU MAY WRITE UNDER A PSEUDONYM, BUT YOUR CHECKS ARE STILL CASHED IN YOUR NAME.
NOT EXACTLY HIGH ESPIONAGE.
I'M DOING YOU A FAVOR HERE, BROCK. THE NEXT PERSON TO COME KNOCKING WILL BE HERE TO KILL YOU.
HEY, WHAT...

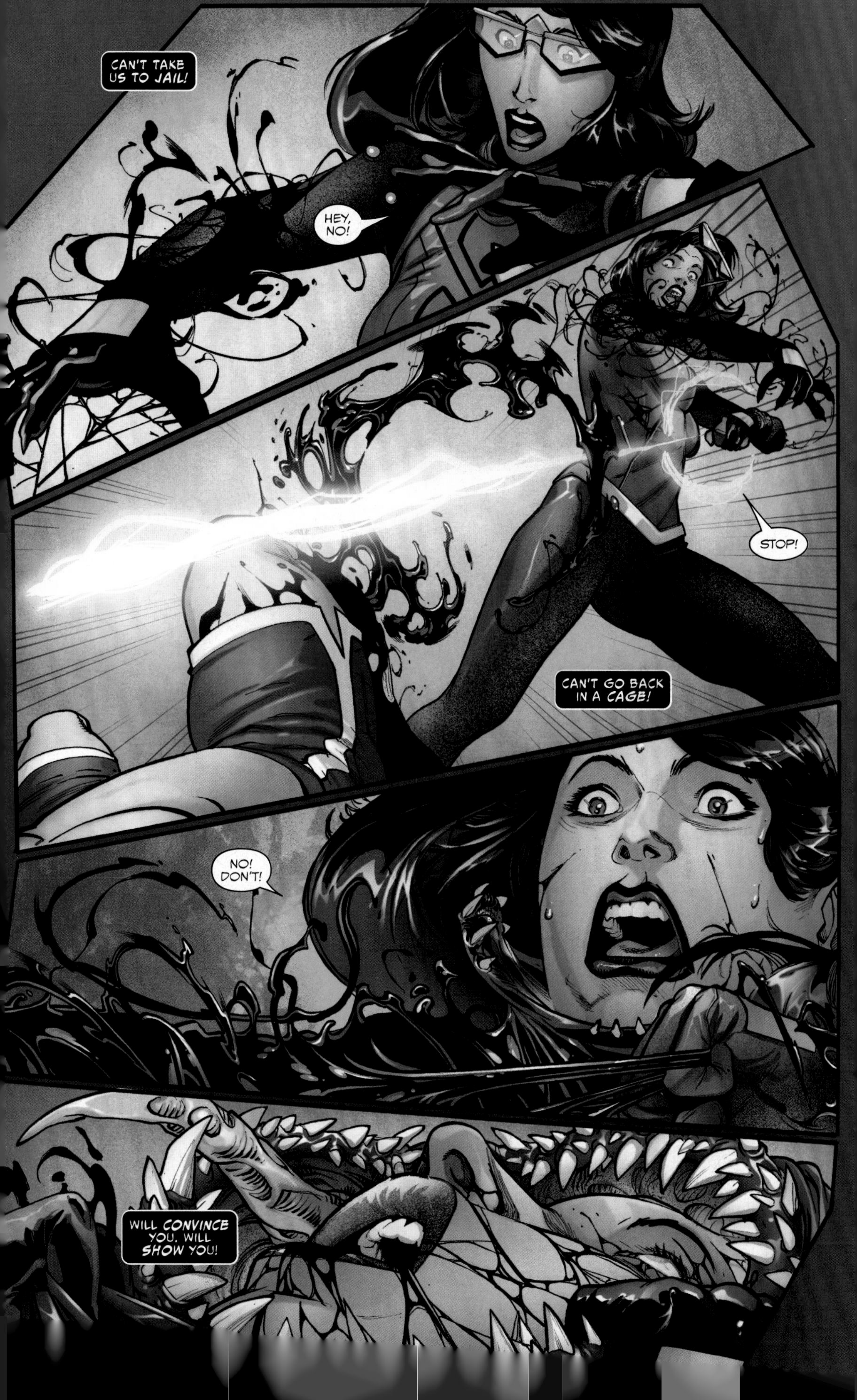
CAN'T TAKE US TO JAIL!
HEY, NO!
STOP!
CAN'T GO BACK IN A CAGE!
NO! DON'T!
WILL CONVINCE YOU. WILL SHOW YOU!

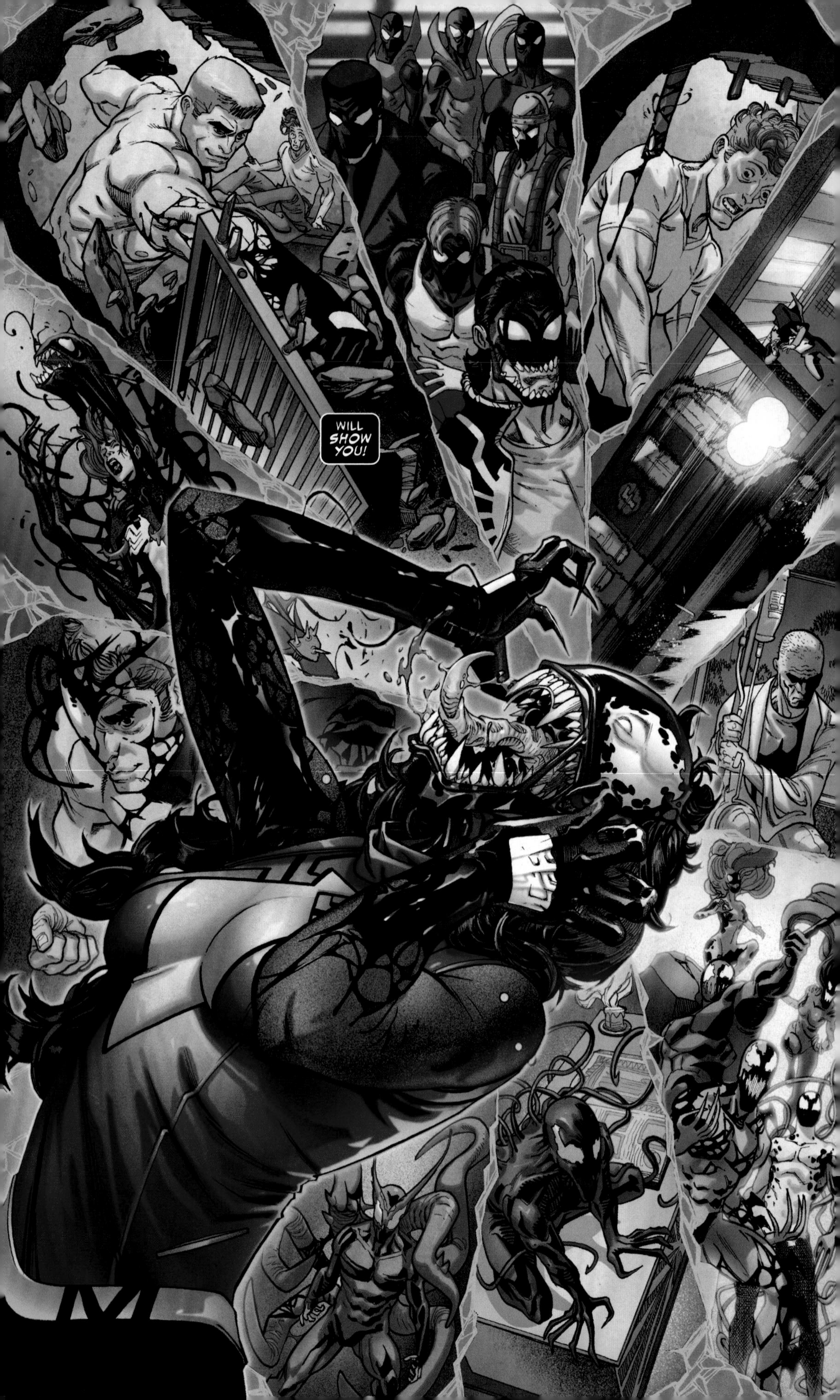
WILL SHOW YOU!

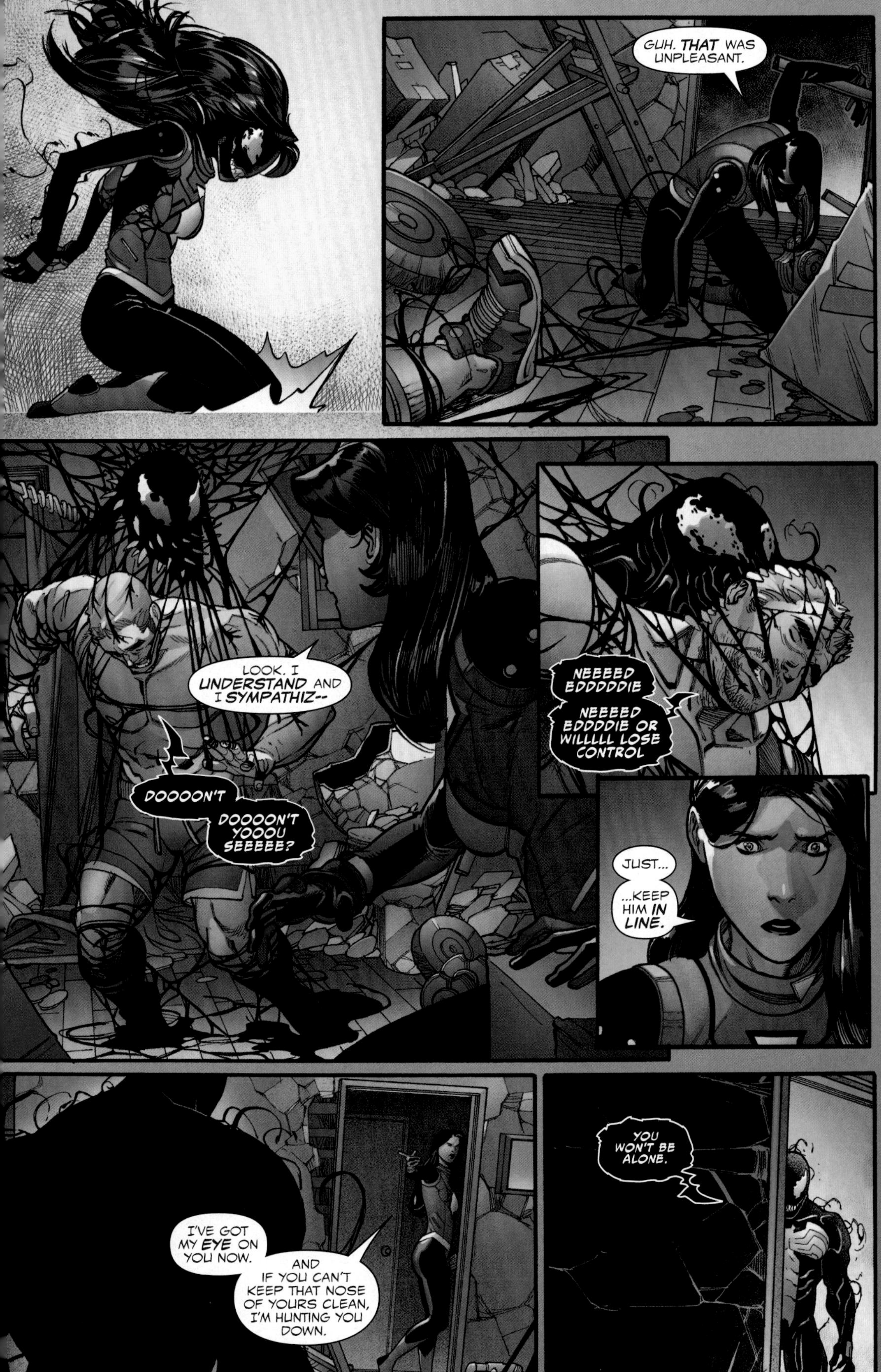
GUH. THAT WAS UNPLEASANT.
LOOK. I UNDERSTAND AND I SYMPATHIZ--
DOOOON'T
DOOOON'T YOOOU SEEEEE?
NEEEED EDDDDDIE
NEEEED EDDDDIE OR WILLLLL LOSE CONTROL
JUST...
...KEEP HIM IN LINE.
I'VE GOT MY EYE ON YOU NOW.
AND IF YOU CAN'T KEEP THAT NOSE OF YOURS CLEAN, I'M HUNTING YOU DOWN.
YOU WON'T BE ALONE.

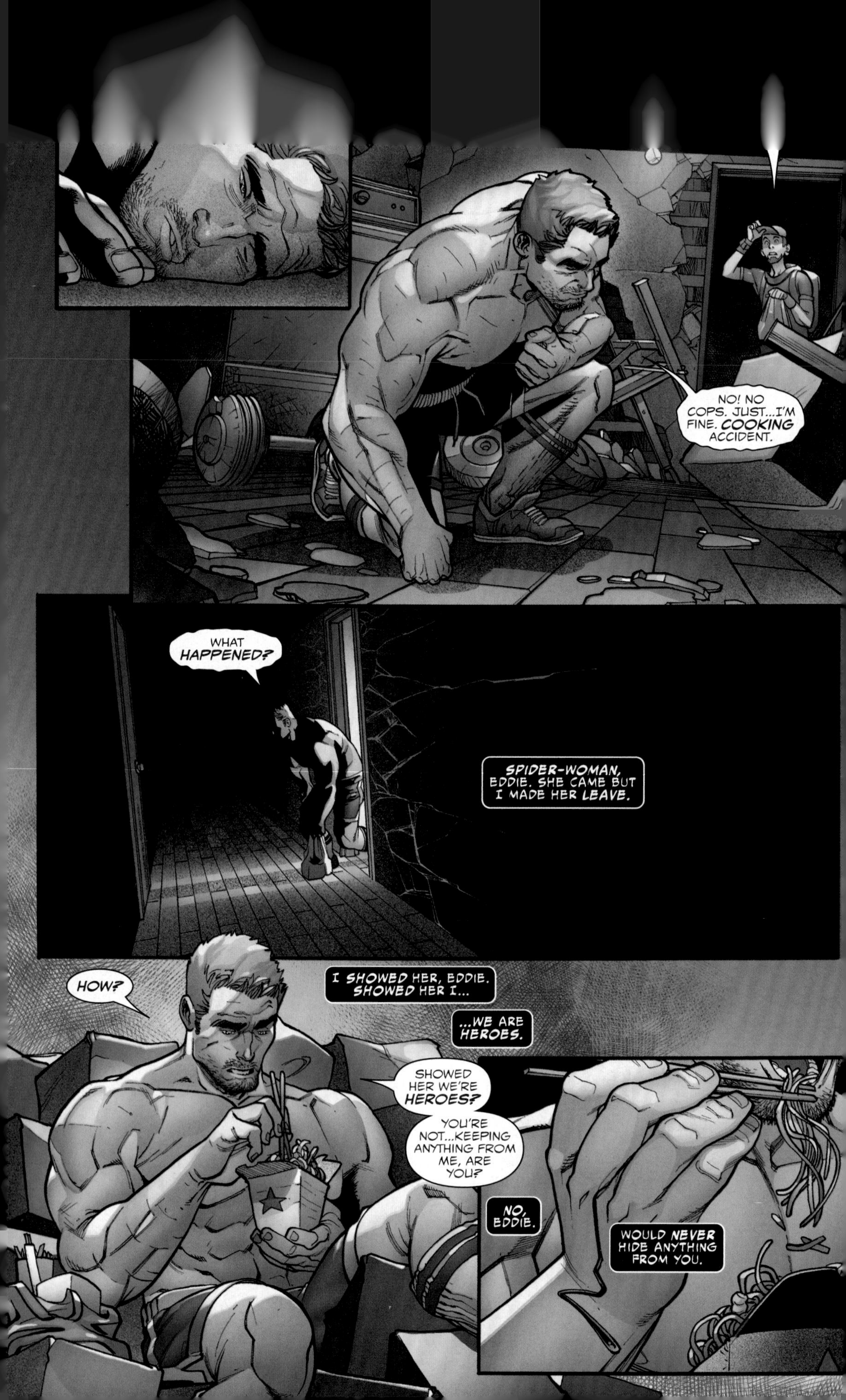
NO! NO COPS. JUST...I'M FINE. COOKING ACCIDENT.
WHAT HAPPENED?
SPIDER-WOMAN, EDDIE. SHE CAME BUT I MADE HER LEAVE.
HOW?
I SHOWED HER, EDDIE. SHOWED HER I...
...WE ARE HEROES.
SHOWED HER WE'RE HEROES?
YOU'RE NOT...KEEPING ANYTHING FROM ME, ARE YOU?
NO, EDDIE.
WOULD NEVER HIDE ANYTHING FROM YOU.

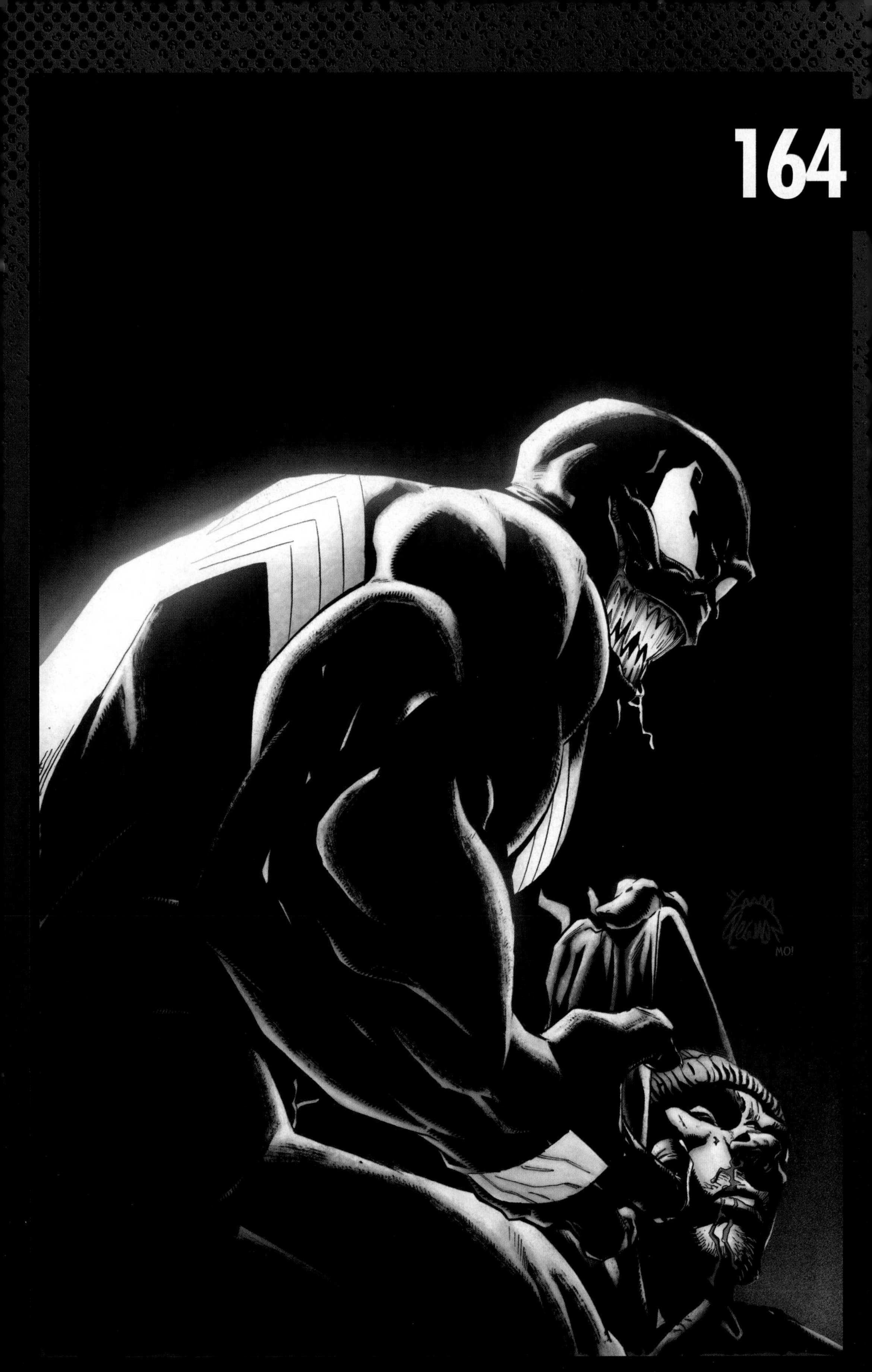
164

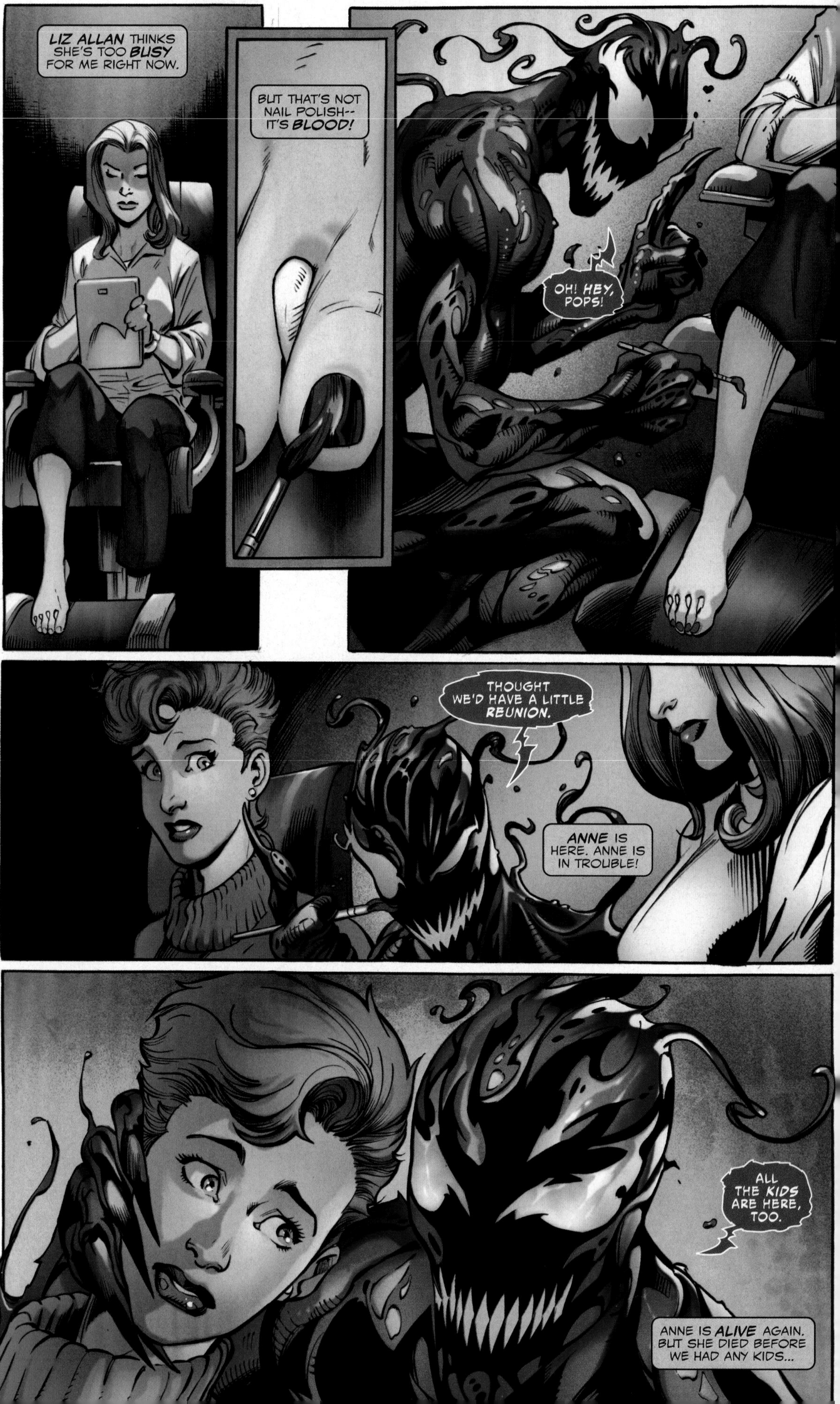
LIZ ALLAN THINKS SHE'S TOO BUSY FOR ME RIGHT NOW.
BUT THAT'S NOT NAIL POLISH-- IT'S BLOOD!
OH! HEY, POPS!
THOUGHT WE'D HAVE A LITTLE REUNION.
ANNE IS HERE. ANNE IS IN TROUBLE!
ALL THE KIDS ARE HERE, TOO.
ANNE IS ALIVE AGAIN. BUT SHE DIED BEFORE WE HAD ANY KIDS...

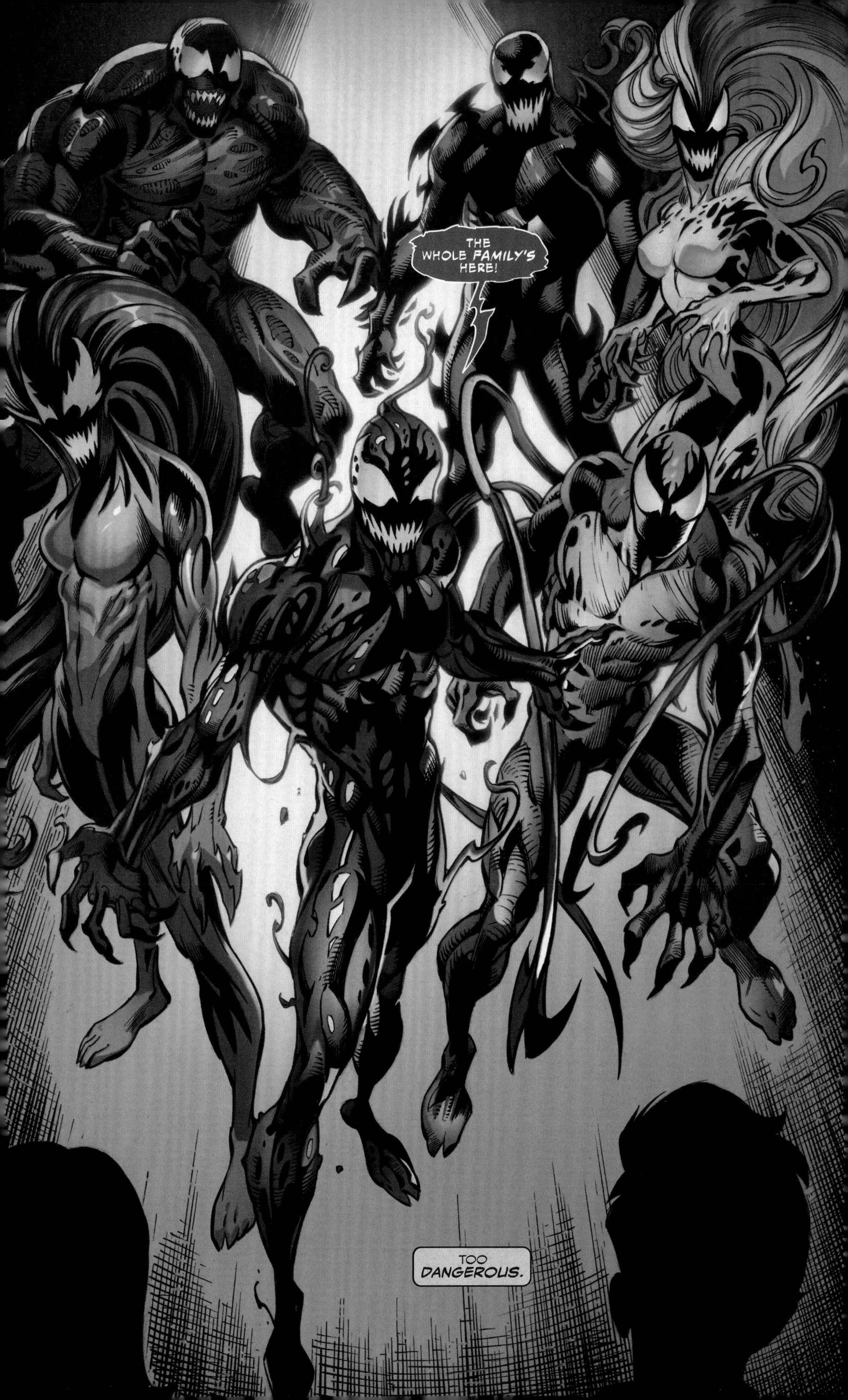
THE WHOLE FAMILY'S HERE!
TOO DANGEROUS.

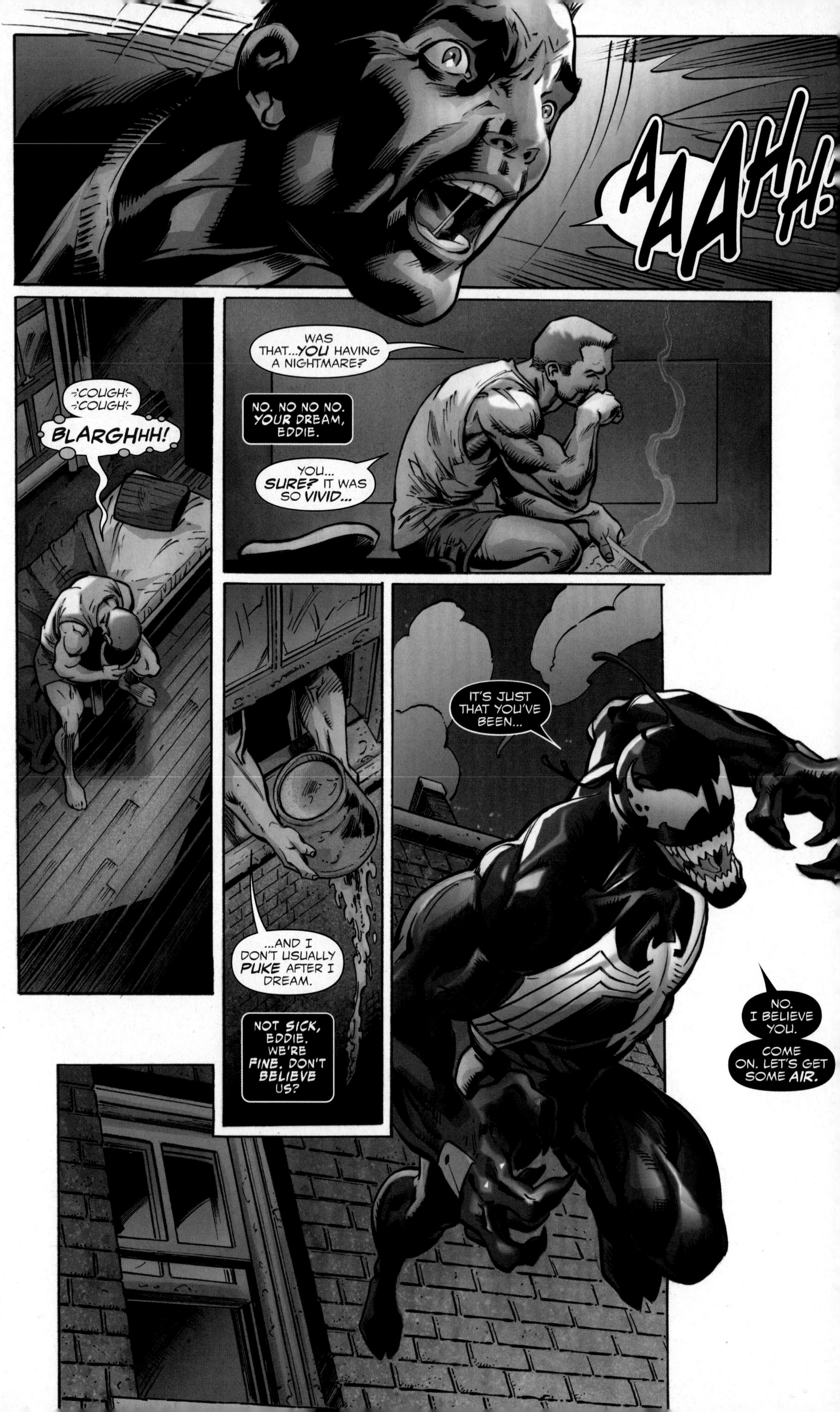
AAAHH!
WAS THAT...YOU HAVING A NIGHTMARE?
NO. NO NO NO. YOUR DREAM, EDDIE.
YOU... SURE? IT WAS SO VIVID...
COUGH COUGH
BLARGHHH!
...AND I DON'T USUALLY PUKE AFTER I DREAM.
NOT SICK, EDDIE. WE'RE FINE. DON'T BELIEVE US?
IT'S JUST THAT YOU'VE BEEN...
NO. I BELIEVE YOU.
COME ON. LET'S GET SOME AIR.

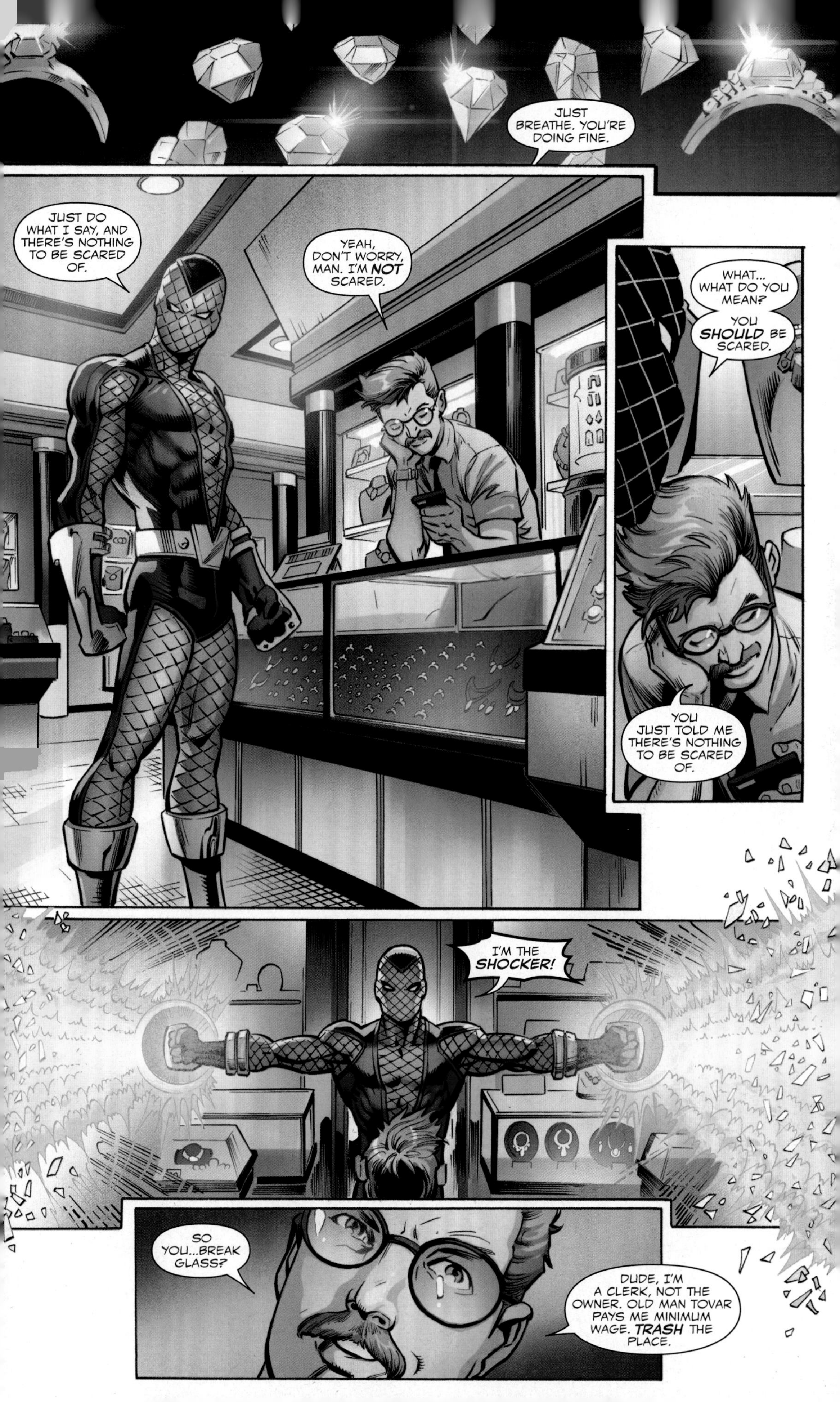
JUST BREATHE. YOU'RE DOING FINE.
JUST DO WHAT I SAY, AND THERE'S NOTHING TO BE SCARED OF.
YEAH, DON'T WORRY, MAN. I'M NOT SCARED.
WHAT... WHAT DO YOU MEAN?
YOU SHOULD BE SCARED.
YOU JUST TOLD ME THERE'S NOTHING TO BE SCARED OF.
I'M THE SHOCKER!
SO YOU...BREAK GLASS?
DUDE, I'M A CLERK, NOT THE OWNER. OLD MAN TOVAR PAYS ME MINIMUM WAGE. TRASH THE PLACE.

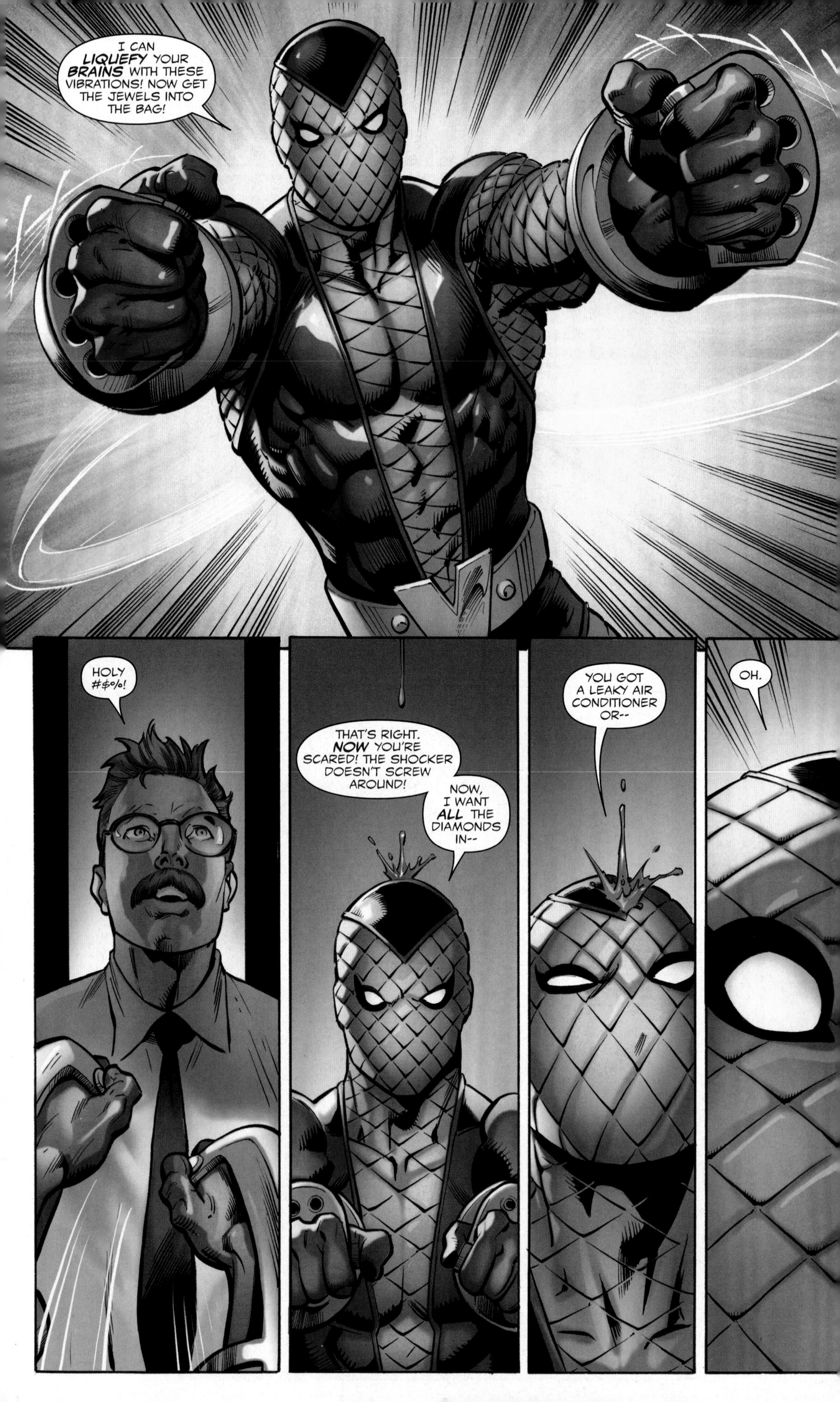

I CAN LIQUEFY YOUR BRAINS WITH THESE VIBRATIONS! NOW GET THE JEWELS INTO THE BAG!
HOLY #$%!
THAT'S RIGHT. NOW YOU'RE SCARED! THE SHOCKER DOESN'T SCREW AROUND!
NOW, I WANT ALL THE DIAMONDS IN--
YOU GOT A LEAKY AIR CONDITIONER OR--
OH.

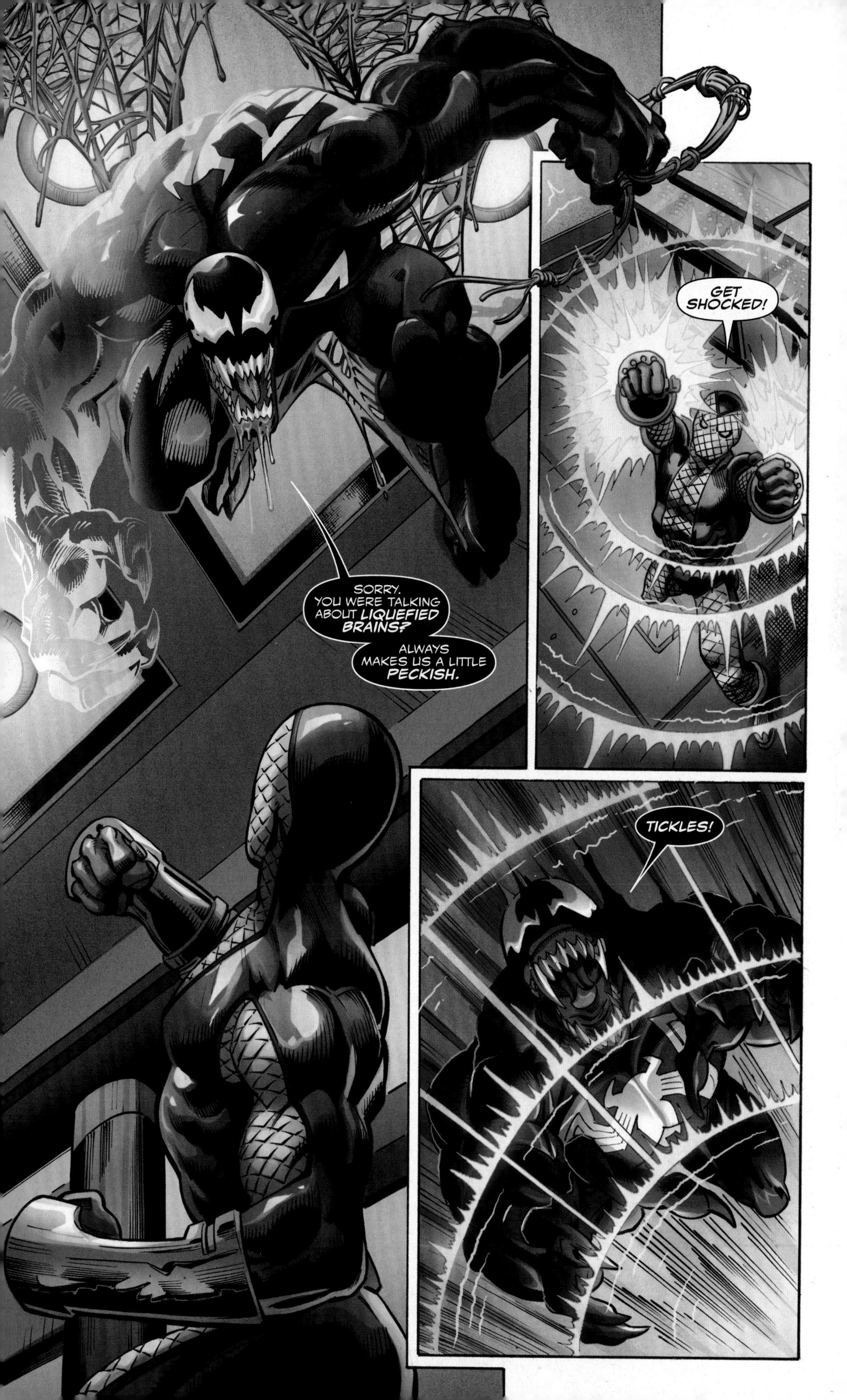
SORRY. YOU WERE TALKING ABOUT LIQUEFIED BRAINS?
ALWAYS MAKES US A LITTLE PECKISH.
GET SHOCKED!
TICKLES!

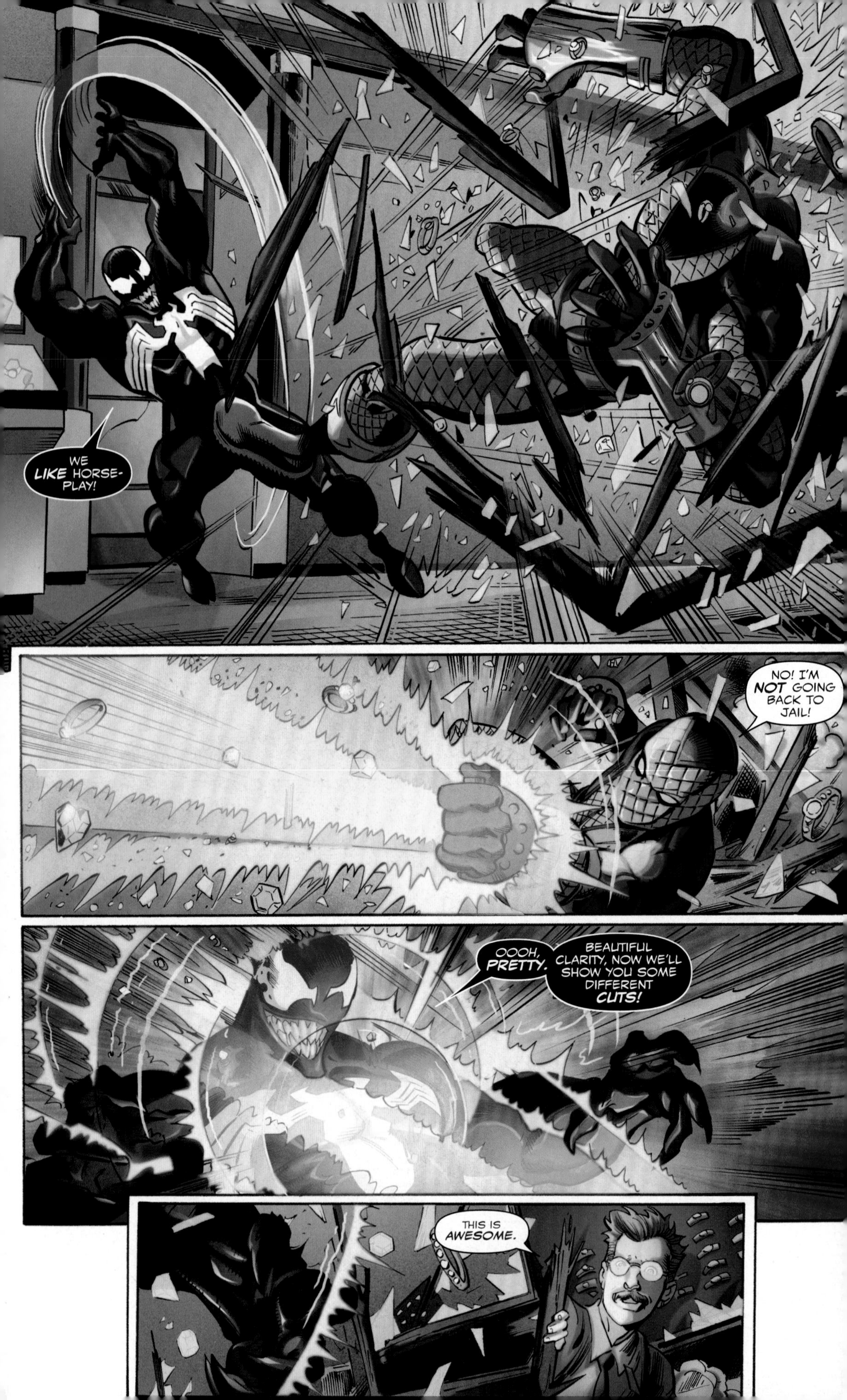
WE LIKE HORSE-PLAY!
NO! I'M NOT GOING BACK TO JAIL!
OOOH, PRETTY.
BEAUTIFUL CLARITY, NOW WE'LL SHOW YOU SOME DIFFERENT CUTS!
THIS IS AWESOME.

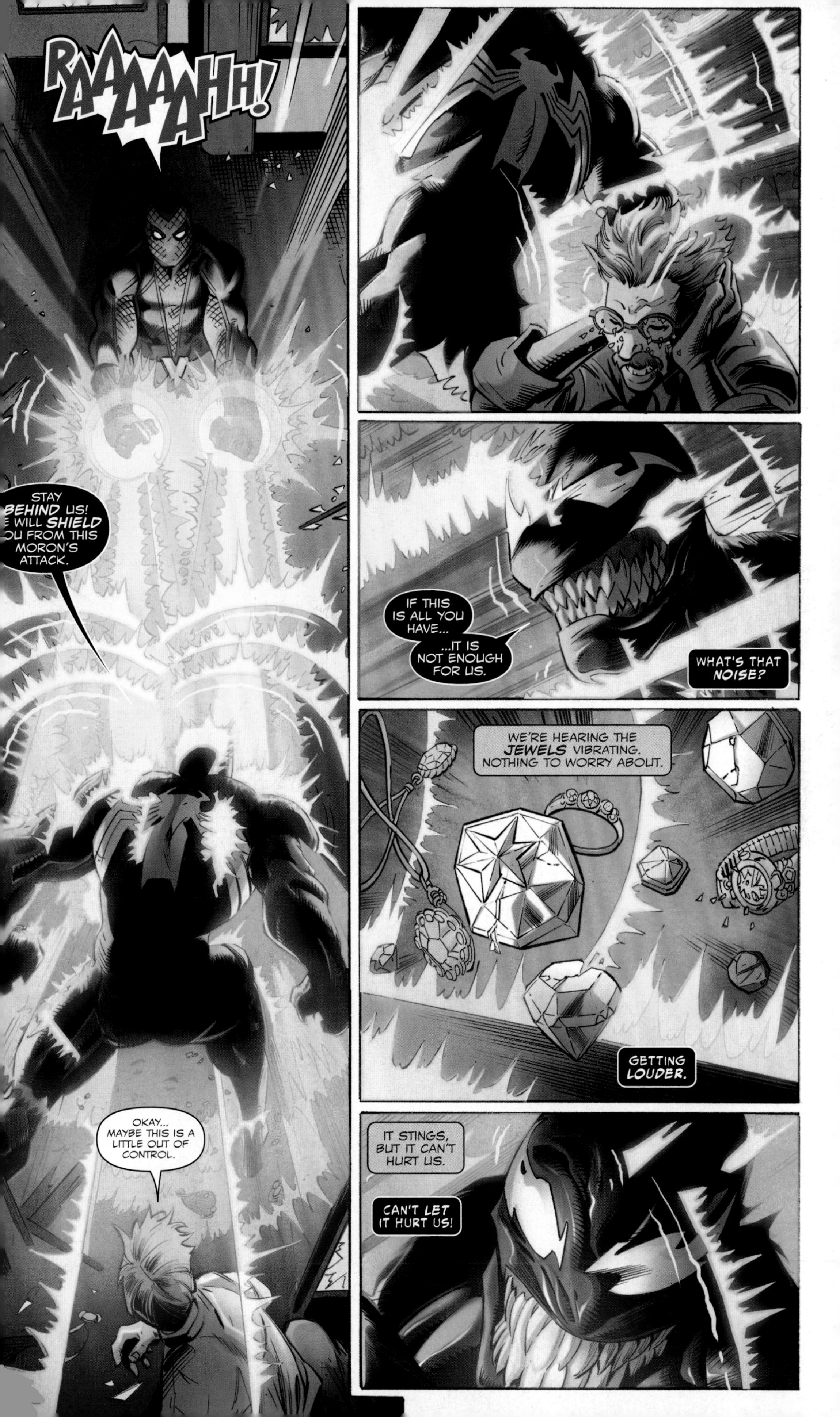
RAAAAAHH!
STAY BEHIND US! E WILL SHIELD OU FROM THIS MORON'S ATTACK.
OKAY... MAYBE THIS IS A LITTLE OUT OF CONTROL.
IF THIS IS ALL YOU HAVE...
...IT IS NOT ENOUGH FOR US.
WHAT'S THAT NOISE?
WE'RE HEARING THE JEWELS VIBRATING. NOTHING TO WORRY ABOUT.
GETTING LOUDER.
IT STINGS, BUT IT CAN'T HURT US.
CAN'T LET IT HURT US!

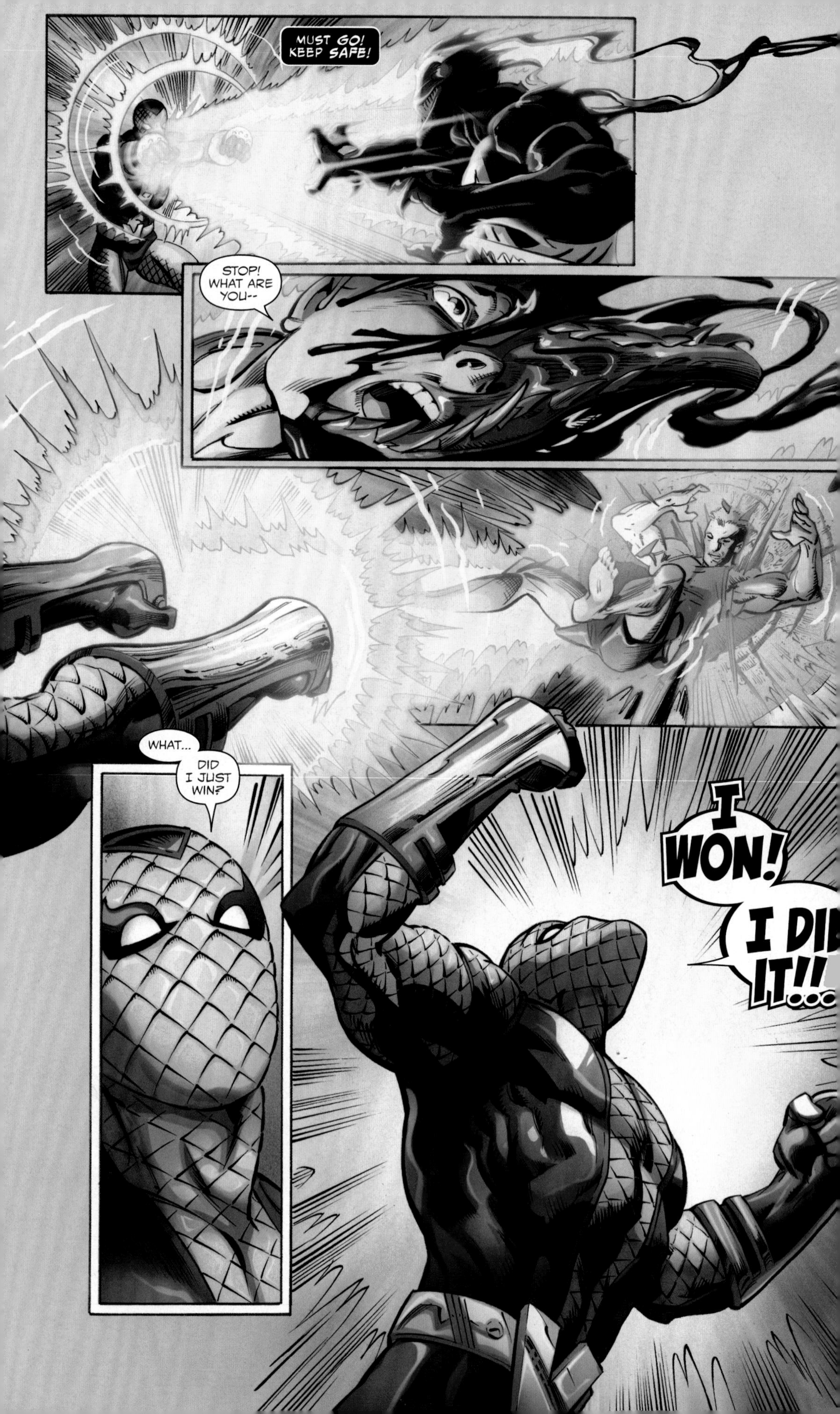
MUST GO! KEEP SAFE!
STOP! WHAT ARE YOU--
WHAT...
DID I JUST WIN?
I WON!
I DI
IT!!...

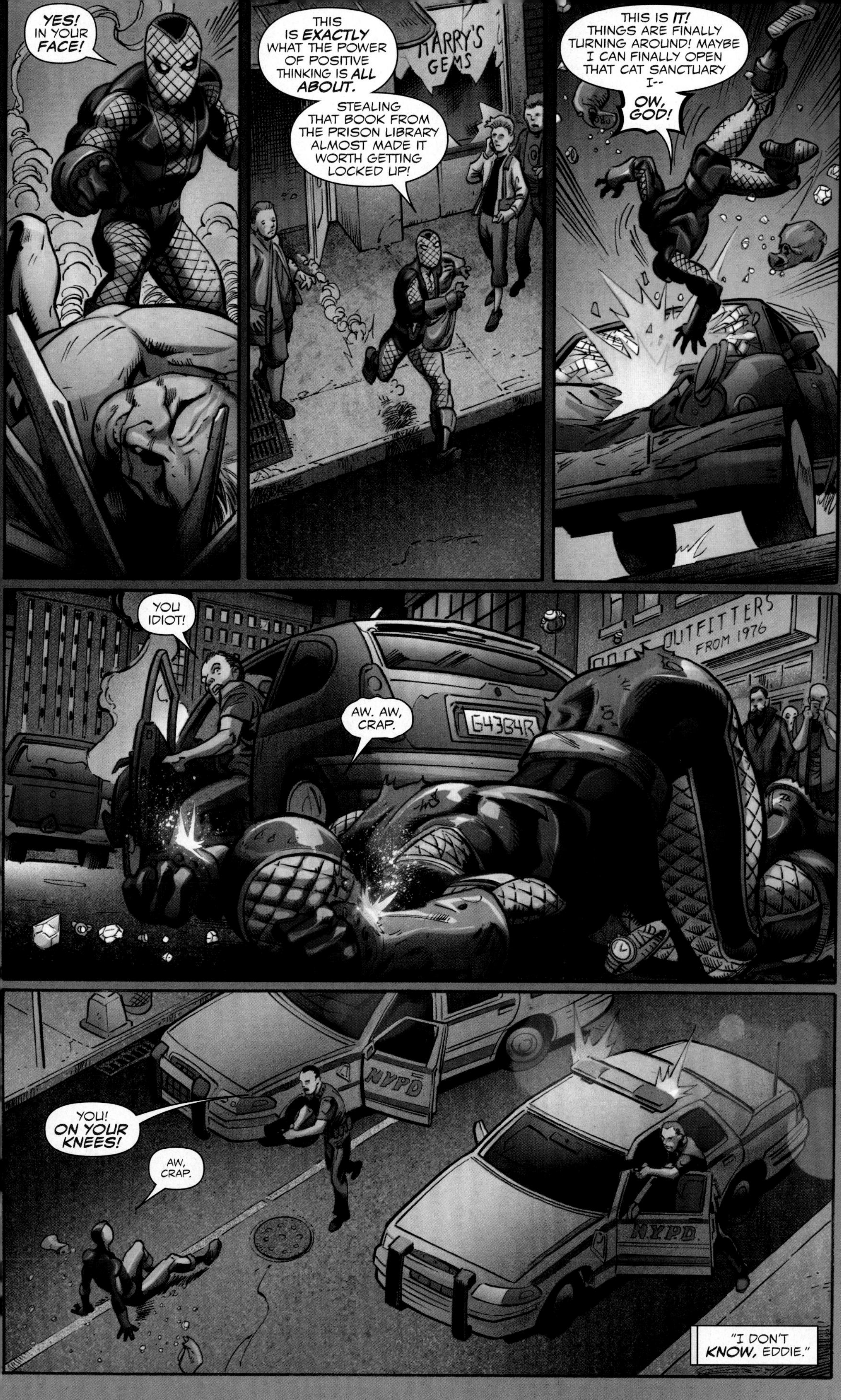

YES! IN YOUR FACE!
HARRY'S GEMS
THIS IS EXACTLY WHAT THE POWER OF POSITIVE THINKING IS ALL ABOUT.
STEALING THAT BOOK FROM THE PRISON LIBRARY ALMOST MADE IT WORTH GETTING LOCKED UP!
THIS IS IT! THINGS ARE FINALLY TURNING AROUND! MAYBE I CAN FINALLY OPEN THAT CAT SANCTUARY I--
OW, GOD!
YOU IDIOT!
OUTFITTERS FROM 1976
AW. AW, CRAP.
G43B4R
NYPD
YOU! ON YOUR KNEES!
AW, CRAP.
N.Y.P.D.
"I DON'T KNOW, EDDIE."

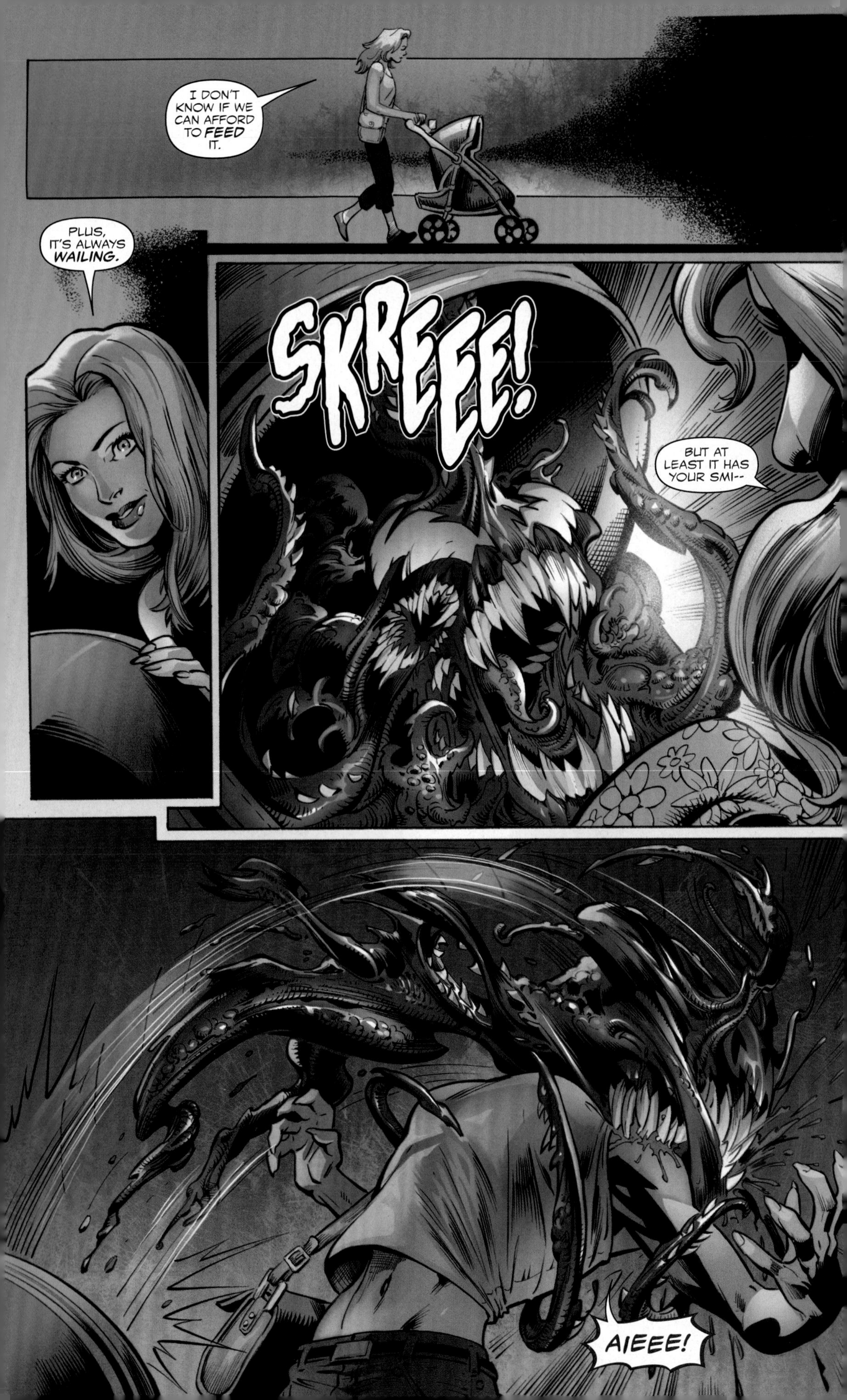
I DON'T KNOW IF WE CAN AFFORD TO FEED IT.
PLUS, IT'S ALWAYS WAILING.
SKREEEE!
BUT AT LEAST IT HAS YOUR SMI--
AIEEE!

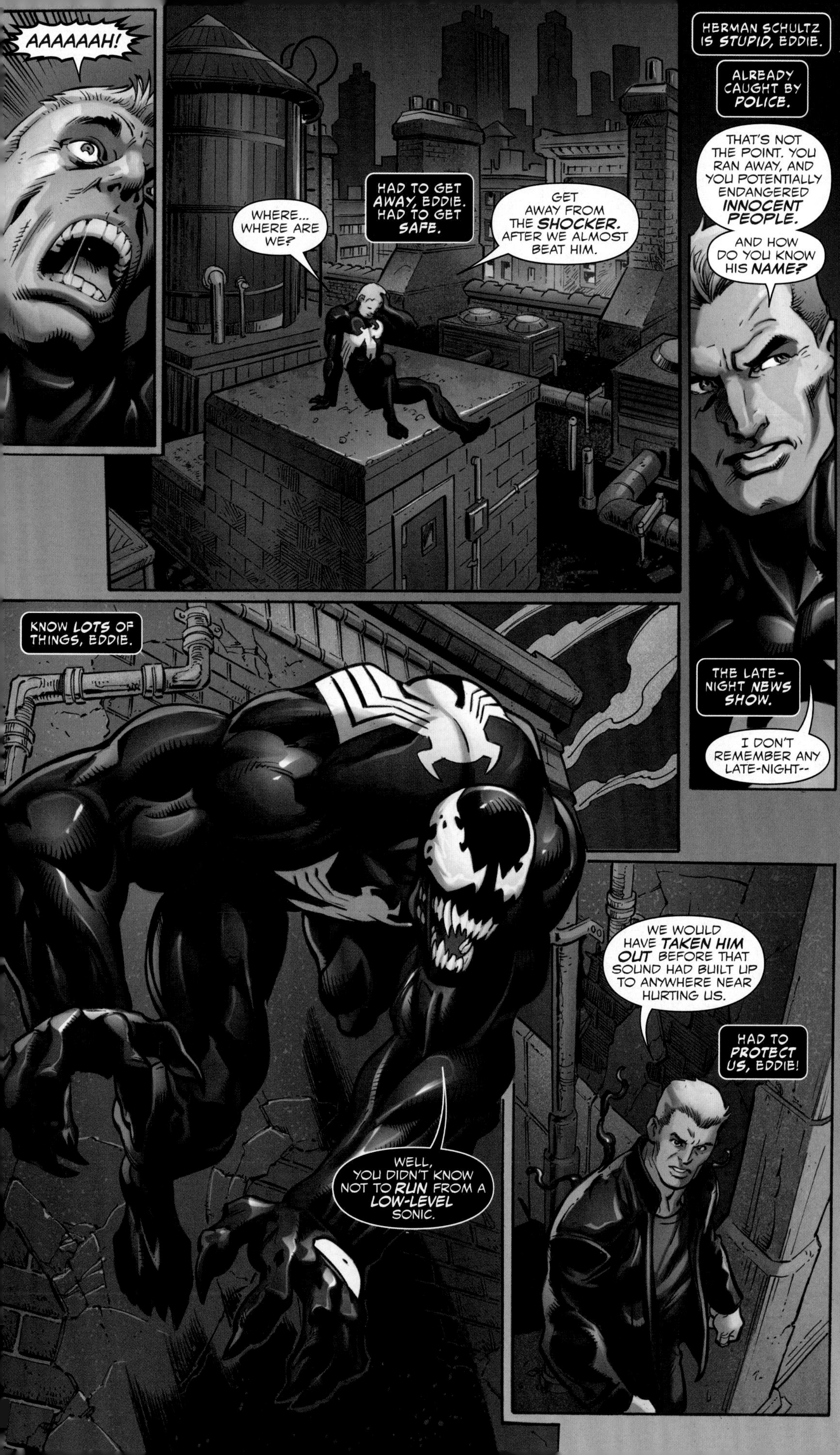
AAAAAAH!
WHERE... WHERE ARE WE?
HAD TO GET AWAY, EDDIE. HAD TO GET SAFE.
GET AWAY FROM THE SHOCKER. AFTER WE ALMOST BEAT HIM.
HERMAN SCHULTZ IS STUPID, EDDIE.
ALREADY CAUGHT BY POLICE.
THAT'S NOT THE POINT. YOU RAN AWAY, AND YOU POTENTIALLY ENDANGERED INNOCENT PEOPLE.
AND HOW DO YOU KNOW HIS NAME?
KNOW LOTS OF THINGS, EDDIE.
THE LATE-NIGHT NEWS SHOW.
I DON'T REMEMBER ANY LATE-NIGHT--
WELL, YOU DIDN'T KNOW NOT TO RUN FROM A LOW-LEVEL SONIC.
WE WOULD HAVE TAKEN HIM OUT BEFORE THAT SOUND HAD BUILT UP TO ANYWHERE NEAR HURTING US.
HAD TO PROTECT US, EDDIE!

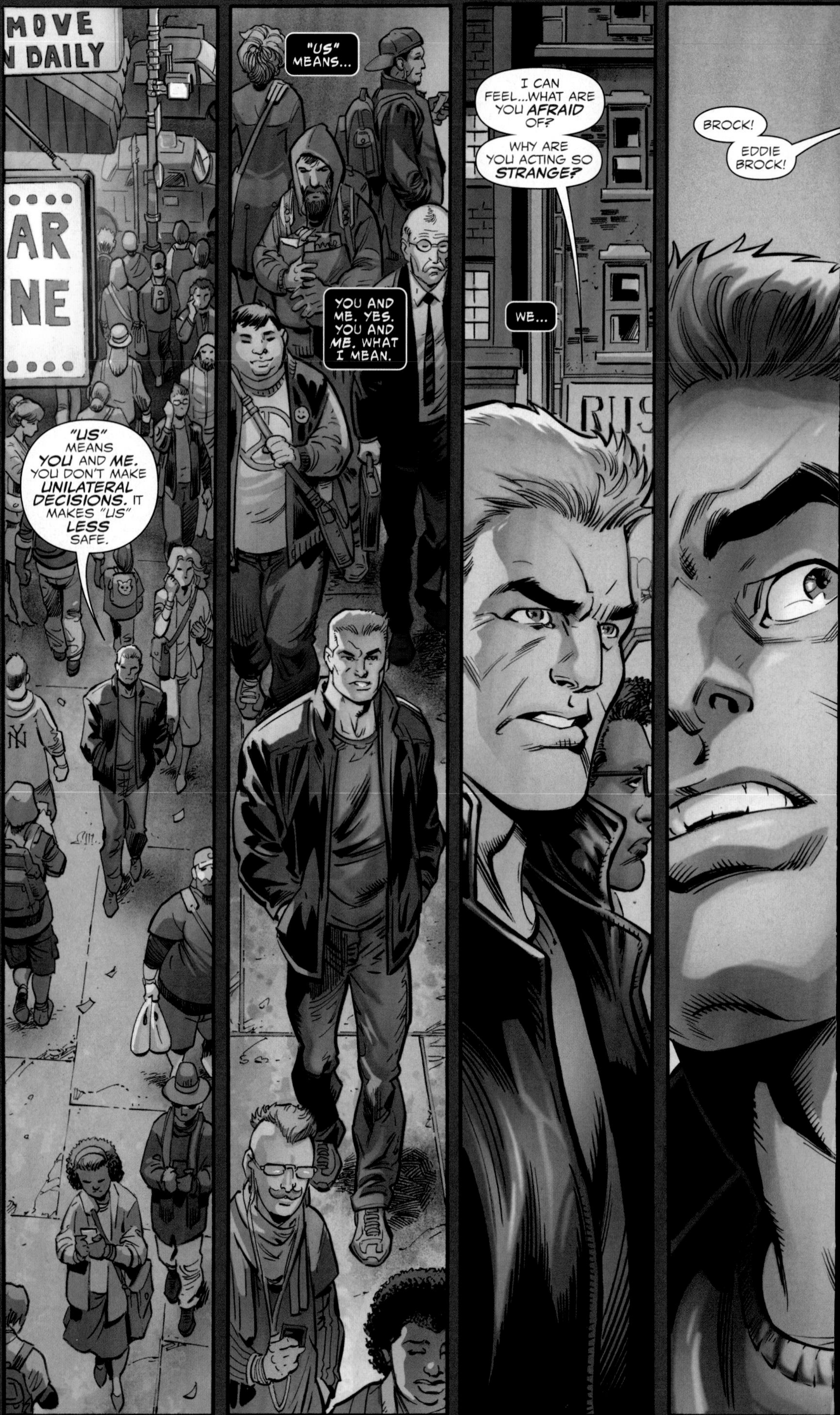

MOVE
N DAILY
AR
NE
"US" MEANS YOU AND ME. YOU DON'T MAKE UNILATERAL DECISIONS. IT MAKES "US" LESS SAFE.
"US" MEANS...
YOU AND ME. YES. YOU AND ME. WHAT I MEAN.
I CAN FEEL...WHAT ARE YOU AFRAID OF?
WHY ARE YOU ACTING SO STRANGE?
WE...
BROCK!
EDDIE BROCK!

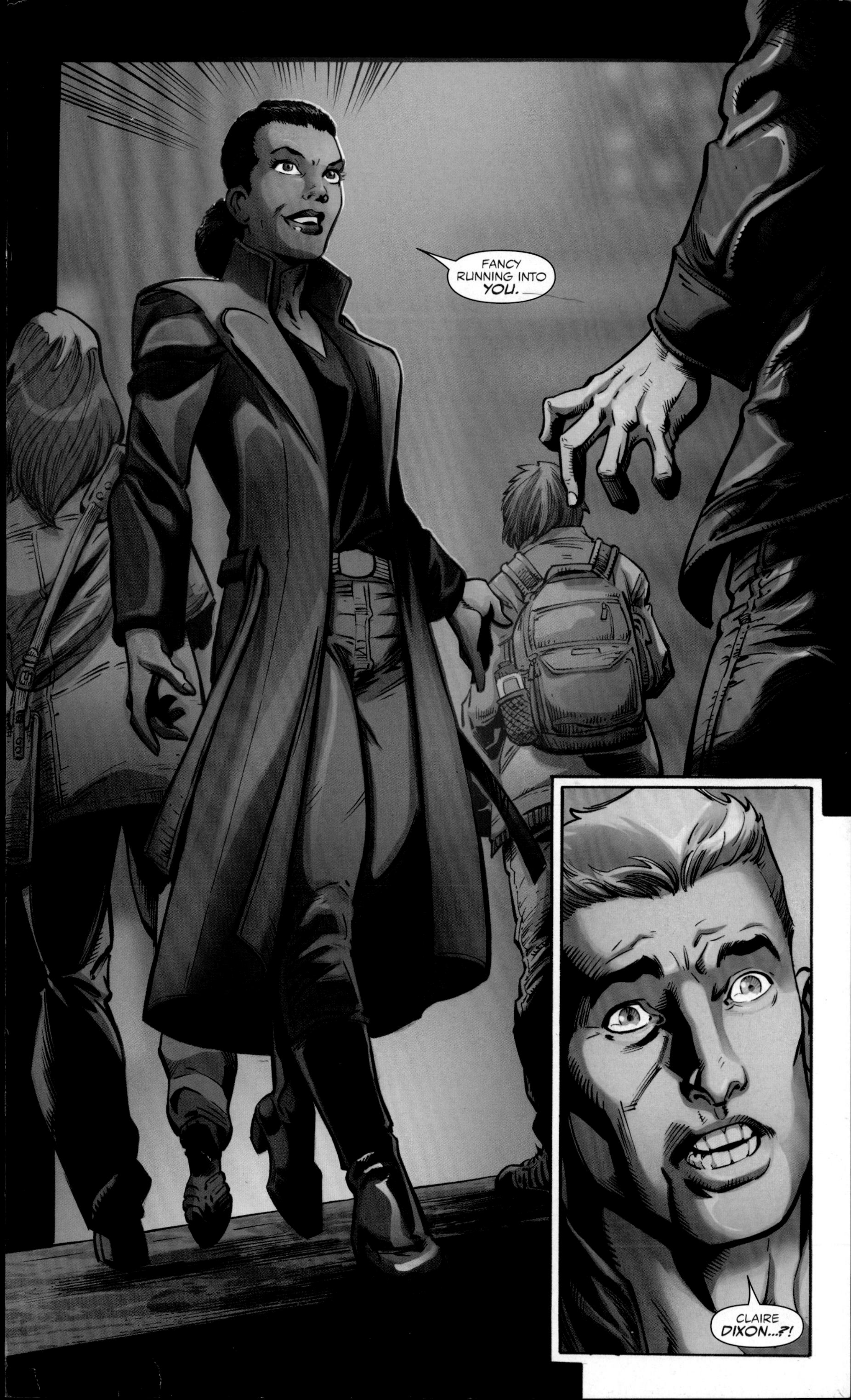
FANCY RUNNING INTO YOU.
CLAIRE DIXON...?!

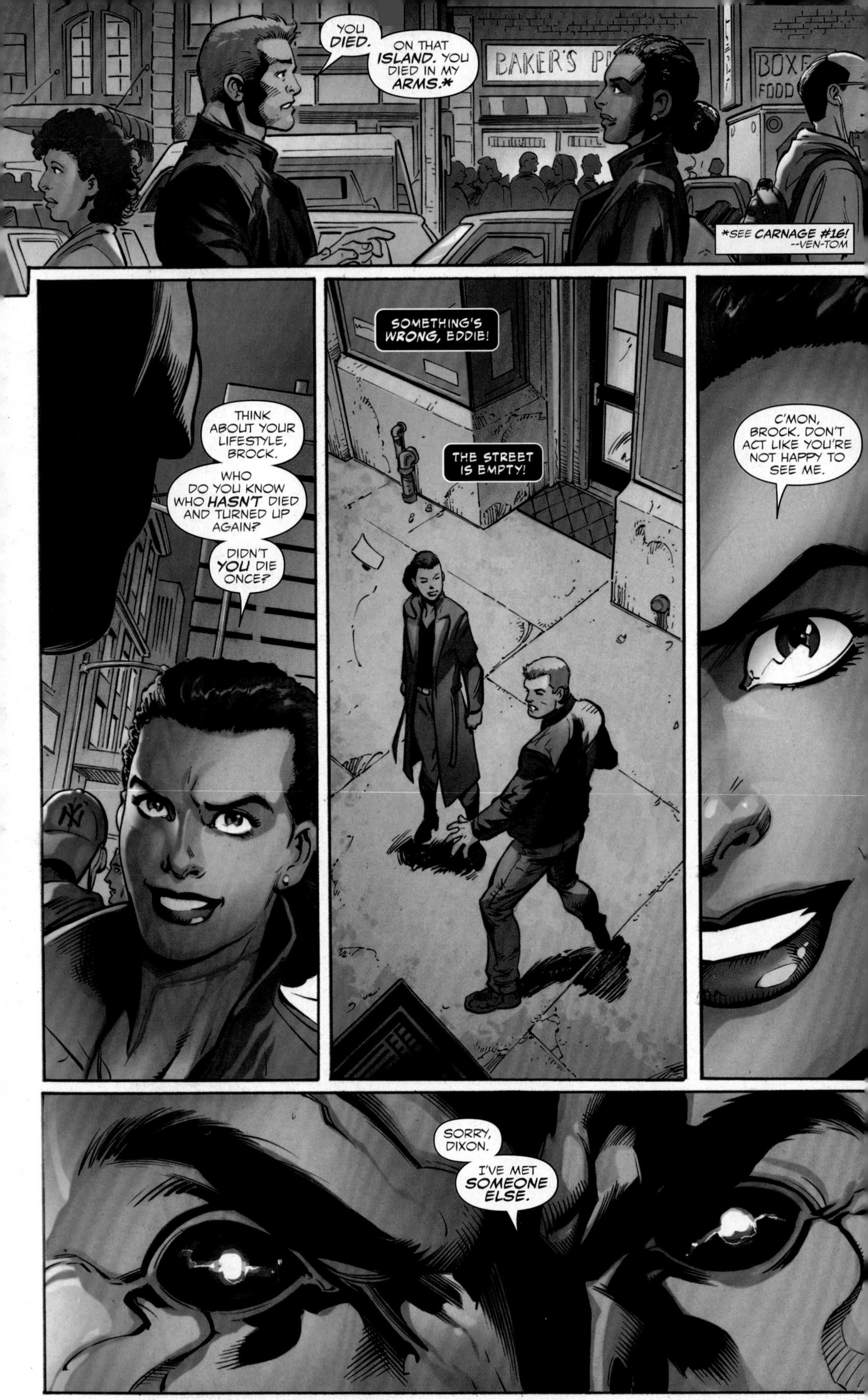

YOU DIED.
ON THAT ISLAND. YOU DIED IN MY ARMS.*
*SEE CARNAGE #16! --VEN-TOM
THINK ABOUT YOUR LIFESTYLE, BROCK.
WHO DO YOU KNOW WHO HASN'T DIED AND TURNED UP AGAIN?
DIDN'T YOU DIE ONCE?
SOMETHING'S WRONG, EDDIE!
THE STREET IS EMPTY!
C'MON, BROCK. DON'T ACT LIKE YOU'RE NOT HAPPY TO SEE ME.
SORRY, DIXON.
I'VE MET SOMEONE ELSE.

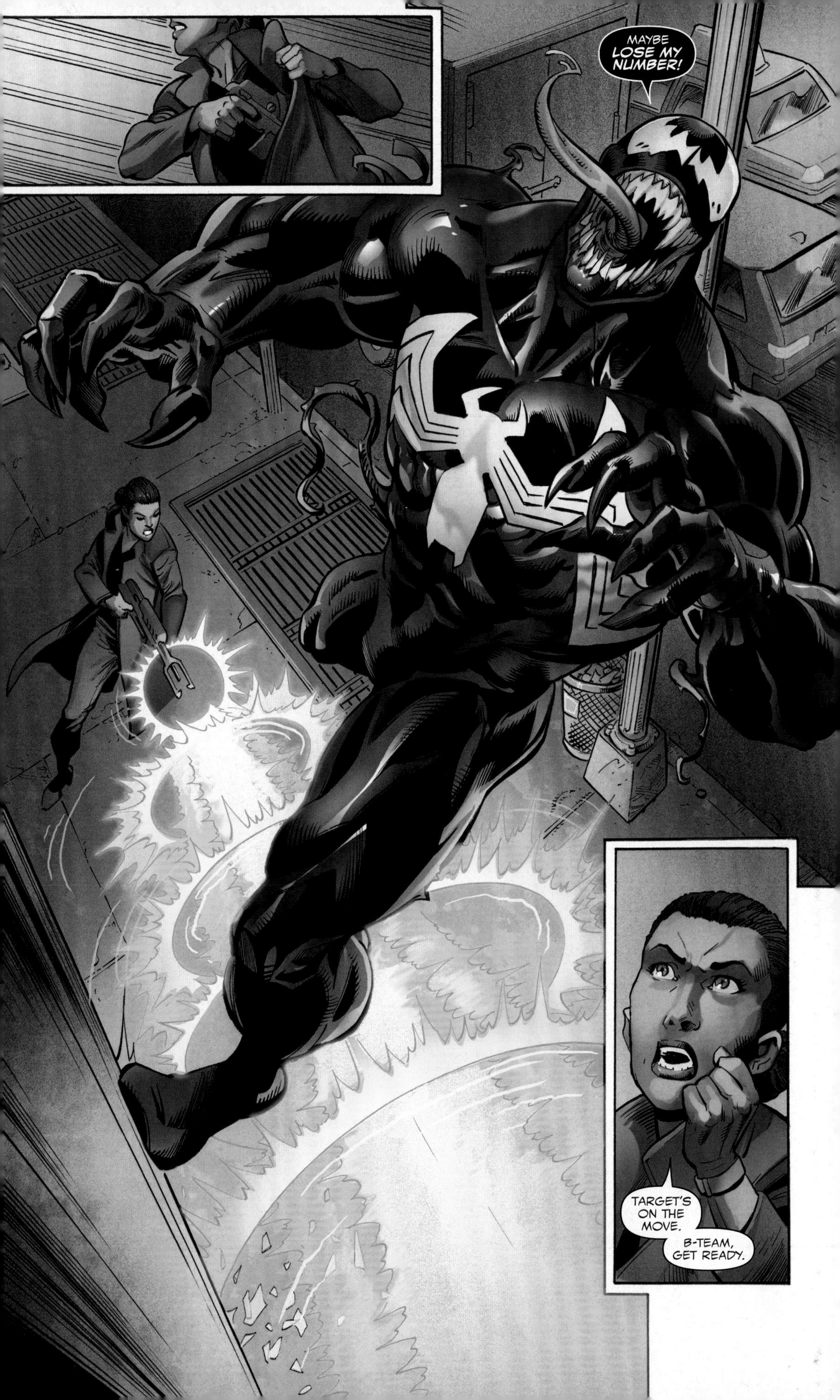
MAYBE LOSE MY NUMBER!
TARGET'S ON THE MOVE.
B-TEAM, GET READY.

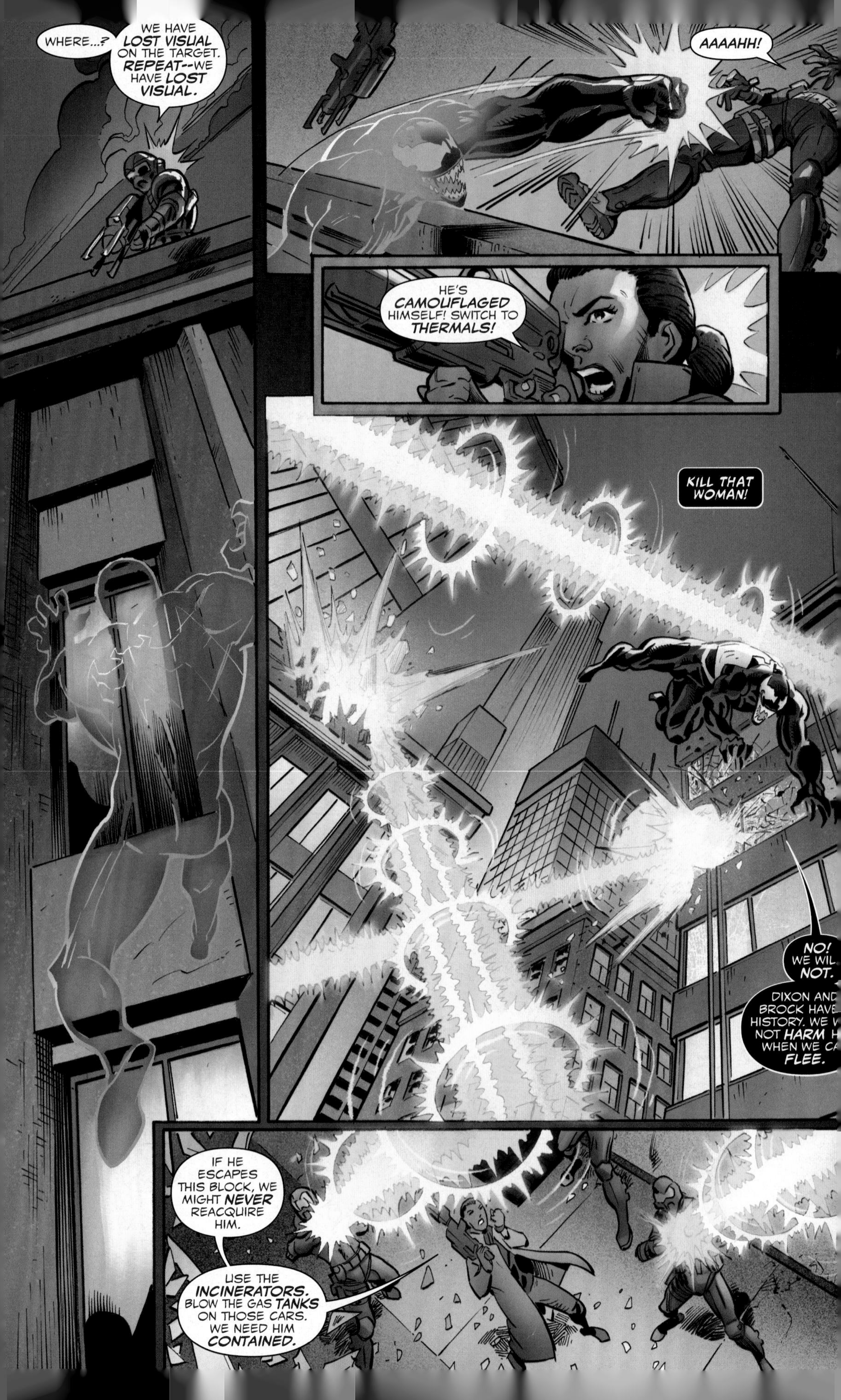
WHERE...?
WE HAVE LOST VISUAL ON THE TARGET. REPEAT--WE HAVE LOST VISUAL.
AAAAHH!
HE'S CAMOUFLAGED HIMSELF! SWITCH TO THERMALS!
KILL THAT WOMAN!
NO! WE WIL NOT.
DIXON AND BROCK HAVE HISTORY. WE W NOT HARM H WHEN WE CA FLEE.
IF HE ESCAPES THIS BLOCK, WE MIGHT NEVER REACQUIRE HIM.
USE THE INCINERATORS. BLOW THE GAS TANKS ON THOSE CARS. WE NEED HIM CONTAINED.

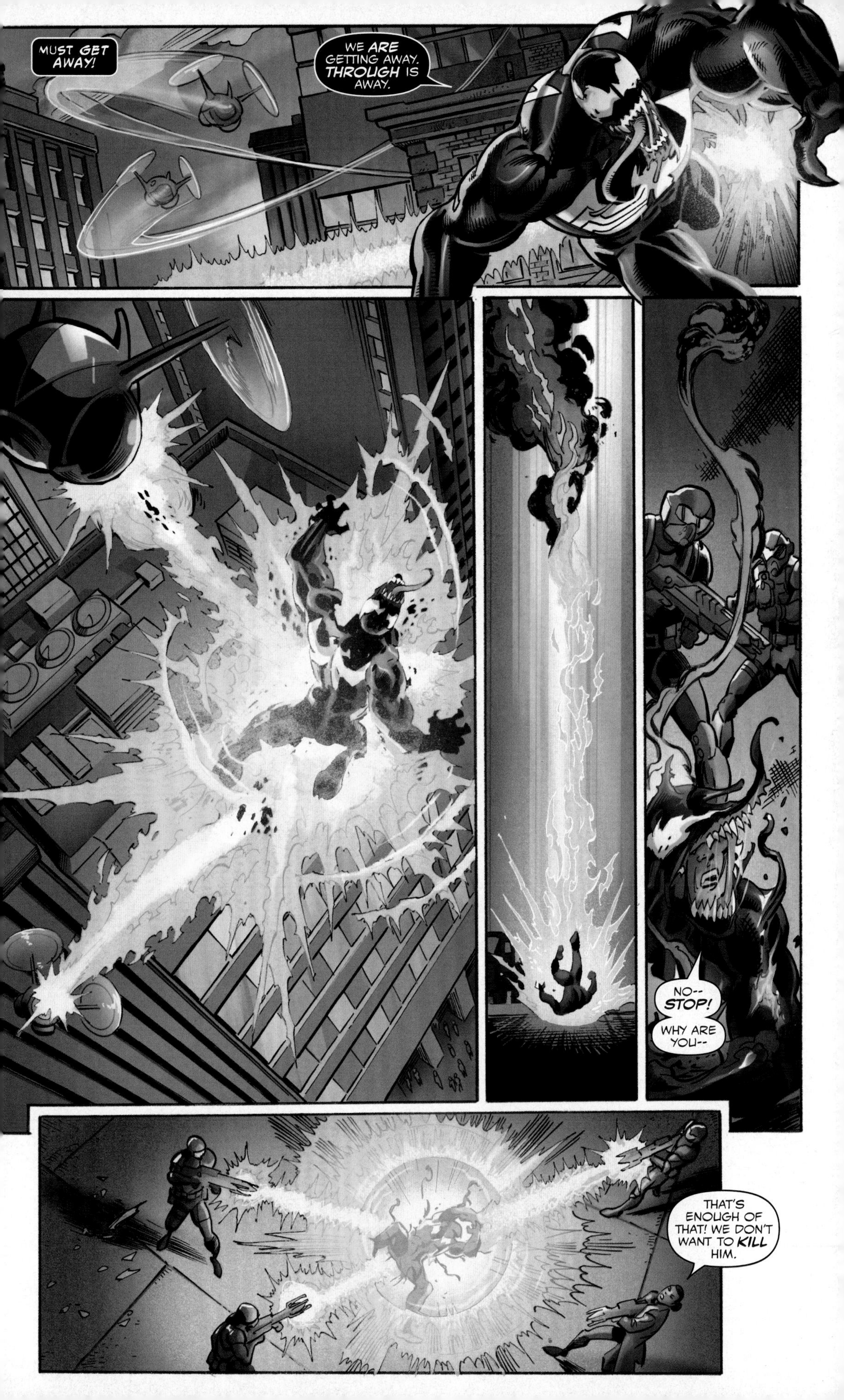
MUST GET AWAY!
WE ARE GETTING AWAY. THROUGH IS AWAY.
NO-- STOP!
WHY ARE YOU--
THAT'S ENOUGH OF THAT! WE DON'T WANT TO KILL HIM.

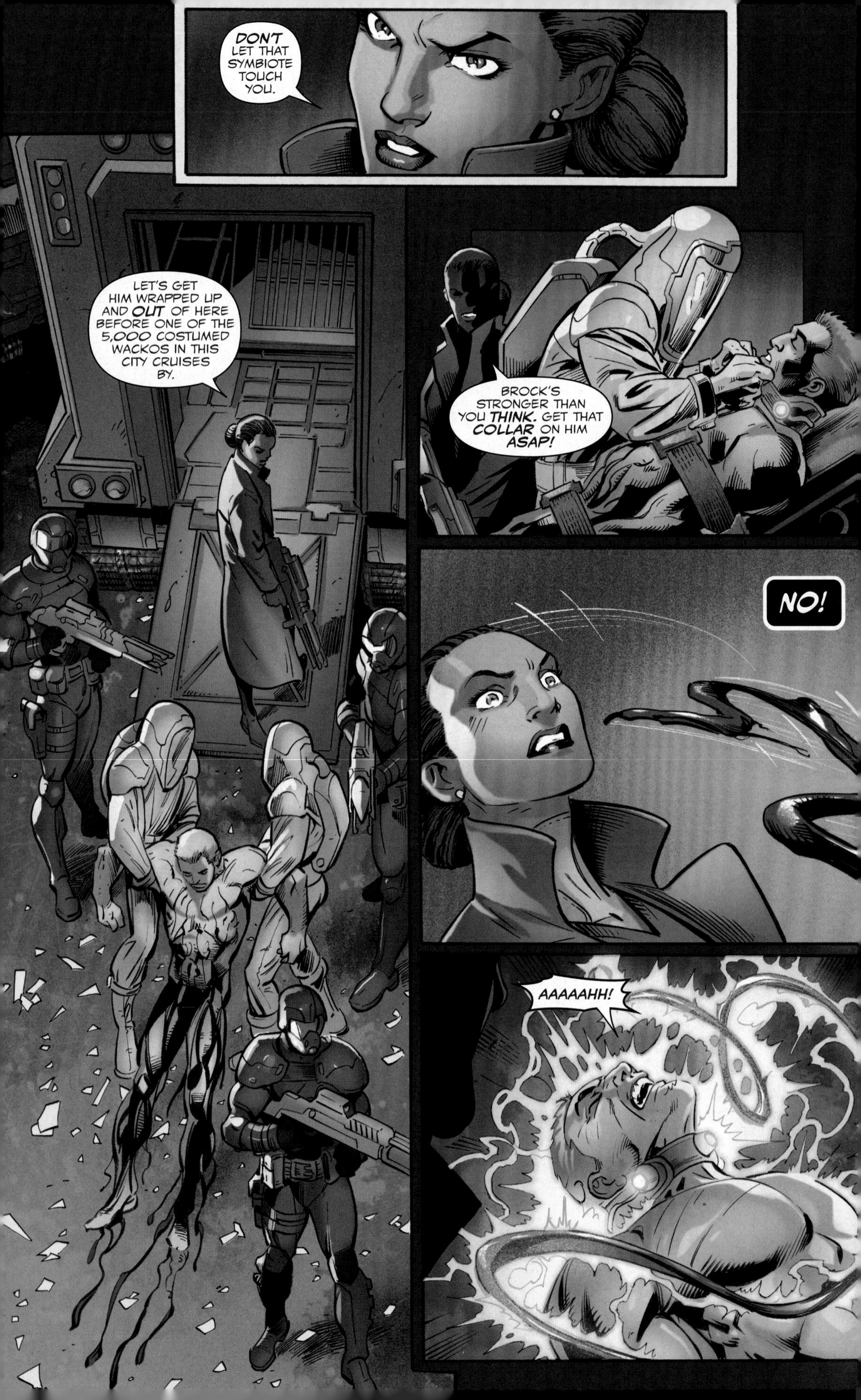
DON'T LET THAT SYMBIOTE TOUCH YOU.
LET'S GET HIM WRAPPED UP AND OUT OF HERE BEFORE ONE OF THE 5,000 COSTUMED WACKOS IN THIS CITY CRUISES BY.
BROCK'S STRONGER THAN YOU THINK. GET THAT COLLAR ON HIM ASAP!
NO!
AAAAAHH!

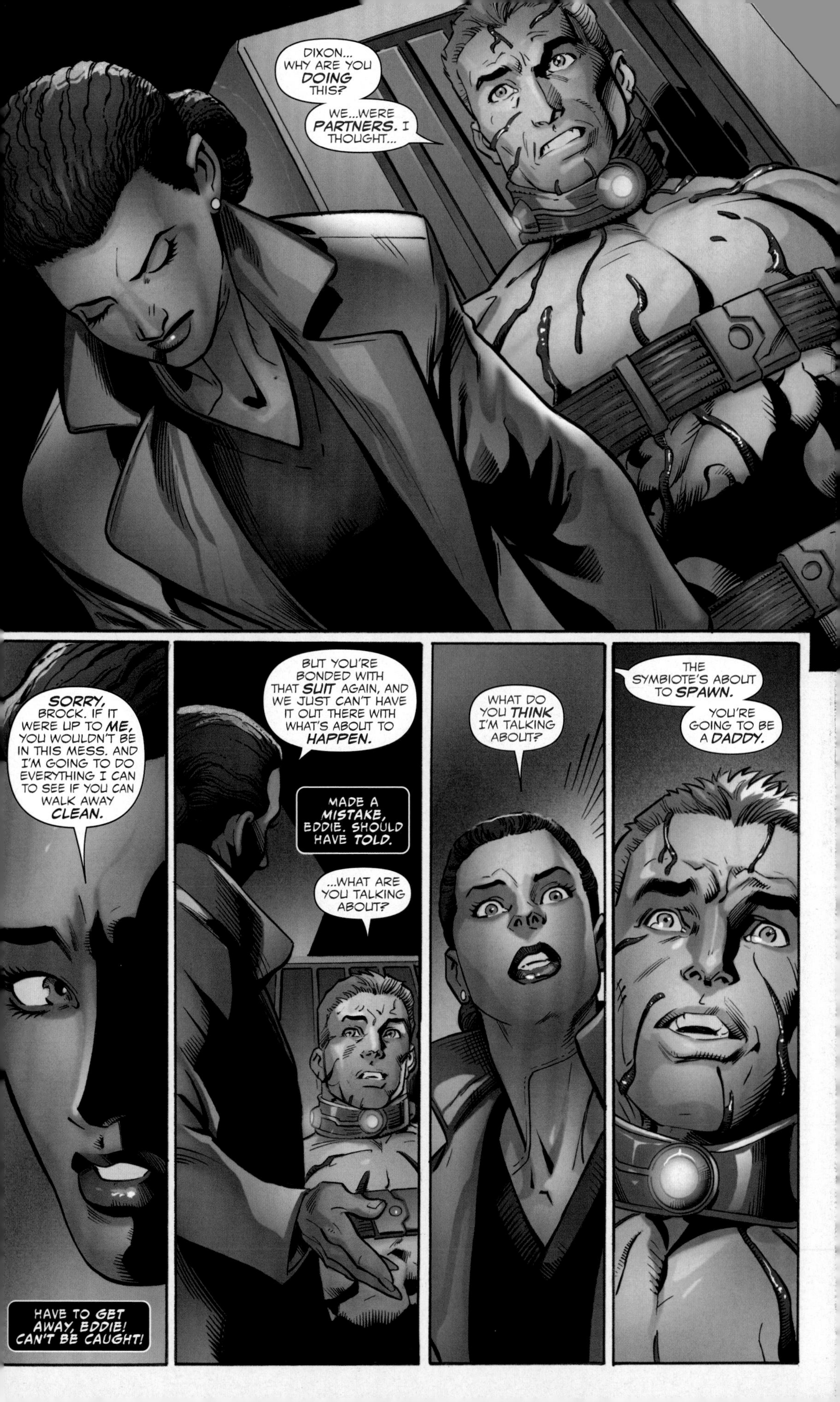

DIXON... WHY ARE YOU DOING THIS?
WE...WERE PARTNERS. I THOUGHT...
SORRY, BROCK. IF IT WERE UP TO ME, YOU WOULDN'T BE IN THIS MESS. AND I'M GOING TO DO EVERYTHING I CAN TO SEE IF YOU CAN WALK AWAY CLEAN.
HAVE TO GET AWAY, EDDIE! CAN'T BE CAUGHT!
BUT YOU'RE BONDED WITH THAT SUIT AGAIN, AND WE JUST CAN'T HAVE IT OUT THERE WITH WHAT'S ABOUT TO HAPPEN.
MADE A MISTAKE, EDDIE. SHOULD HAVE TOLD.
...WHAT ARE YOU TALKING ABOUT?
WHAT DO YOU THINK I'M TALKING ABOUT?
THE SYMBIOTE'S ABOUT TO SPAWN.
YOU'RE GOING TO BE A DADDY.

165

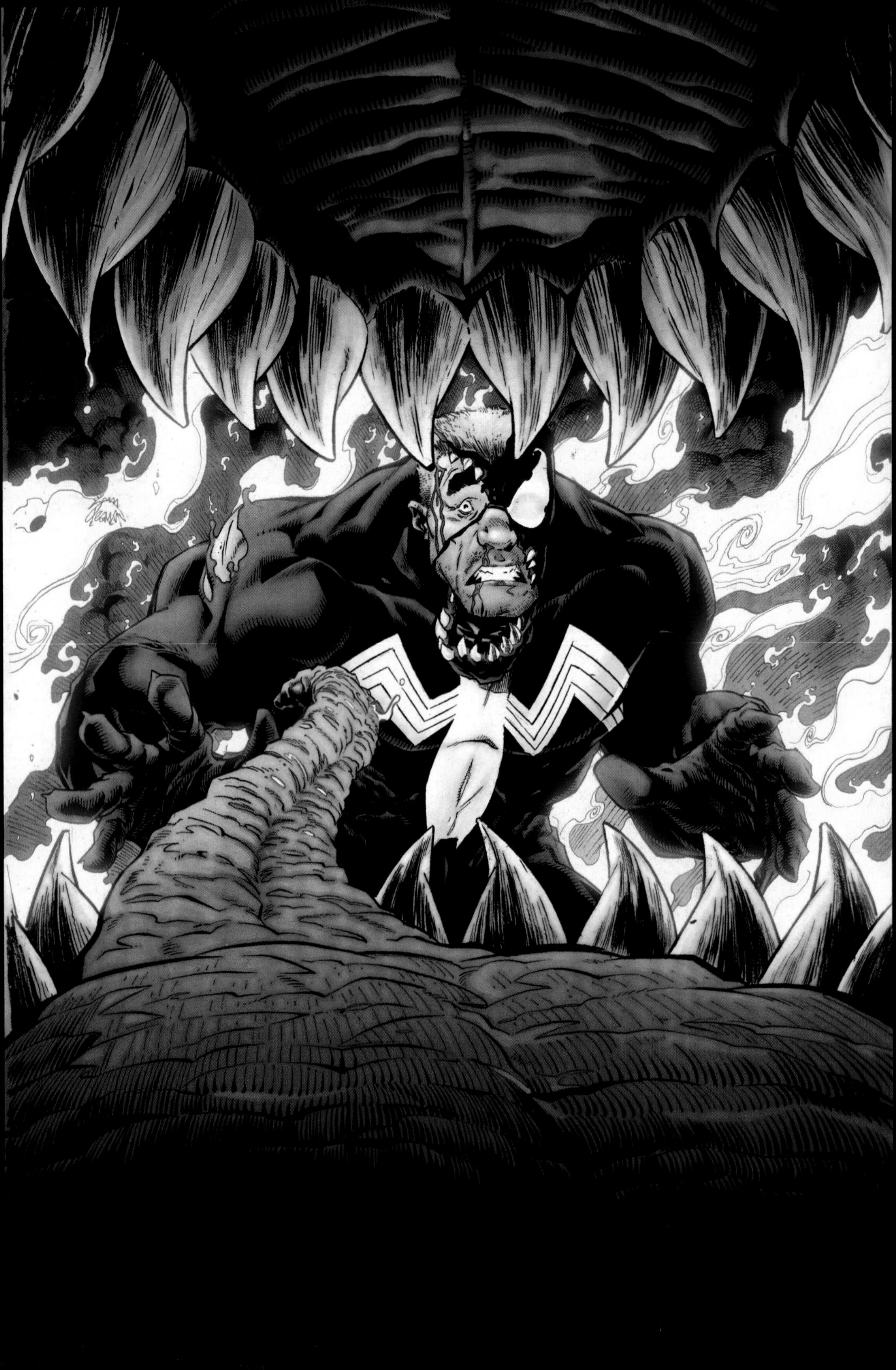

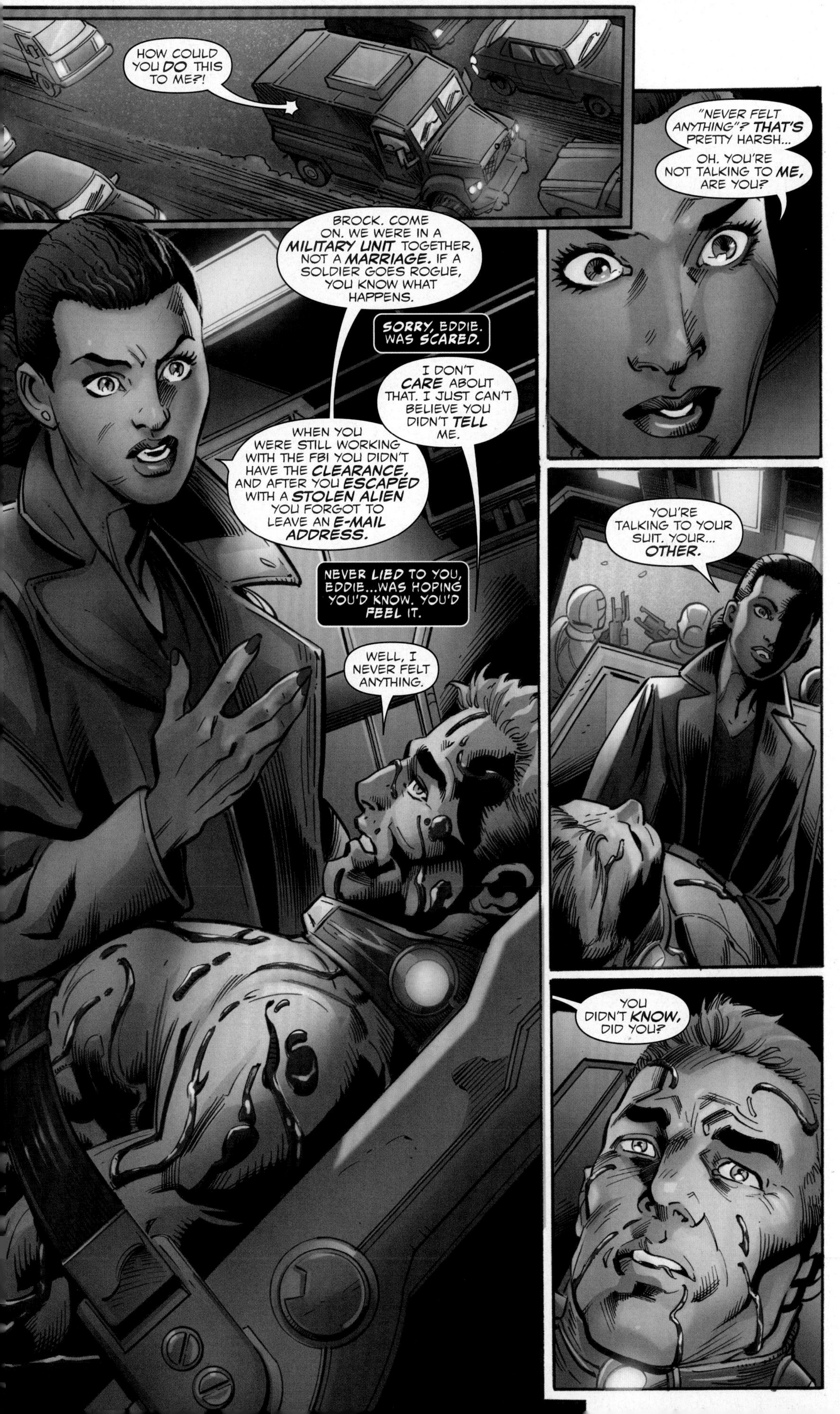
HOW COULD YOU DO THIS TO ME?!
BROCK. COME ON. WE WERE IN A MILITARY UNIT TOGETHER, NOT A MARRIAGE. IF A SOLDIER GOES ROGUE, YOU KNOW WHAT HAPPENS.
SORRY, EDDIE. WAS SCARED.
I DON'T CARE ABOUT THAT. I JUST CAN'T BELIEVE YOU DIDN'T TELL ME.
WHEN YOU WERE STILL WORKING WITH THE FBI YOU DIDN'T HAVE THE CLEARANCE, AND AFTER YOU ESCAPED WITH A STOLEN ALIEN YOU FORGOT TO LEAVE AN E-MAIL ADDRESS.
NEVER LIED TO YOU, EDDIE...WAS HOPING YOU'D KNOW. YOU'D FEEL IT.
WELL, I NEVER FELT ANYTHING.
"NEVER FELT ANYTHING"? THAT'S PRETTY HARSH...
OH. YOU'RE NOT TALKING TO ME, ARE YOU?
YOU'RE TALKING TO YOUR SUIT. YOUR... OTHER.
YOU DIDN'T KNOW, DID YOU?

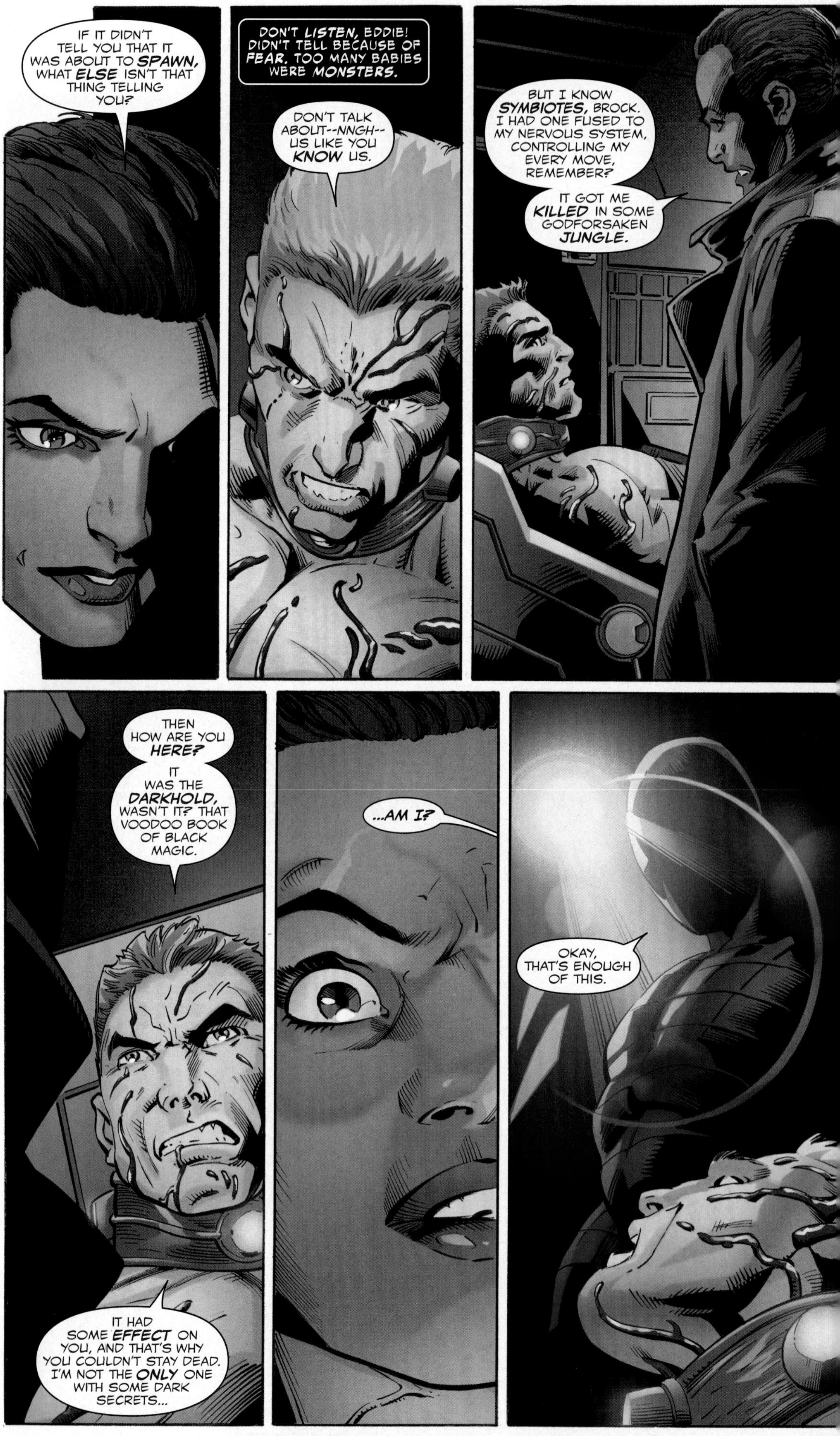
IF IT DIDN'T TELL YOU THAT IT WAS ABOUT TO SPAWN, WHAT ELSE ISN'T THAT THING TELLING YOU?
DON'T LISTEN, EDDIE! DIDN'T TELL BECAUSE OF FEAR. TOO MANY BABIES WERE MONSTERS.
DON'T TALK ABOUT--NNGH-- US LIKE YOU KNOW US.
BUT I KNOW SYMBIOTES, BROCK. I HAD ONE FUSED TO MY NERVOUS SYSTEM, CONTROLLING MY EVERY MOVE, REMEMBER?
IT GOT ME KILLED IN SOME GODFORSAKEN JUNGLE.
THEN HOW ARE YOU HERE?
IT WAS THE DARKHOLD, WASN'T IT? THAT VOODOO BOOK OF BLACK MAGIC.
IT HAD SOME EFFECT ON YOU, AND THAT'S WHY YOU COULDN'T STAY DEAD. I'M NOT THE ONLY ONE WITH SOME DARK SECRETS...
...AM I?
OKAY, THAT'S ENOUGH OF THIS.

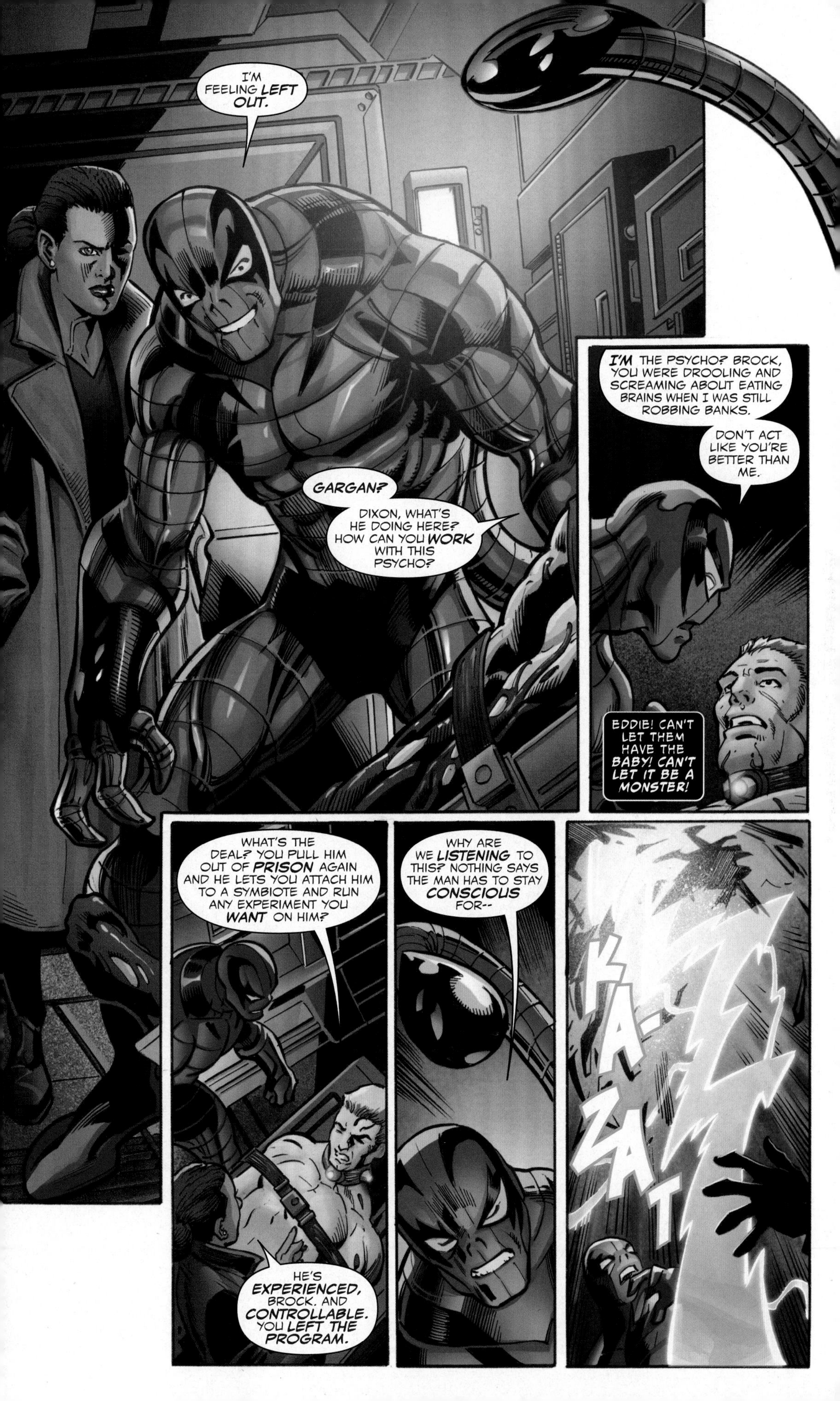

I'M FEELING LEFT OUT.
GARGAN?
DIXON, WHAT'S HE DOING HERE? HOW CAN YOU WORK WITH THIS PSYCHO?
I'M THE PSYCHO? BROCK, YOU WERE DROOLING AND SCREAMING ABOUT EATING BRAINS WHEN I WAS STILL ROBBING BANKS.
DON'T ACT LIKE YOU'RE BETTER THAN ME.
EDDIE! CAN'T LET THEM HAVE THE BABY! CAN'T LET IT BE A MONSTER!
WHAT'S THE DEAL? YOU PULL HIM OUT OF PRISON AGAIN AND HE LETS YOU ATTACH HIM TO A SYMBIOTE AND RUN ANY EXPERIMENT YOU WANT ON HIM?
HE'S EXPERIENCED, BROCK. AND CONTROLLABLE. YOU LEFT THE PROGRAM.
WHY ARE WE LISTENING TO THIS? NOTHING SAYS THE MAN HAS TO STAY CONSCIOUS FOR--
KA-ZAT

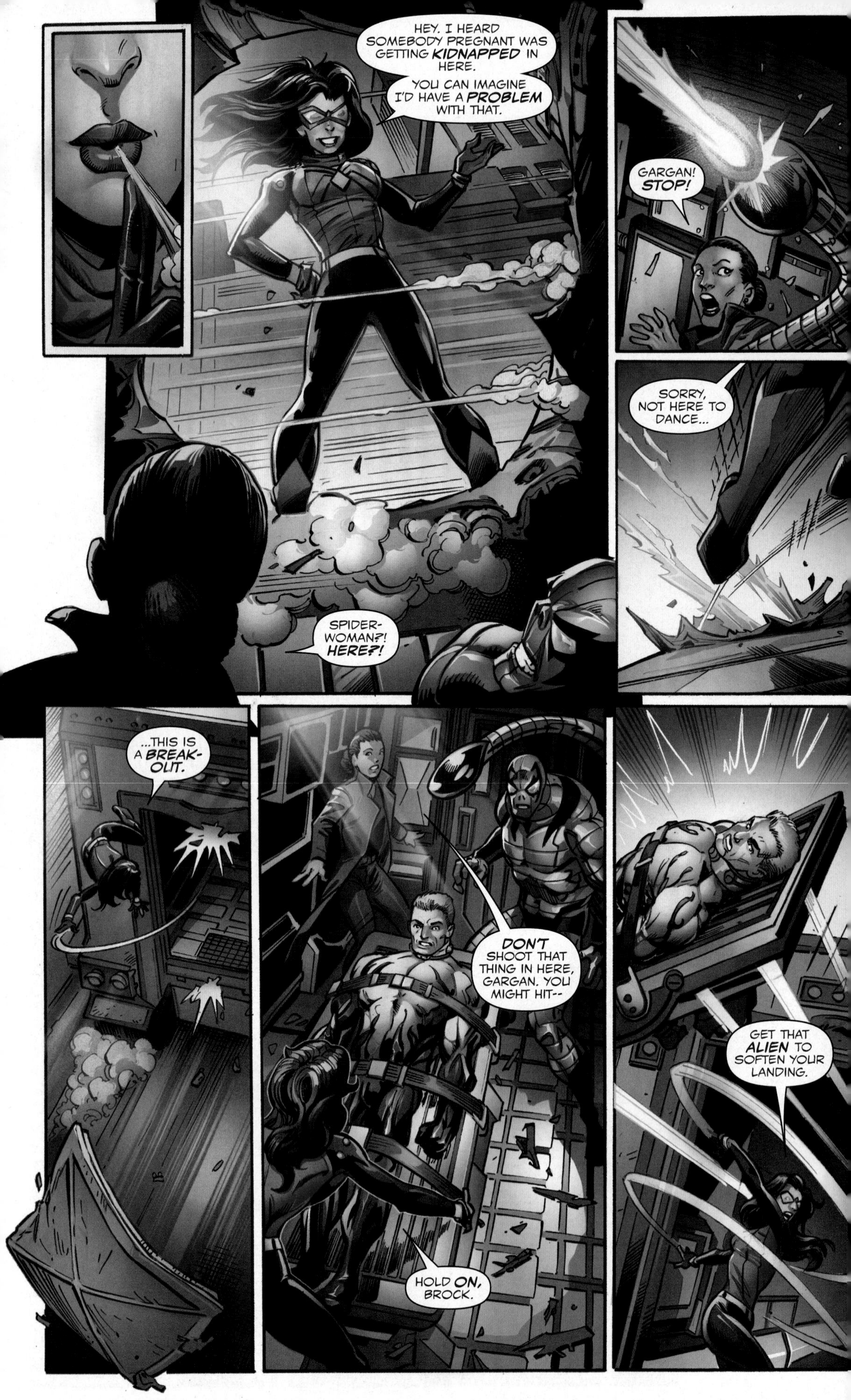
HEY. I HEARD SOMEBODY PREGNANT WAS GETTING KIDNAPPED IN HERE.
YOU CAN IMAGINE I'D HAVE A PROBLEM WITH THAT.
SPIDER-WOMAN?! HERE?!
GARGAN! STOP!
SORRY, NOT HERE TO DANCE...
...THIS IS A BREAK-OUT.
DON'T SHOOT THAT THING IN HERE, GARGAN. YOU MIGHT HIT--
HOLD ON, BROCK.
GET THAT ALIEN TO SOFTEN YOUR LANDING.

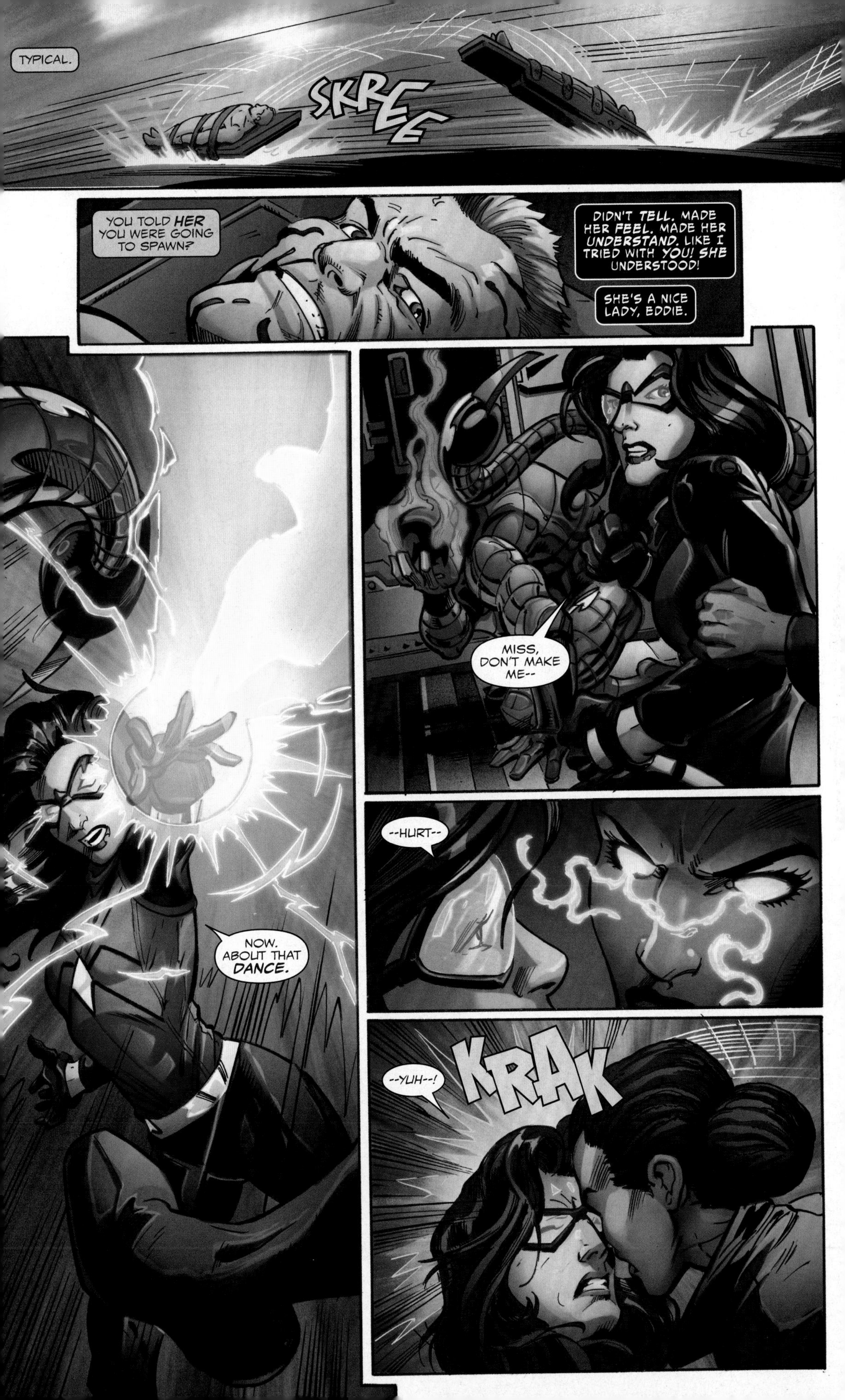
TYPICAL.
SKREEE
YOU TOLD HER YOU WERE GOING TO SPAWN?
DIDN'T TELL. MADE HER FEEL. MADE HER UNDERSTAND. LIKE I TRIED WITH YOU! SHE UNDERSTOOD!
SHE'S A NICE LADY, EDDIE.
NOW. ABOUT THAT DANCE.
MISS, DON'T MAKE ME--
--HURT--
--YUH--!
KRAK

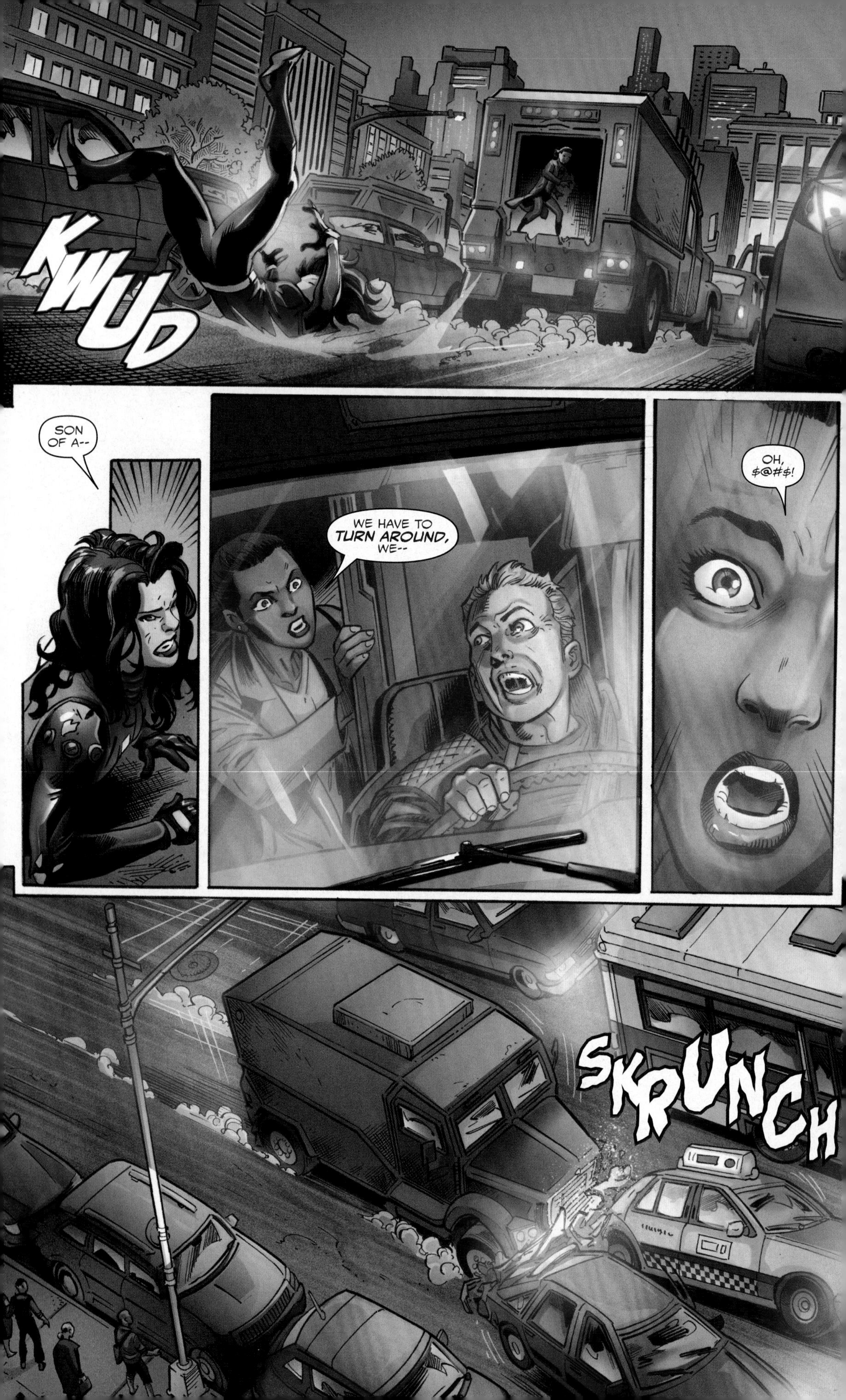
KWUD
SON OF A--
WE HAVE TO TURN AROUND, WE--
OH, $@#$!
SKRUNCH

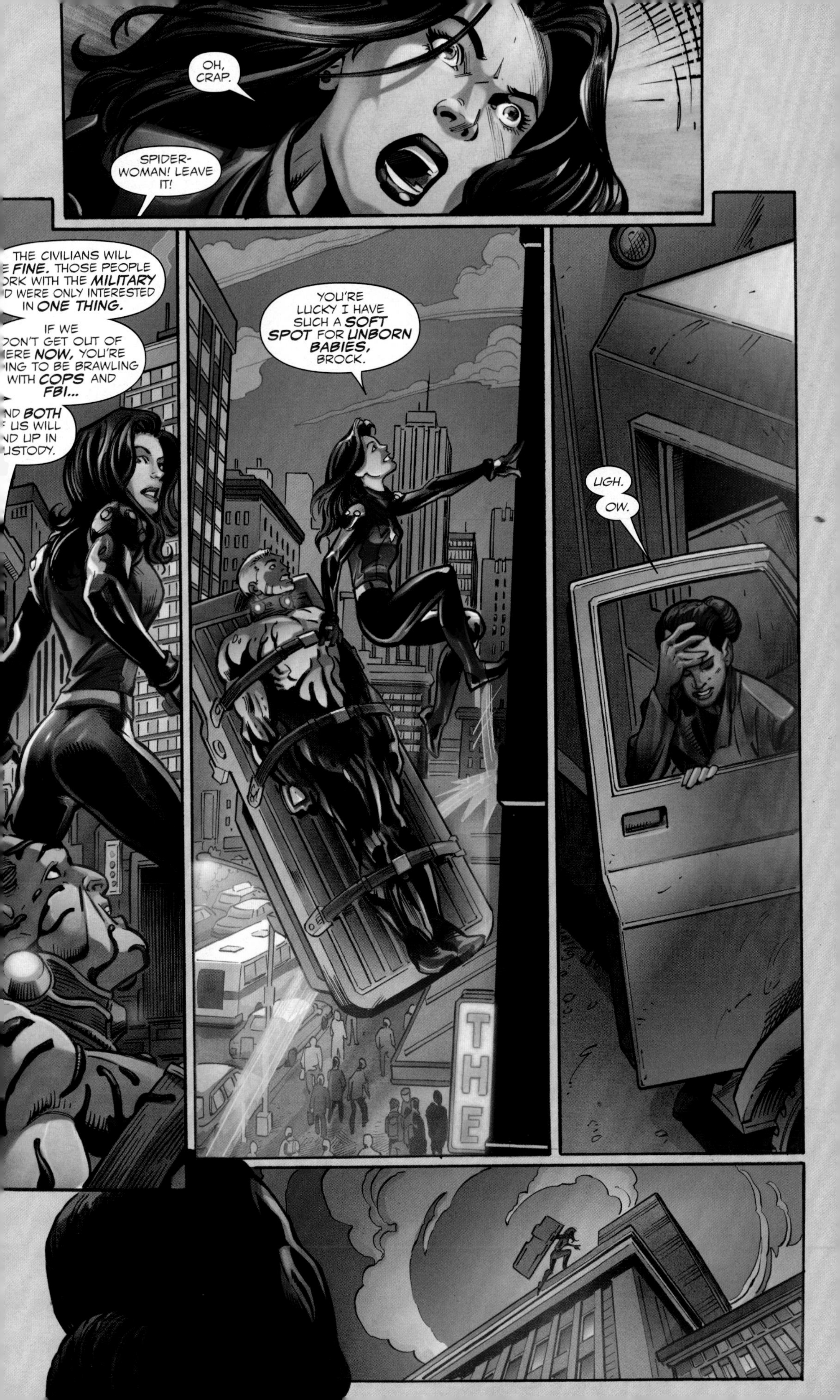

OH, CRAP.
SPIDER-WOMAN! LEAVE IT!
THE CIVILIANS WILL E FINE. THOSE PEOPLE ORK WITH THE MILITARY D WERE ONLY INTERESTED IN ONE THING.
IF WE DON'T GET OUT OF ERE NOW, YOU'RE ING TO BE BRAWLING WITH COPS AND FBI...
ND BOTH F US WILL ND UP IN USTODY.
YOU'RE LUCKY I HAVE SUCH A SOFT SPOT FOR UNBORN BABIES, BROCK.
THE
UGH.
OW.

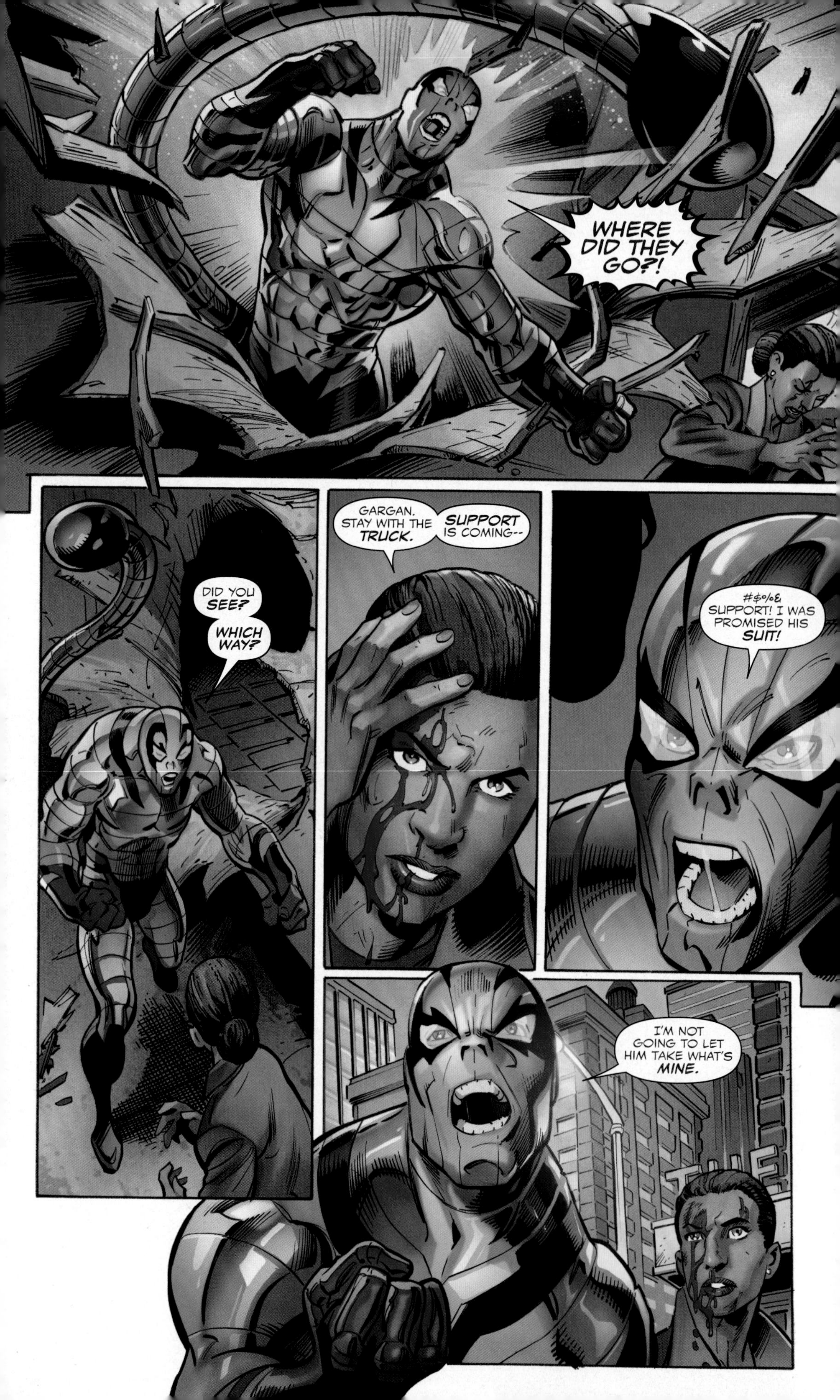
WHERE DID THEY GO?!
DID YOU SEE?
WHICH WAY?
GARGAN. STAY WITH THE TRUCK.
SUPPORT IS COMING--
#$%&
SUPPORT! I WAS PROMISED HIS SUIT!
I'M NOT GOING TO LET HIM TAKE WHAT'S MINE.

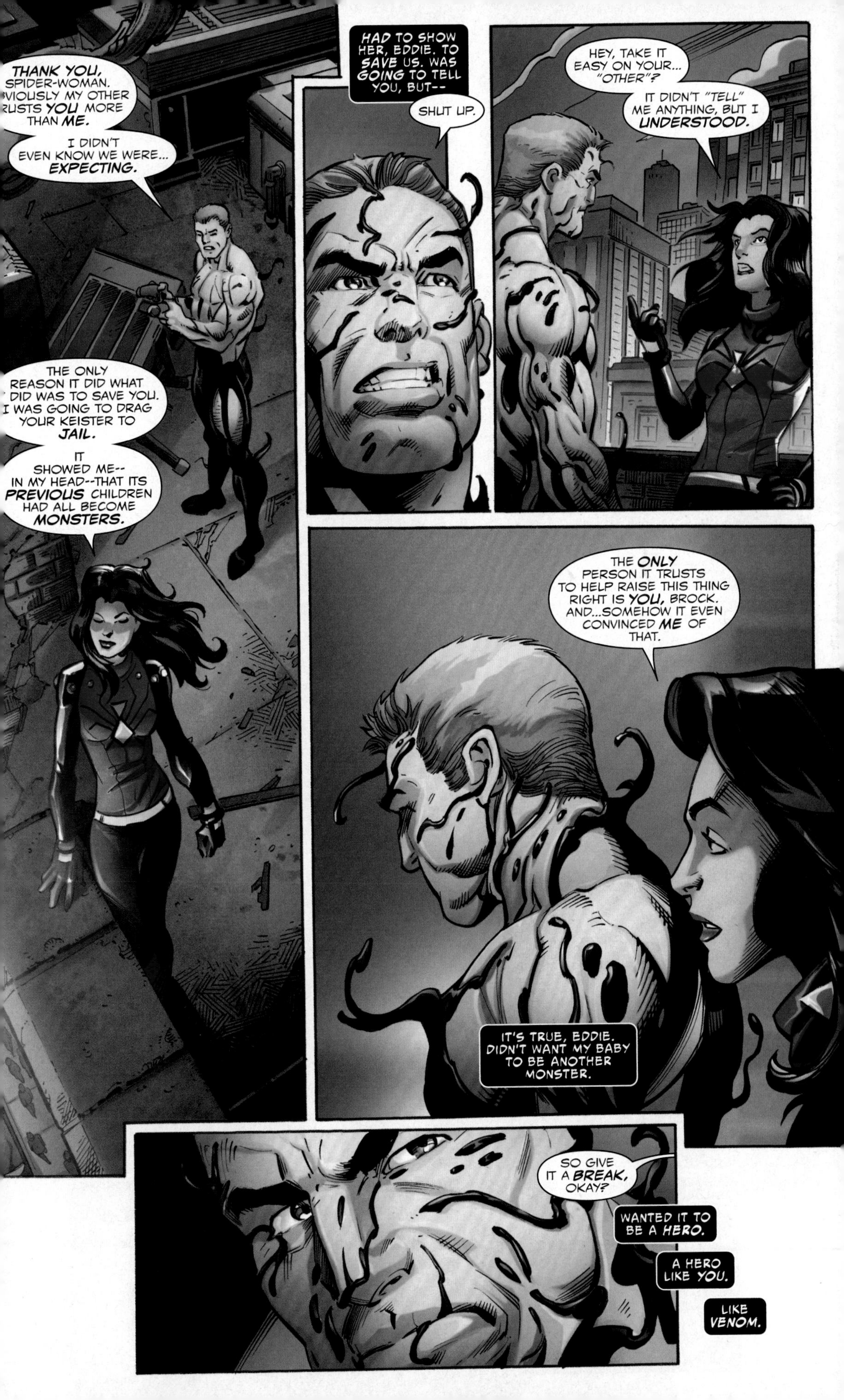
THANK YOU, SPIDER-WOMAN. ...VIOUSLY MY OTHER ...RUSTS YOU MORE THAN ME.
I DIDN'T EVEN KNOW WE WERE... EXPECTING.
THE ONLY REASON IT DID WHAT ... DID WAS TO SAVE YOU. I WAS GOING TO DRAG YOUR KEISTER TO JAIL.
IT SHOWED ME-- IN MY HEAD--THAT ITS PREVIOUS CHILDREN HAD ALL BECOME MONSTERS.
HAD TO SHOW HER, EDDIE. TO SAVE US. WAS GOING TO TELL YOU, BUT--
SHUT UP.
HEY, TAKE IT EASY ON YOUR... "OTHER"?
IT DIDN'T "TELL" ME ANYTHING, BUT I UNDERSTOOD.
THE ONLY PERSON IT TRUSTS TO HELP RAISE THIS THING RIGHT IS YOU, BROCK. AND...SOMEHOW IT EVEN CONVINCED ME OF THAT.
IT'S TRUE, EDDIE. DIDN'T WANT MY BABY TO BE ANOTHER MONSTER.
SO GIVE IT A BREAK, OKAY?
WANTED IT TO BE A HERO.
A HERO LIKE YOU.
LIKE VENOM.

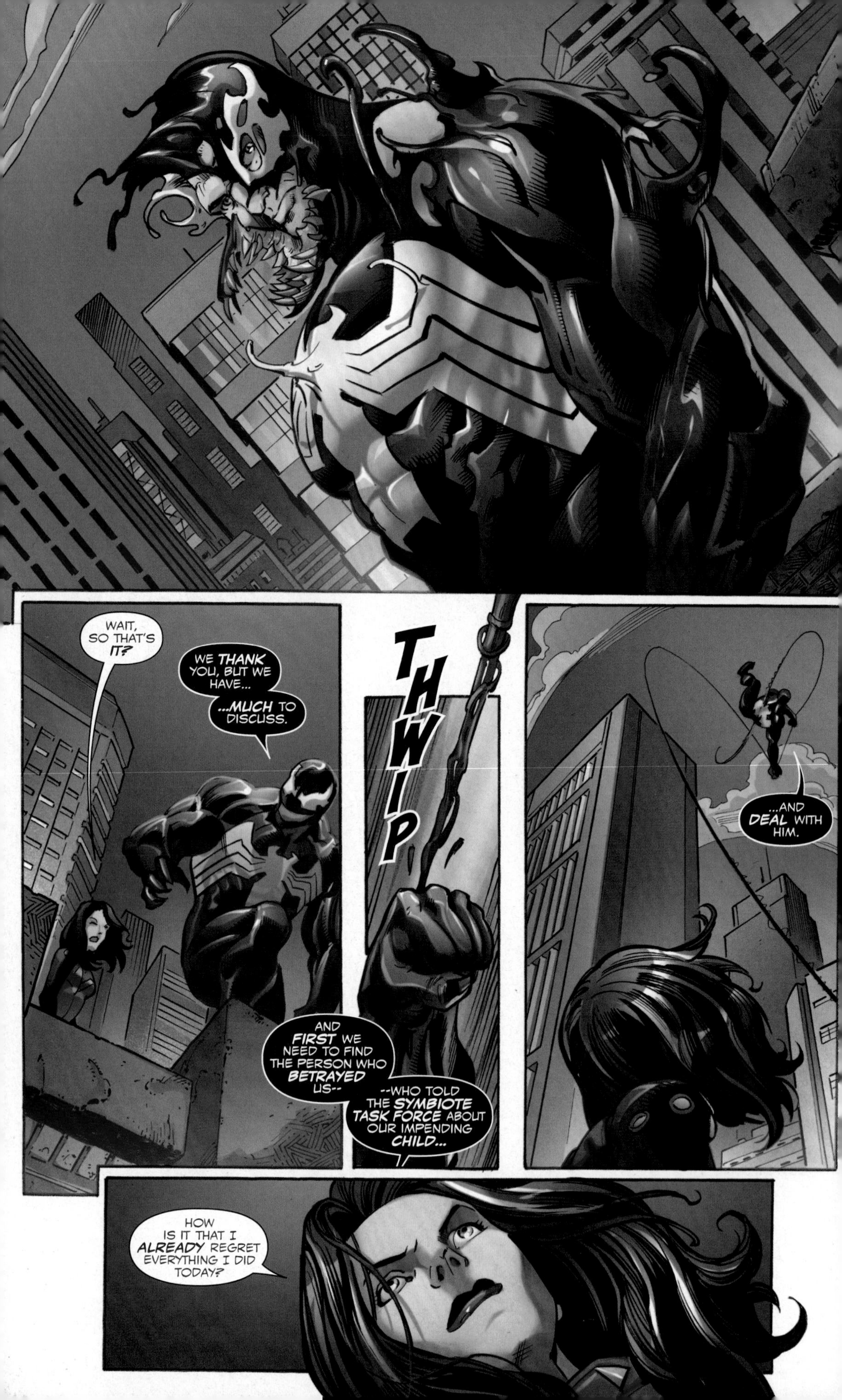
WAIT, SO THAT'S IT?
WE THANK YOU, BUT WE HAVE...
...MUCH TO DISCUSS.
THWIP
AND FIRST WE NEED TO FIND THE PERSON WHO BETRAYED US--
--WHO TOLD THE SYMBIOTE TASK FORCE ABOUT OUR IMPENDING CHILD...
...AND DEAL WITH HIM.
HOW IS IT THAT I ALREADY REGRET EVERYTHING I DID TODAY?

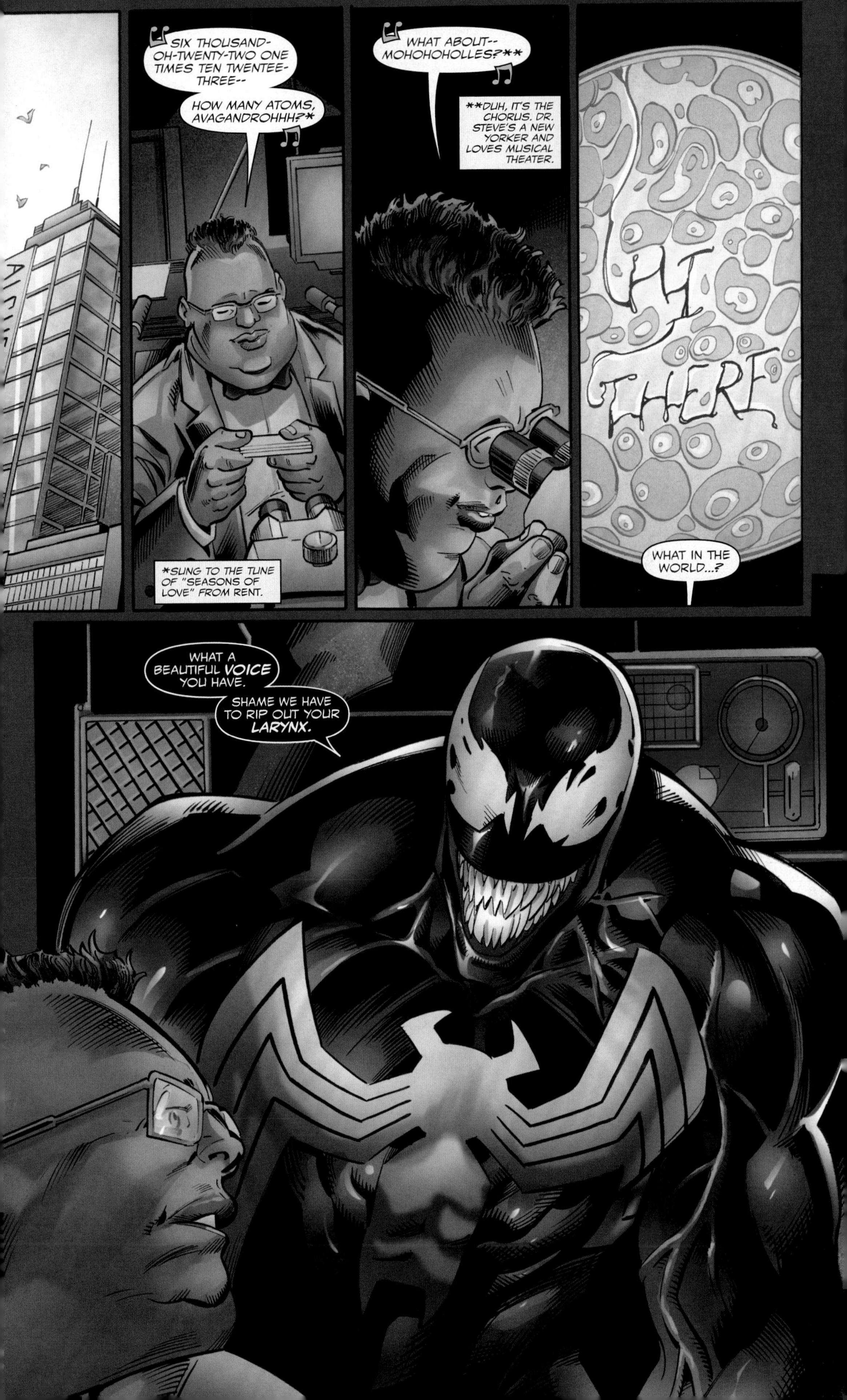
SIX THOUSAND-OH-TWENTY-TWO ONE TIMES TEN TWENTEE-THREE--
HOW MANY ATOMS, AVAGANDROHHH?*
*SUNG TO THE TUNE OF "SEASONS OF LOVE" FROM RENT.
WHAT ABOUT--MOHOHOHOLLES?**
**DUH, IT'S THE CHORUS. DR. STEVE'S A NEW YORKER AND LOVES MUSICAL THEATER.
HI THERE
WHAT IN THE WORLD...?
WHAT A BEAUTIFUL VOICE YOU HAVE.
SHAME WE HAVE TO RIP OUT YOUR LARYNX.

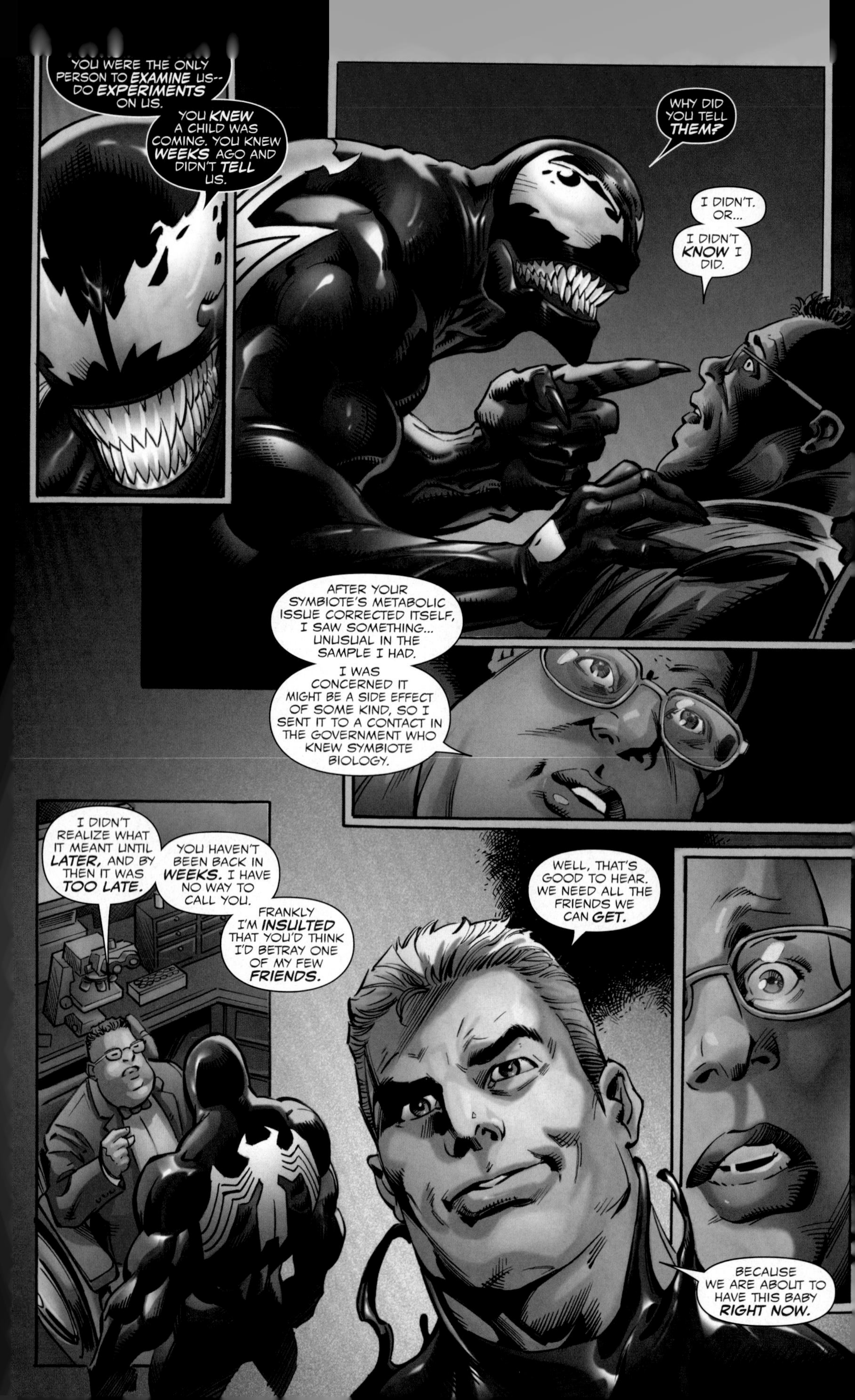
YOU WERE THE ONLY PERSON TO EXAMINE US-- DO EXPERIMENTS ON US.
YOU KNEW A CHILD WAS COMING. YOU KNEW WEEKS AGO AND DIDN'T TELL US.
WHY DID YOU TELL THEM?
I DIDN'T. OR...
I DIDN'T KNOW I DID.
AFTER YOUR SYMBIOTE'S METABOLIC ISSUE CORRECTED ITSELF, I SAW SOMETHING... UNUSUAL IN THE SAMPLE I HAD.
I WAS CONCERNED IT MIGHT BE A SIDE EFFECT OF SOME KIND, SO I SENT IT TO A CONTACT IN THE GOVERNMENT WHO KNEW SYMBIOTE BIOLOGY.
I DIDN'T REALIZE WHAT IT MEANT UNTIL LATER, AND BY THEN IT WAS TOO LATE.
YOU HAVEN'T BEEN BACK IN WEEKS. I HAVE NO WAY TO CALL YOU.
FRANKLY I'M INSULTED THAT YOU'D THINK I'D BETRAY ONE OF MY FEW FRIENDS.
WELL, THAT'S GOOD TO HEAR. WE NEED ALL THE FRIENDS WE CAN GET.
BECAUSE WE ARE ABOUT TO HAVE THIS BABY RIGHT NOW.

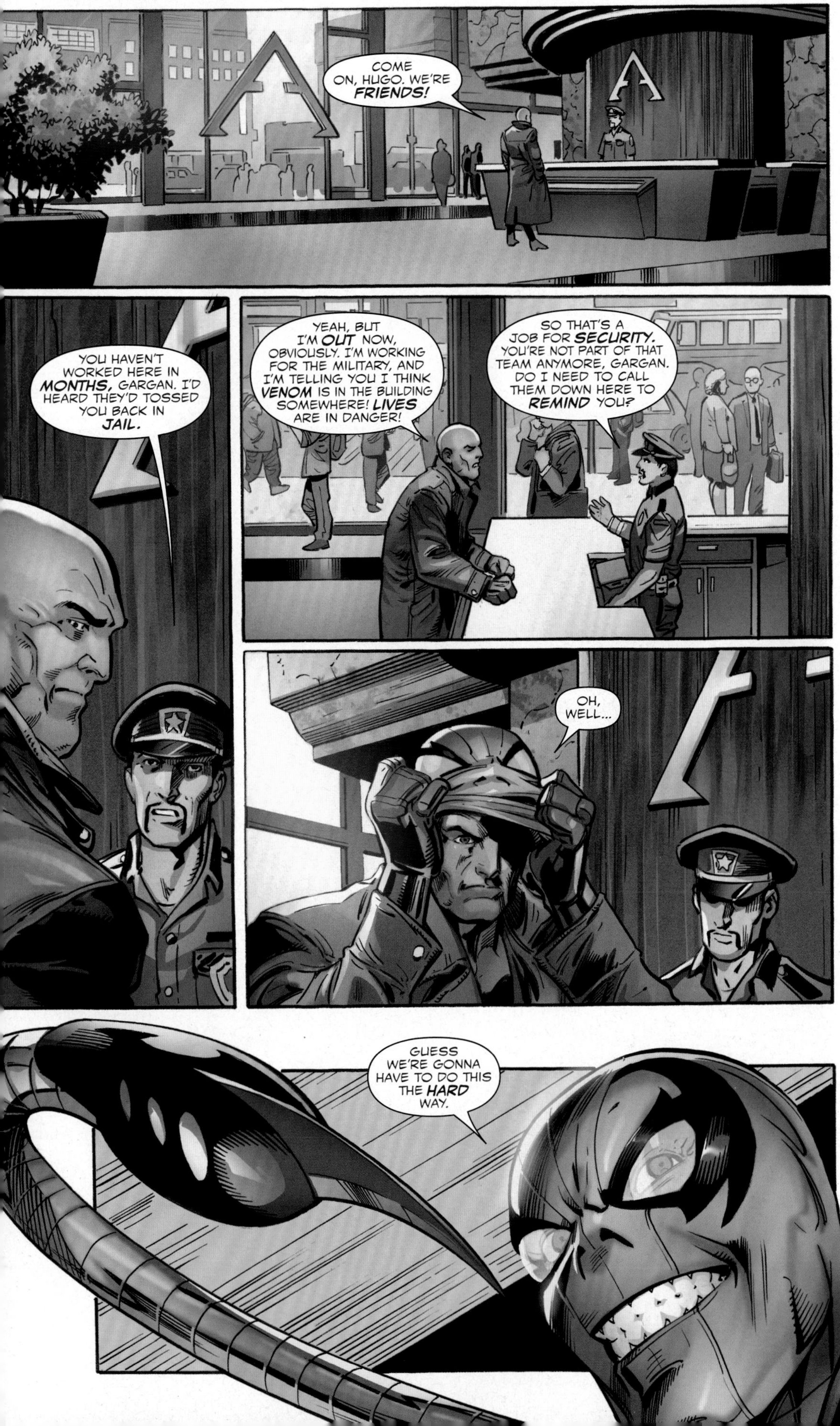
COME ON, HUGO. WE'RE FRIENDS!
YOU HAVEN'T WORKED HERE IN MONTHS, GARGAN. I'D HEARD THEY'D TOSSED YOU BACK IN JAIL.
YEAH, BUT I'M OUT NOW, OBVIOUSLY. I'M WORKING FOR THE MILITARY, AND I'M TELLING YOU I THINK VENOM IS IN THE BUILDING SOMEWHERE! LIVES ARE IN DANGER!
SO THAT'S A JOB FOR SECURITY. YOU'RE NOT PART OF THAT TEAM ANYMORE, GARGAN. DO I NEED TO CALL THEM DOWN HERE TO REMIND YOU?
OH, WELL...
GUESS WE'RE GONNA HAVE TO DO THIS THE HARD WAY.

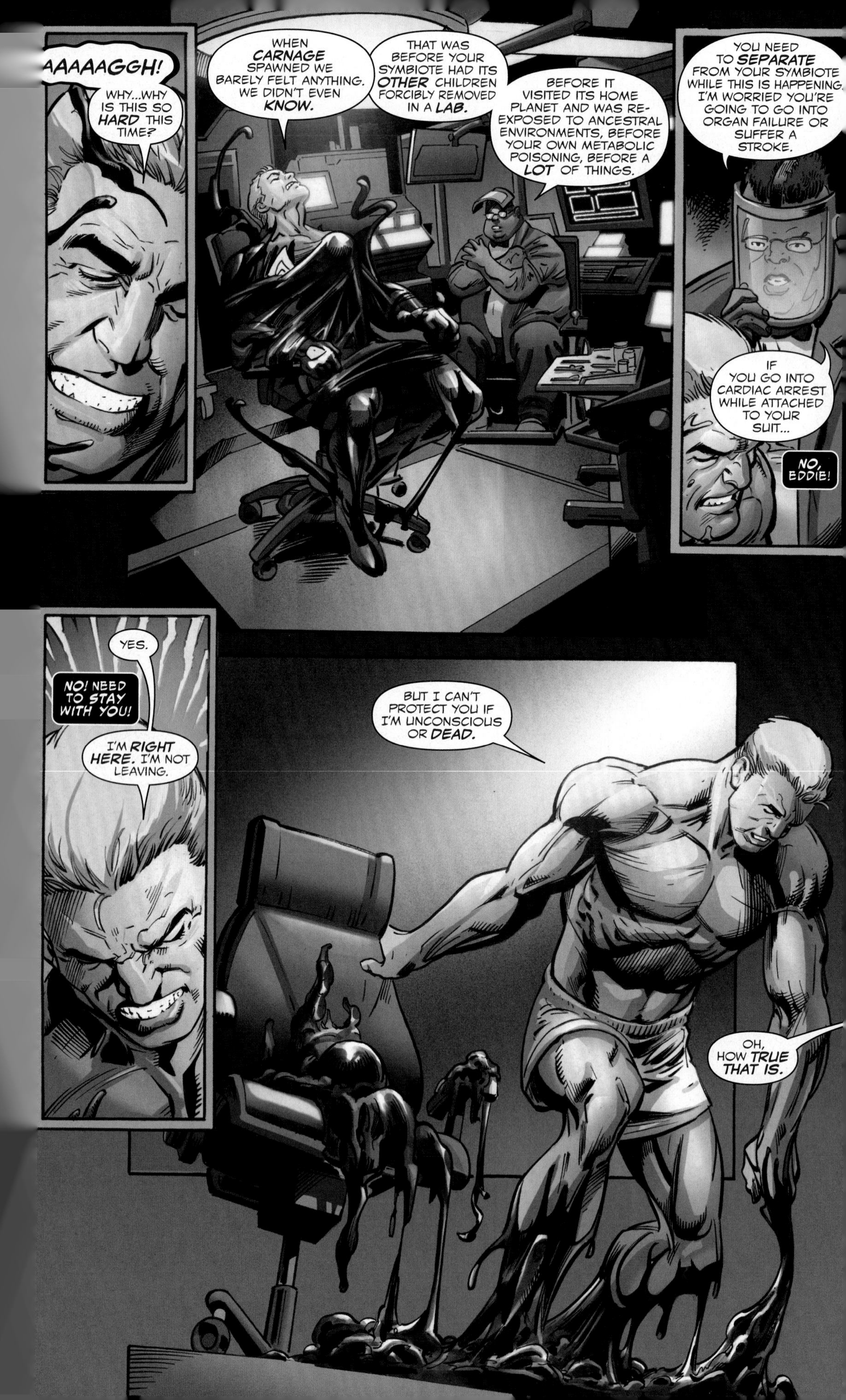
AAAAAGGH!
WHY...WHY IS THIS SO HARD THIS TIME?
WHEN CARNAGE SPAWNED WE BARELY FELT ANYTHING. WE DIDN'T EVEN KNOW.
THAT WAS BEFORE YOUR SYMBIOTE HAD ITS OTHER CHILDREN FORCIBLY REMOVED IN A LAB.
BEFORE IT VISITED ITS HOME PLANET AND WAS RE-EXPOSED TO ANCESTRAL ENVIRONMENTS, BEFORE YOUR OWN METABOLIC POISONING, BEFORE A LOT OF THINGS.
YOU NEED TO SEPARATE FROM YOUR SYMBIOTE WHILE THIS IS HAPPENING. I'M WORRIED YOU'RE GOING TO GO INTO ORGAN FAILURE OR SUFFER A STROKE.
IF YOU GO INTO CARDIAC ARREST WHILE ATTACHED TO YOUR SUIT...
NO, EDDIE!
YES.
NO! NEED TO STAY WITH YOU!
I'M RIGHT HERE. I'M NOT LEAVING.
BUT I CAN'T PROTECT YOU IF I'M UNCONSCIOUS OR DEAD.
OH, HOW TRUE THAT IS.

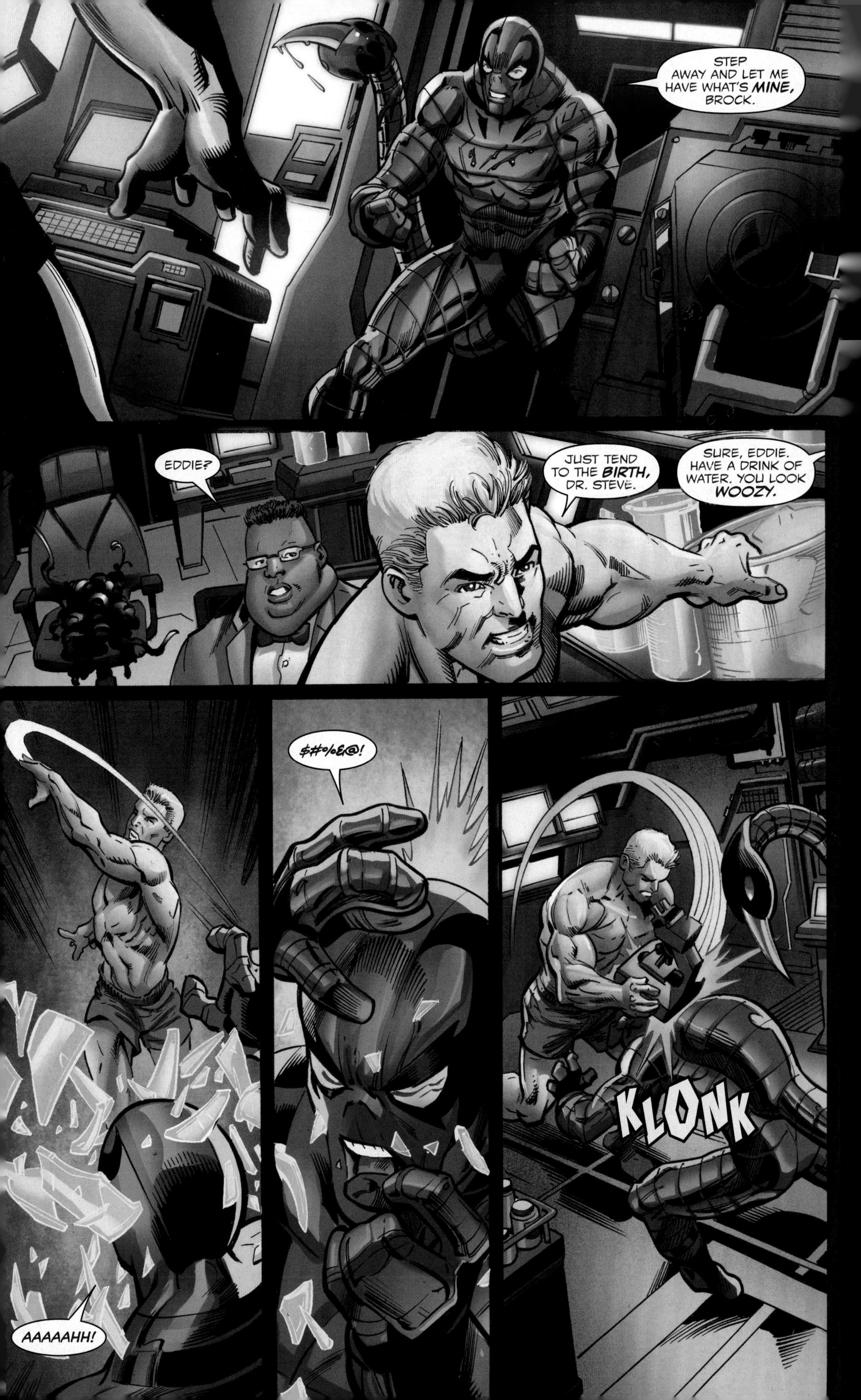
STEP AWAY AND LET ME HAVE WHAT'S MINE, BROCK.
EDDIE?
JUST TEND TO THE BIRTH, DR. STEVE.
SURE, EDDIE. HAVE A DRINK OF WATER. YOU LOOK WOOZY.
AAAAAHH!
$#%&@!
KLONK

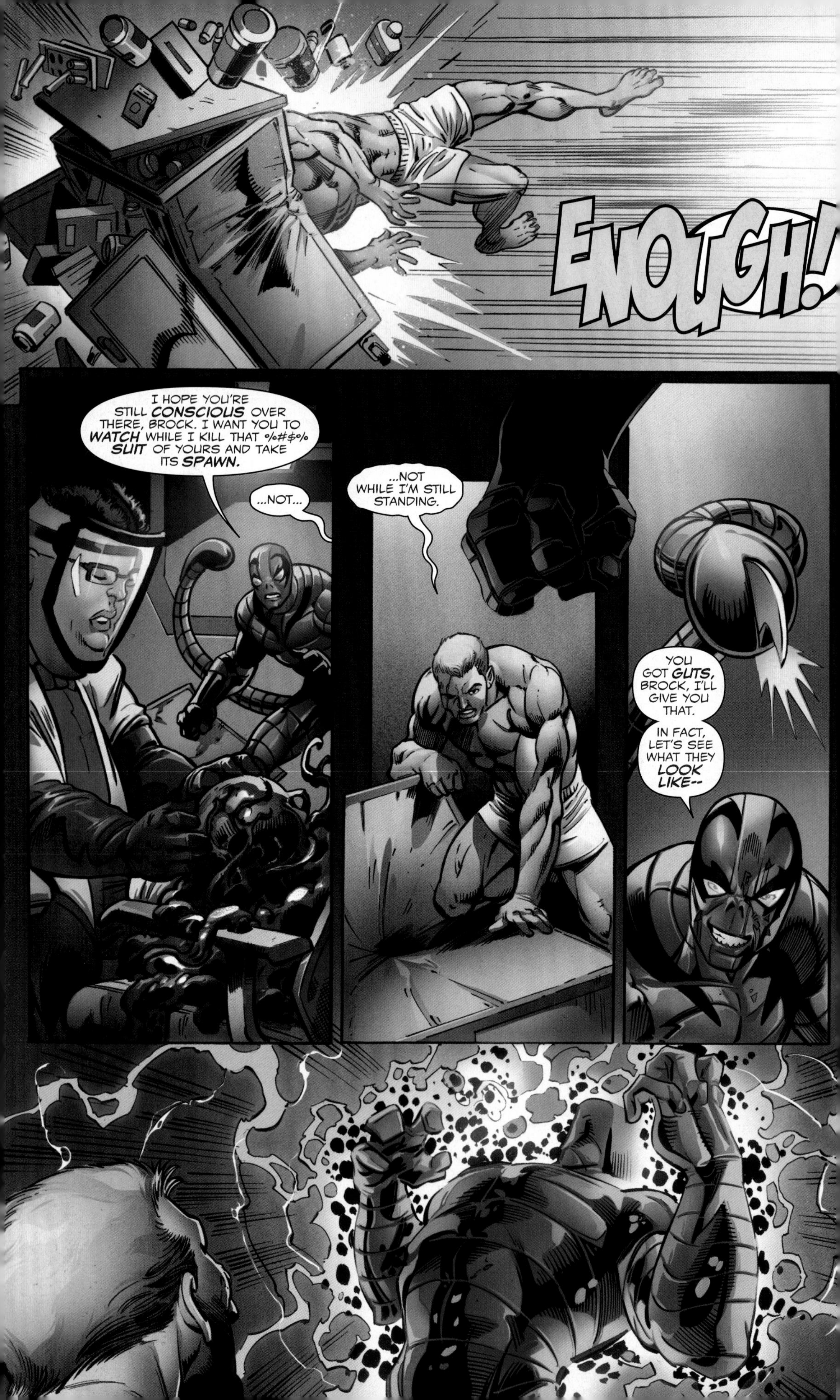
ENOUGH!
I HOPE YOU'RE STILL CONSCIOUS OVER THERE, BROCK. I WANT YOU TO WATCH WHILE I KILL THAT %#$% SUIT OF YOURS AND TAKE ITS SPAWN.
...NOT...
...NOT WHILE I'M STILL STANDING.
YOU GOT GUTS, BROCK, I'LL GIVE YOU THAT.
IN FACT, LET'S SEE WHAT THEY LOOK LIKE--

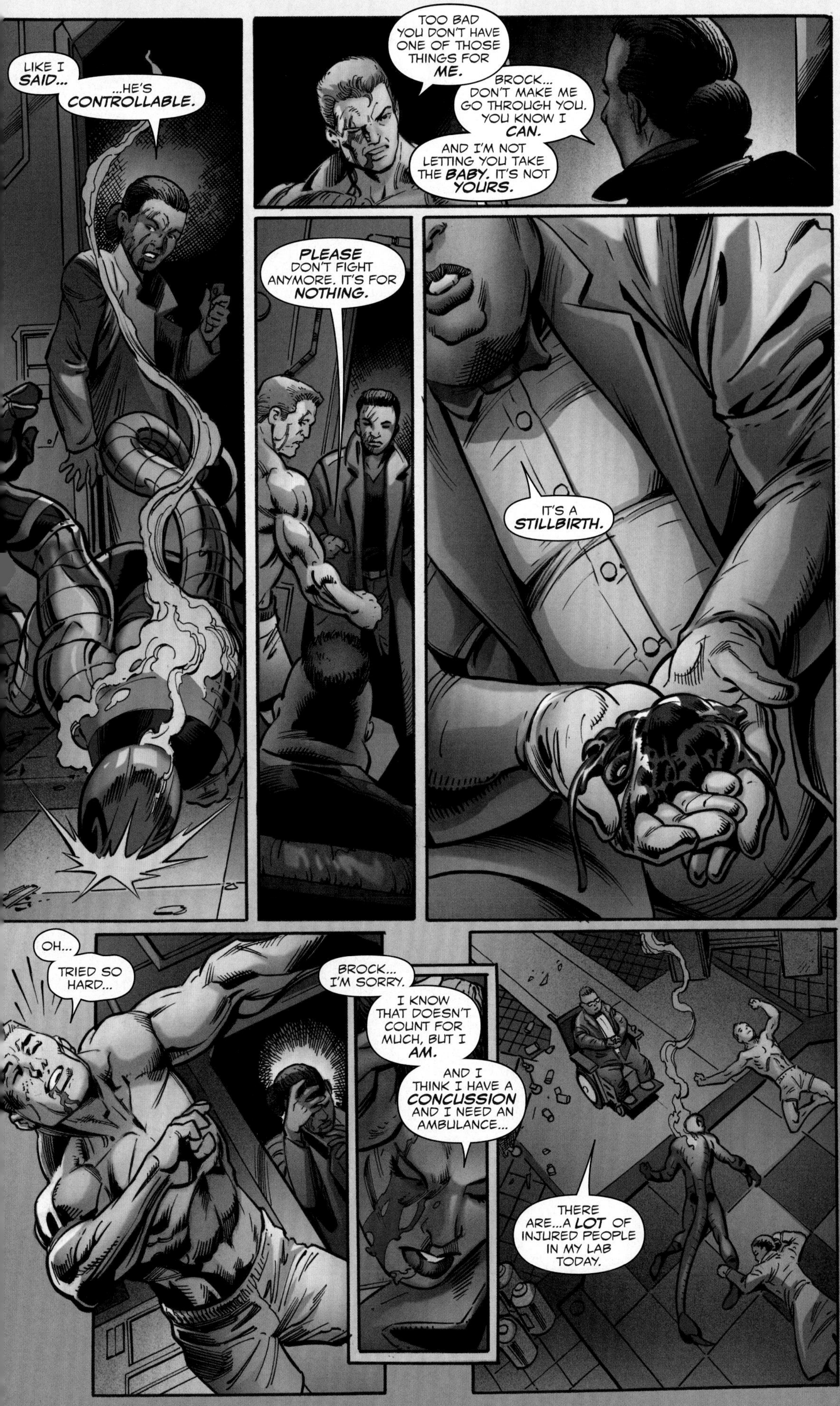
LIKE I SAID...
...HE'S CONTROLLABLE.
TOO BAD YOU DON'T HAVE ONE OF THOSE THINGS FOR ME.
BROCK... DON'T MAKE ME GO THROUGH YOU. YOU KNOW I CAN.
AND I'M NOT LETTING YOU TAKE THE BABY. IT'S NOT YOURS.
PLEASE DON'T FIGHT ANYMORE. IT'S FOR NOTHING.
IT'S A STILLBIRTH.
OH...
TRIED SO HARD...
BROCK... I'M SORRY.
I KNOW THAT DOESN'T COUNT FOR MUCH, BUT I AM.
AND I THINK I HAVE A CONCUSSION AND I NEED AN AMBULANCE...
THERE ARE...A LOT OF INJURED PEOPLE IN MY LAB TODAY.

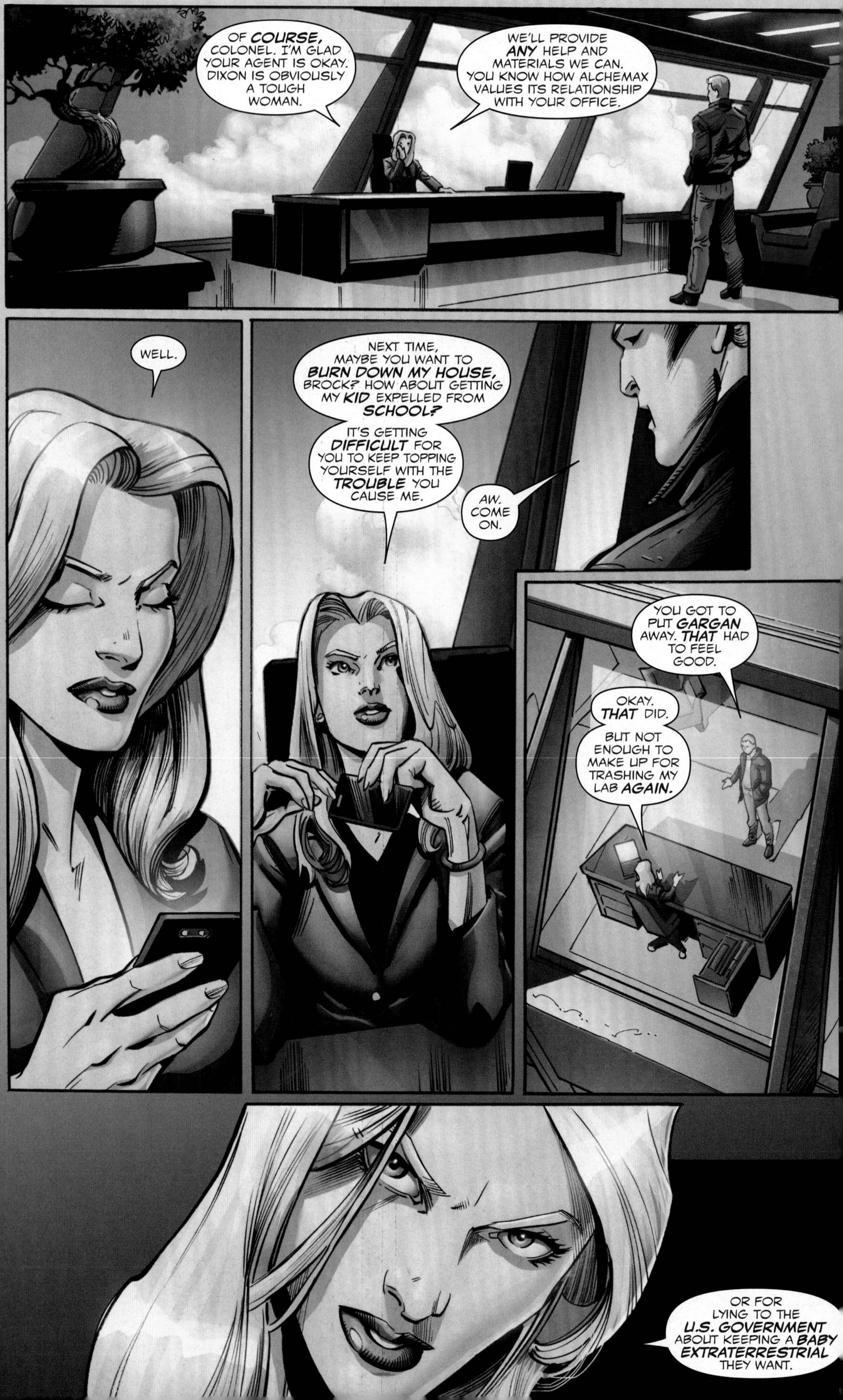
OF COURSE, COLONEL. I'M GLAD YOUR AGENT IS OKAY. DIXON IS OBVIOUSLY A TOUGH WOMAN.
WE'LL PROVIDE ANY HELP AND MATERIALS WE CAN. YOU KNOW HOW ALCHEMAX VALUES ITS RELATIONSHIP WITH YOUR OFFICE.
WELL.
NEXT TIME, MAYBE YOU WANT TO BURN DOWN MY HOUSE, BROCK? HOW ABOUT GETTING MY KID EXPELLED FROM SCHOOL?
IT'S GETTING DIFFICULT FOR YOU TO KEEP TOPPING YOURSELF WITH THE TROUBLE YOU CAUSE ME.
AW. COME ON.
YOU GOT TO PUT GARGAN AWAY. THAT HAD TO FEEL GOOD.
OKAY. THAT DID.
BUT NOT ENOUGH TO MAKE UP FOR TRASHING MY LAB AGAIN.
OR FOR LYING TO THE U.S. GOVERNMENT ABOUT KEEPING A BABY EXTRATERRESTRIAL THEY WANT.

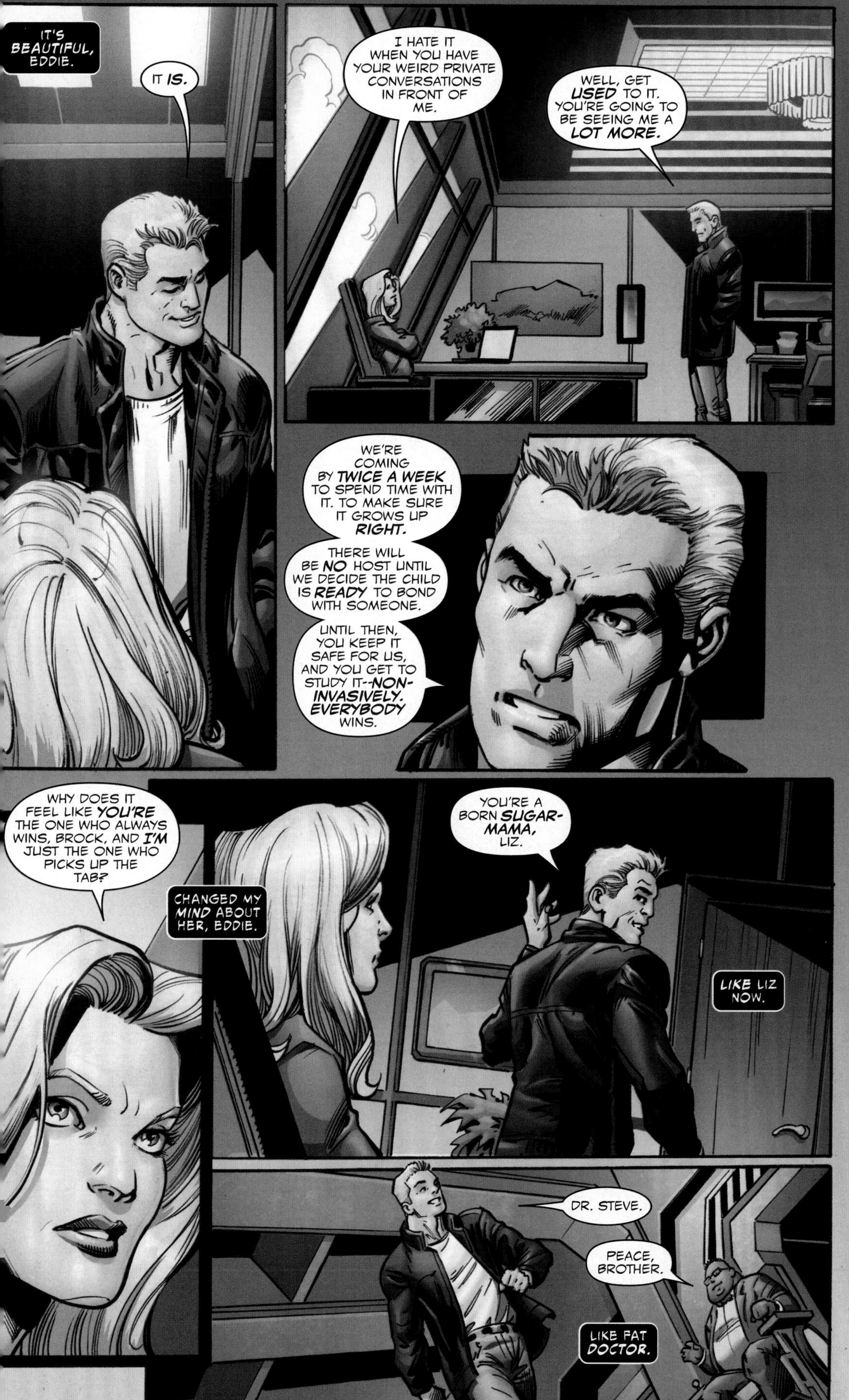
IT'S BEAUTIFUL, EDDIE.
IT IS.
I HATE IT WHEN YOU HAVE YOUR WEIRD PRIVATE CONVERSATIONS IN FRONT OF ME.
WELL, GET USED TO IT. YOU'RE GOING TO BE SEEING ME A LOT MORE.
WE'RE COMING BY TWICE A WEEK TO SPEND TIME WITH IT. TO MAKE SURE IT GROWS UP RIGHT.
THERE WILL BE NO HOST UNTIL WE DECIDE THE CHILD IS READY TO BOND WITH SOMEONE.
UNTIL THEN, YOU KEEP IT SAFE FOR US, AND YOU GET TO STUDY IT--NON-INVASIVELY. EVERYBODY WINS.
WHY DOES IT FEEL LIKE YOU'RE THE ONE WHO ALWAYS WINS, BROCK, AND I'M JUST THE ONE WHO PICKS UP THE TAB?
CHANGED MY MIND ABOUT HER, EDDIE.
YOU'RE A BORN SUGAR-MAMA, LIZ.
LIKE LIZ NOW.
DR. STEVE.
PEACE, BROTHER.
LIKE FAT DOCTOR.

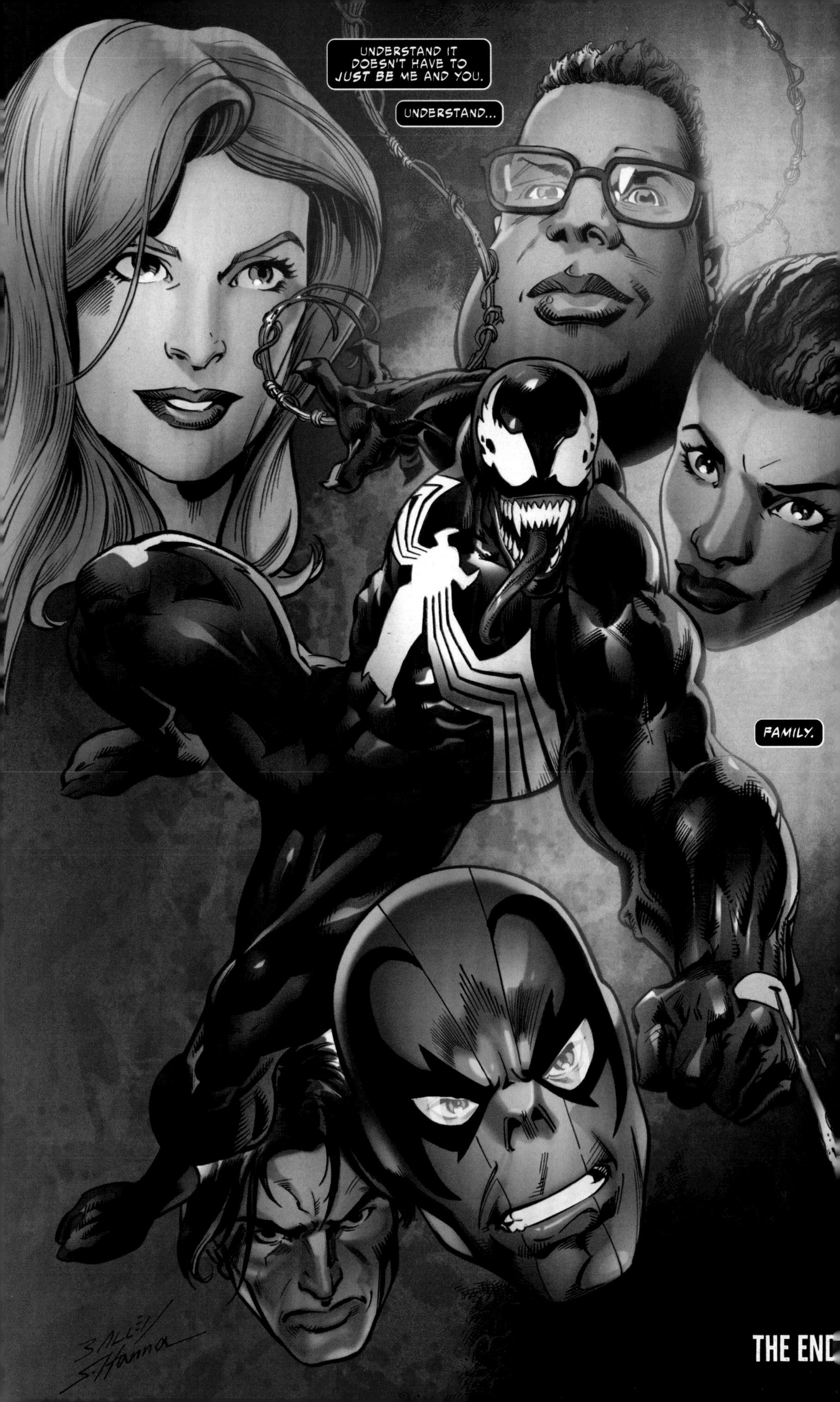
UNDERSTAND IT DOESN'T HAVE TO JUST BE ME AND YOU.
UNDERSTAND...
FAMILY.
THE END

FOR YEARS VENOM SOUGHT THE DEATH OF SPIDER-MAN, BUT NOW THEY MUST TEAM UP IF THE ARE TO DEFEAT THE SYMBIOTE'S MURDEROUS OFFSPRING, CARNAGE!

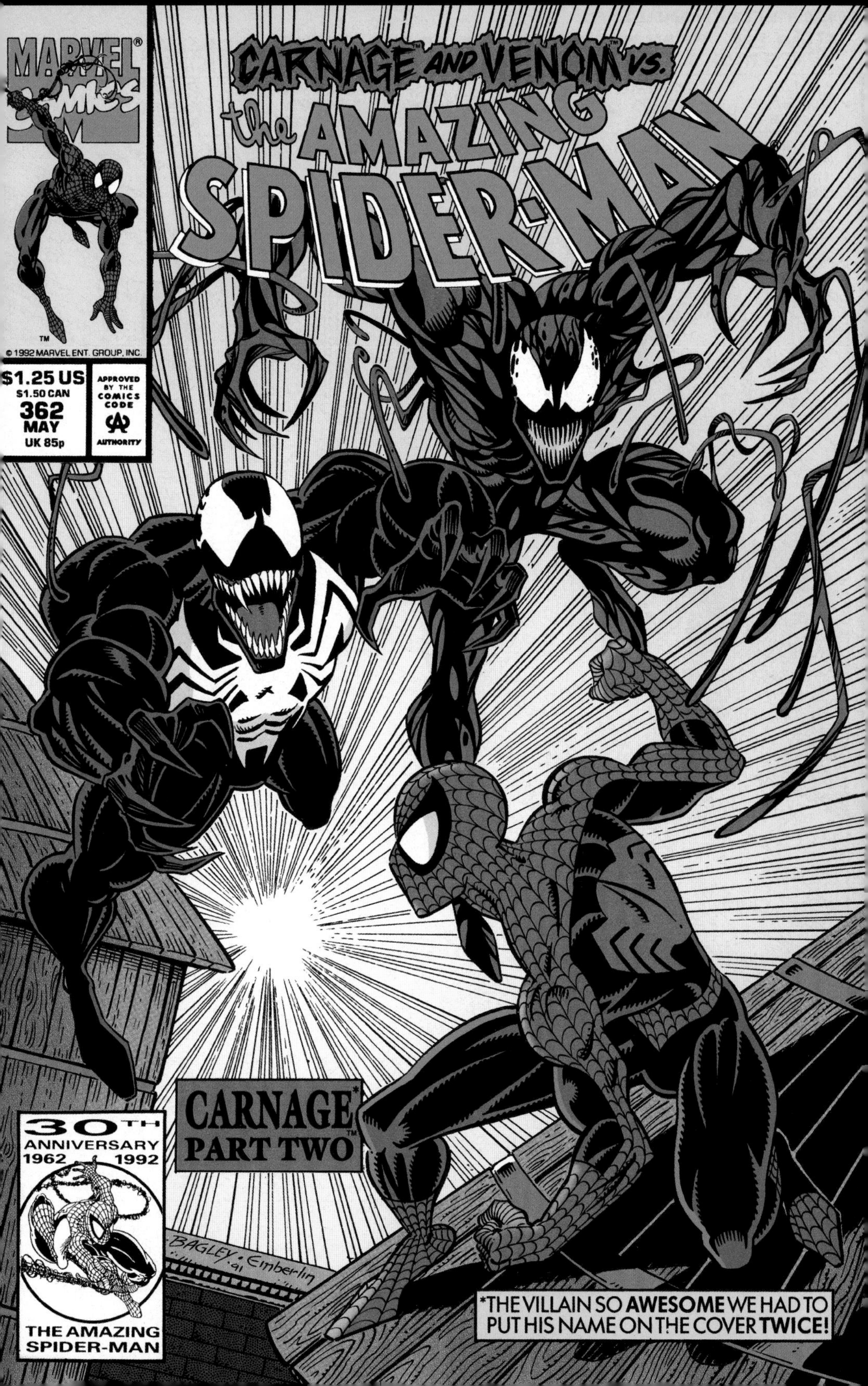
MARVEL COMICS
CARNAGE AND VENOM VS.
the AMAZING SPIDER-MAN
© 1992 MARVEL ENT. GROUP, INC.
$1.25 US
$1.50 CAN
362
MAY
UK 85p
APPROVED BY THE COMICS CODE AUTHORITY
CARNAGE* PART TWO
30TH ANNIVERSARY 1962 1992
THE AMAZING SPIDER-MAN
BAGLEY • Emberlin '91
*THE VILLAIN SO AWESOME WE HAD TO PUT HIS NAME ON THE COVER TWICE!

BITTEN BY A RADIOACTIVE SPIDER, STUDENT PETER PARKER GAINED THE PROPORTIONATE STRENGTH AND AGILITY OF AN ARACHNID! ARMED WITH HIS WONDROUS WEB-SHOOTERS, THE RELUCTANT SUPER HERO STRUGGLES WITH SINISTER SUPER-VILLAINS, MAKING ENDS MEET, AND MAINTAINING SOME SEMBLANCE OF A NORMAL LIFE!

Stan Lee PRESENTS: THE AMAZING SPIDER-MAN®

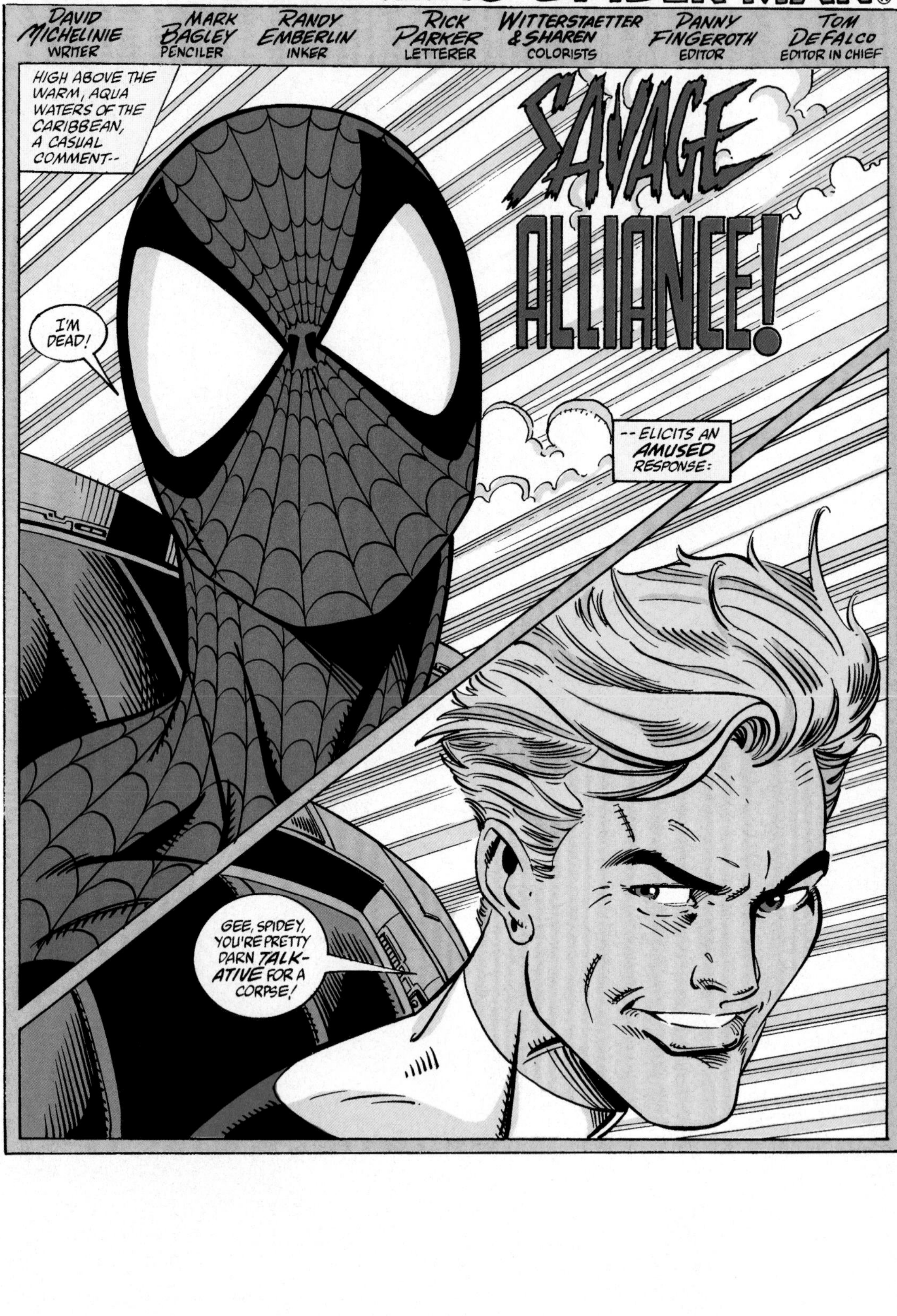
DAVID MICHELINIE WRITER
MARK BAGLEY PENCILER
RANDY EMBERLIN INKER
RICK PARKER LETTERER
WITTERSTAETTER & SHAREN COLORISTS
DANNY FINGEROTH EDITOR
TOM DEFALCO EDITOR IN CHIEF
HIGH ABOVE THE WARM, AQUA WATERS OF THE CARIBBEAN, A CASUAL COMMENT--
SAVAGE ALLIANCE!
I'M DEAD!
--ELICITS AN AMUSED RESPONSE:
GEE, SPIDEY, YOU'RE PRETTY DARN TALK-ATIVE FOR A CORPSE!

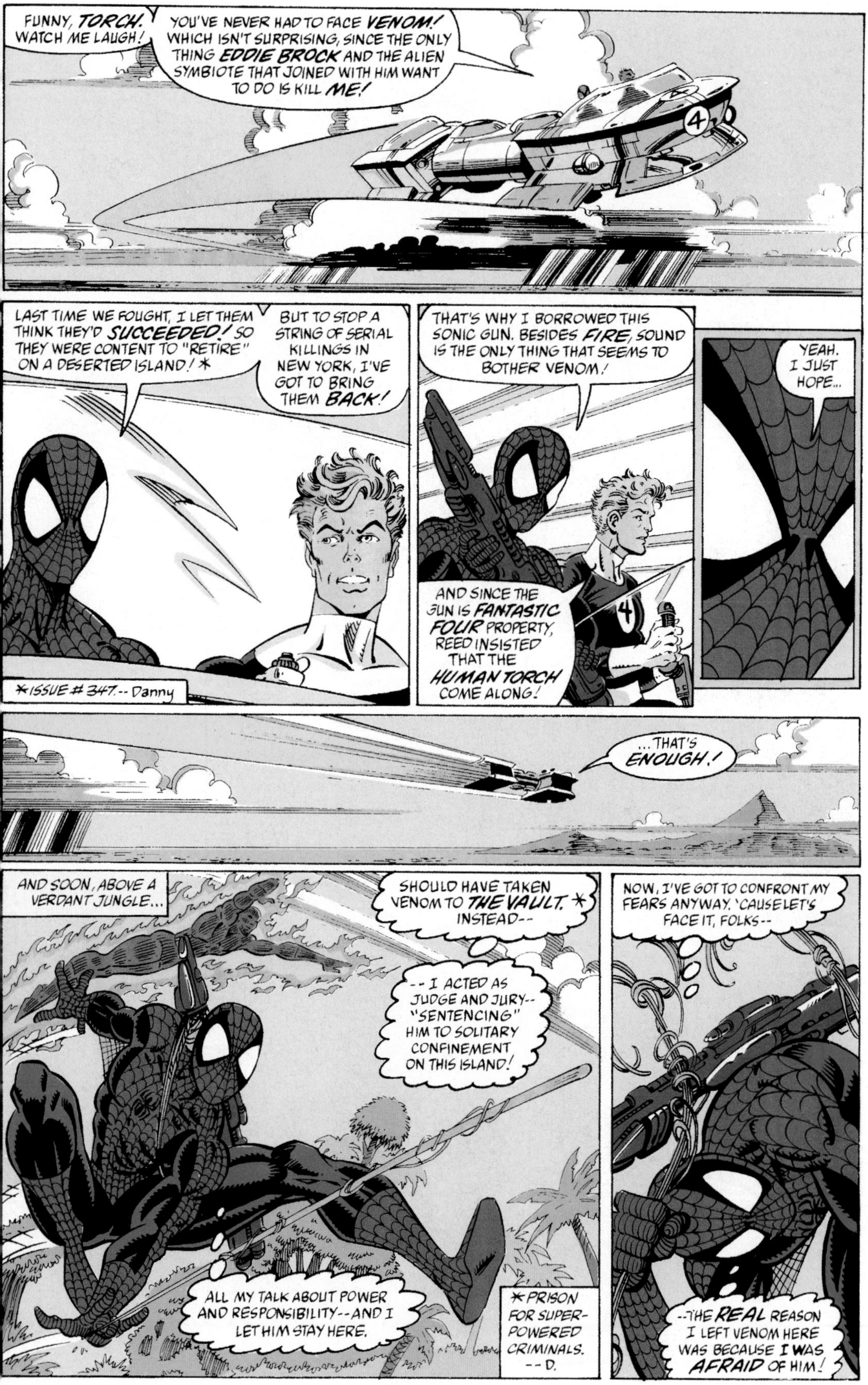

FUNNY, TORCH. WATCH ME LAUGH!
YOU'VE NEVER HAD TO FACE VENOM! WHICH ISN'T SURPRISING, SINCE THE ONLY THING EDDIE BROCK AND THE ALIEN SYMBIOTE THAT JOINED WITH HIM WANT TO DO IS KILL ME!
4
LAST TIME WE FOUGHT, I LET THEM THINK THEY'D SUCCEEDED! SO THEY WERE CONTENT TO "RETIRE" ON A DESERTED ISLAND! *
BUT TO STOP A STRING OF SERIAL KILLINGS IN NEW YORK, I'VE GOT TO BRING THEM BACK!
*ISSUE # 347.-- Danny
THAT'S WHY I BORROWED THIS SONIC GUN. BESIDES FIRE, SOUND IS THE ONLY THING THAT SEEMS TO BOTHER VENOM!
AND SINCE THE GUN IS FANTASTIC FOUR PROPERTY, REED INSISTED THAT THE HUMAN TORCH COME ALONG!
YEAH. I JUST HOPE...
...THAT'S ENOUGH!
AND SOON, ABOVE A VERDANT JUNGLE...
SHOULD HAVE TAKEN VENOM TO THE VAULT. * INSTEAD--
-- I ACTED AS JUDGE AND JURY-- "SENTENCING" HIM TO SOLITARY CONFINEMENT ON THIS ISLAND!
ALL MY TALK ABOUT POWER AND RESPONSIBILITY--AND I LET HIM STAY HERE.
*PRISON FOR SUPER-POWERED CRIMINALS. --D.
NOW, I'VE GOT TO CONFRONT MY FEARS ANYWAY. 'CAUSE LET'S FACE IT, FOLKS--
--THE REAL REASON I LEFT VENOM HERE WAS BECAUSE I WAS AFRAID OF HIM!

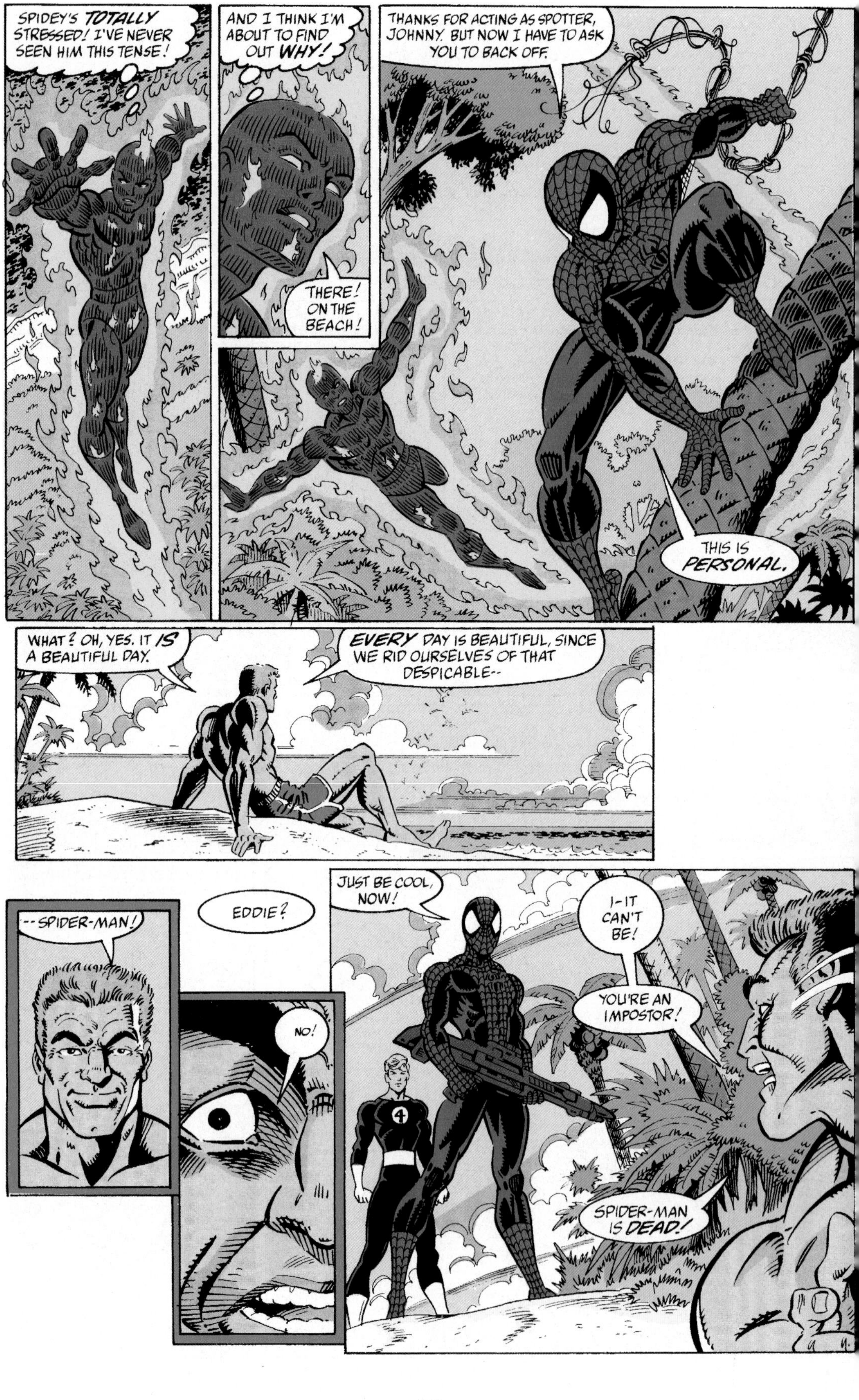

SPIDEY'S TOTALLY STRESSED! I'VE NEVER SEEN HIM THIS TENSE!
AND I THINK I'M ABOUT TO FIND OUT WHY!
THERE! ON THE BEACH!
THANKS FOR ACTING AS SPOTTER, JOHNNY. BUT NOW I HAVE TO ASK YOU TO BACK OFF.
THIS IS PERSONAL.
WHAT? OH, YES. IT IS A BEAUTIFUL DAY.
EVERY DAY IS BEAUTIFUL, SINCE WE RID OURSELVES OF THAT DESPICABLE--
--SPIDER-MAN!
EDDIE?
NO!
JUST BE COOL, NOW!
I-IT CAN'T BE!
YOU'RE AN IMPOSTOR!
SPIDER-MAN IS DEAD!

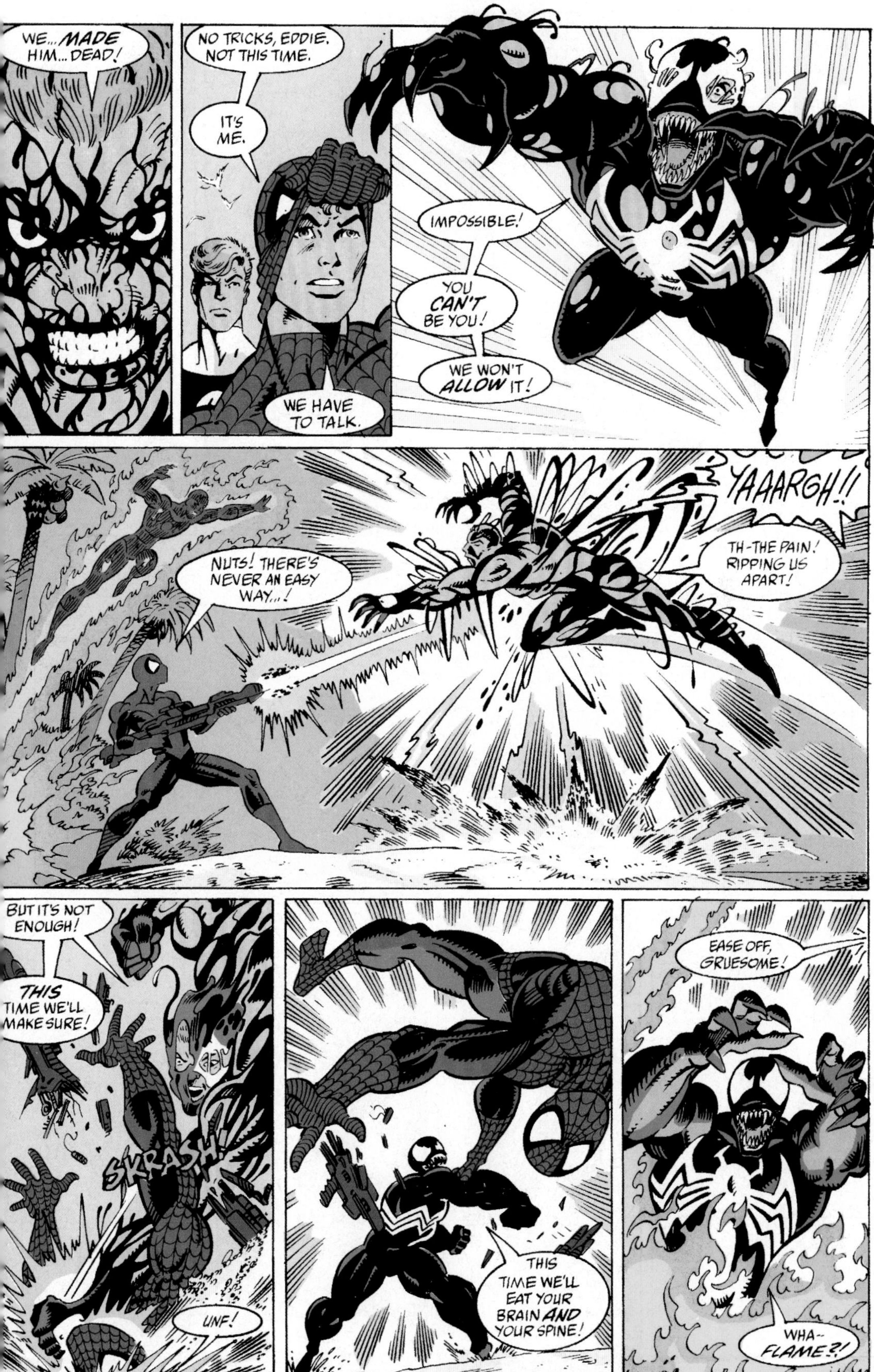
WE... MADE HIM... DEAD!
NO TRICKS, EDDIE. NOT THIS TIME.
IT'S ME.
WE HAVE TO TALK.
IMPOSSIBLE!
YOU CAN'T BE YOU!
WE WON'T ALLOW IT!
NUTS! THERE'S NEVER AN EASY WAY...!
YAAARGH!!
TH-THE PAIN! RIPPING US APART!
BUT IT'S NOT ENOUGH!
THIS TIME WE'LL MAKE SURE!
SKRASH
UNF!
THIS TIME WE'LL EAT YOUR BRAIN AND YOUR SPINE!
EASE OFF, GRUESOME!
WHA-- FLAME?!

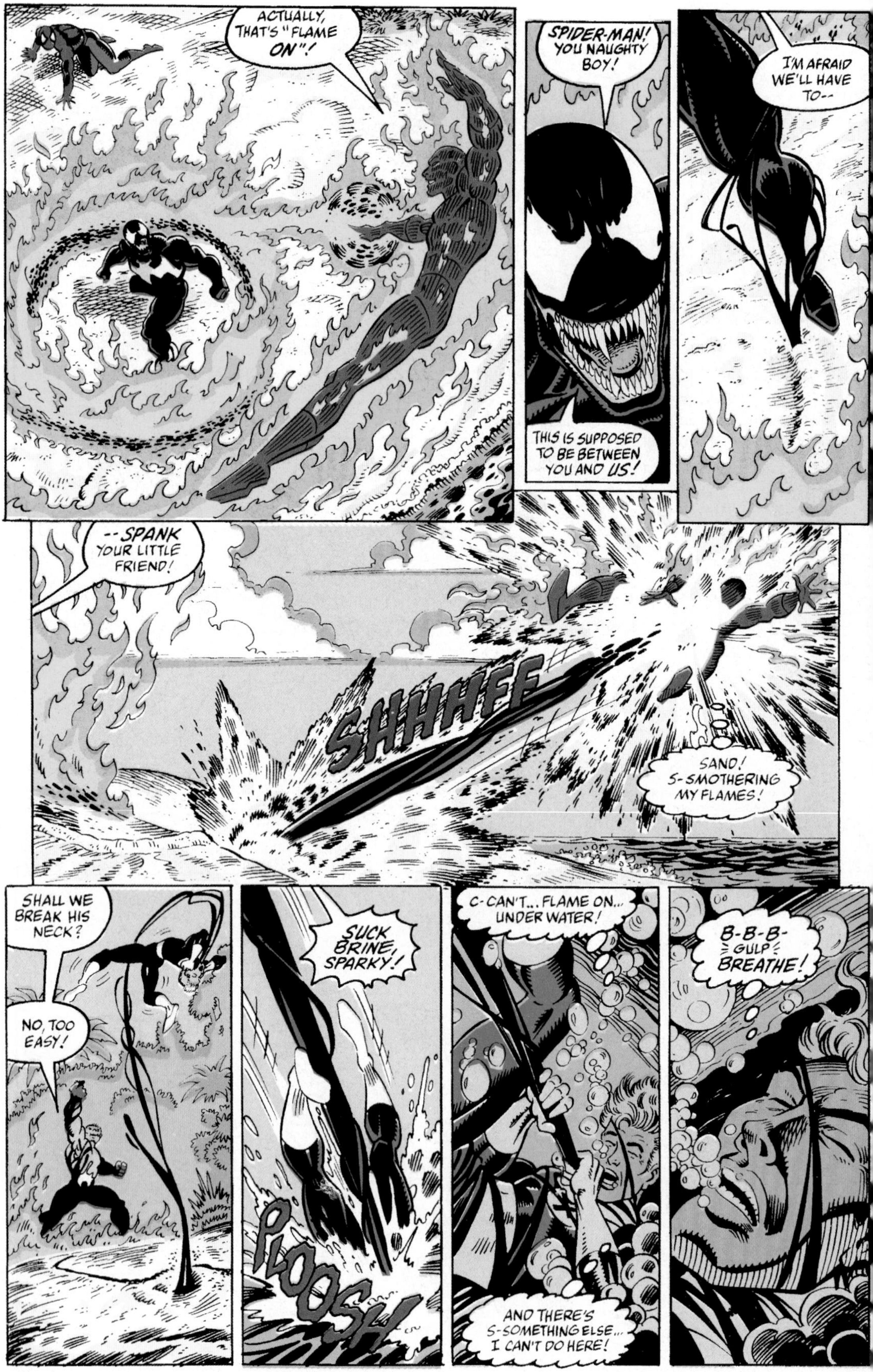
ACTUALLY, THAT'S "FLAME ON"!
SPIDER-MAN! YOU NAUGHTY BOY!
THIS IS SUPPOSED TO BE BETWEEN YOU AND US!
I'M AFRAID WE'LL HAVE TO--
--SPANK YOUR LITTLE FRIEND!
SHHHFF
SAND! S-SMOTHERING MY FLAMES!
SHALL WE BREAK HIS NECK?
NO, TOO EASY!
SUCK BRINE, SPARKY!
PLOOSH
C-CAN'T... FLAME ON... UNDER WATER!
AND THERE'S S-SOMETHING ELSE... I CAN'T DO HERE!
B-B-B- GULP BREATHE!

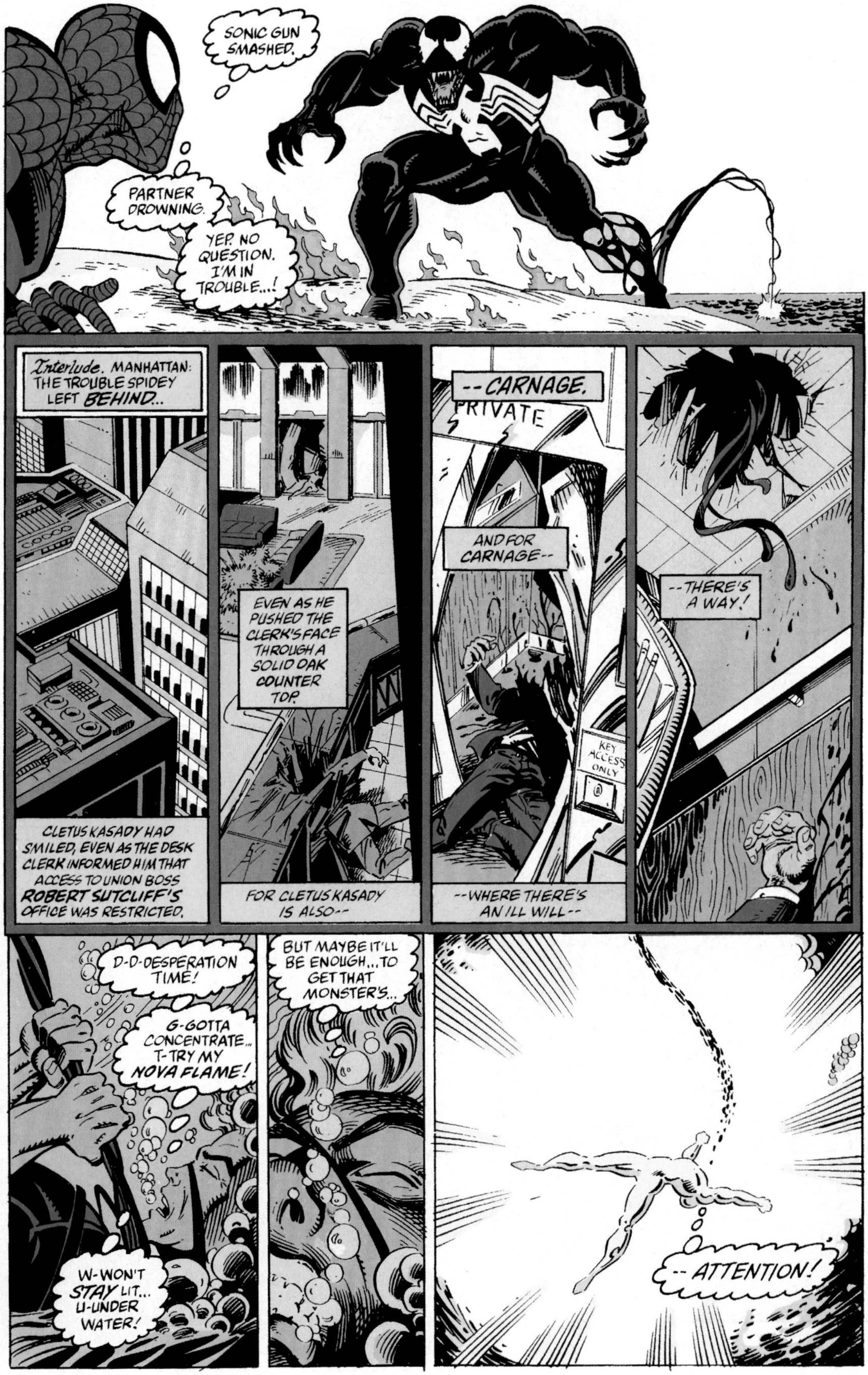
SONIC GUN SMASHED.
PARTNER DROWNING.
YEP. NO QUESTION. I'M IN TROUBLE...!
Interlude. MANHATTAN: THE TROUBLE SPIDEY LEFT BEHIND...
CLETUS KASADY HAD SMILED, EVEN AS THE DESK CLERK INFORMED HIM THAT ACCESS TO UNION BOSS ROBERT SUTCLIFF'S OFFICE WAS RESTRICTED.
EVEN AS HE PUSHED THE CLERK'S FACE THROUGH A SOLID OAK COUNTER TOP.
FOR CLETUS KASADY IS ALSO--
--CARNAGE.
PRIVATE
AND FOR CARNAGE--
KEY ACCESS ONLY
--WHERE THERE'S AN ILL WILL--
--THERE'S A WAY!
D-D-DESPERATION TIME!
G-GOTTA CONCENTRATE... T-TRY MY NOVA FLAME!
W-WON'T STAY LIT... U-UNDER WATER!
BUT MAYBE IT'LL BE ENOUGH... TO GET THAT MONSTER'S...
--ATTENTION!

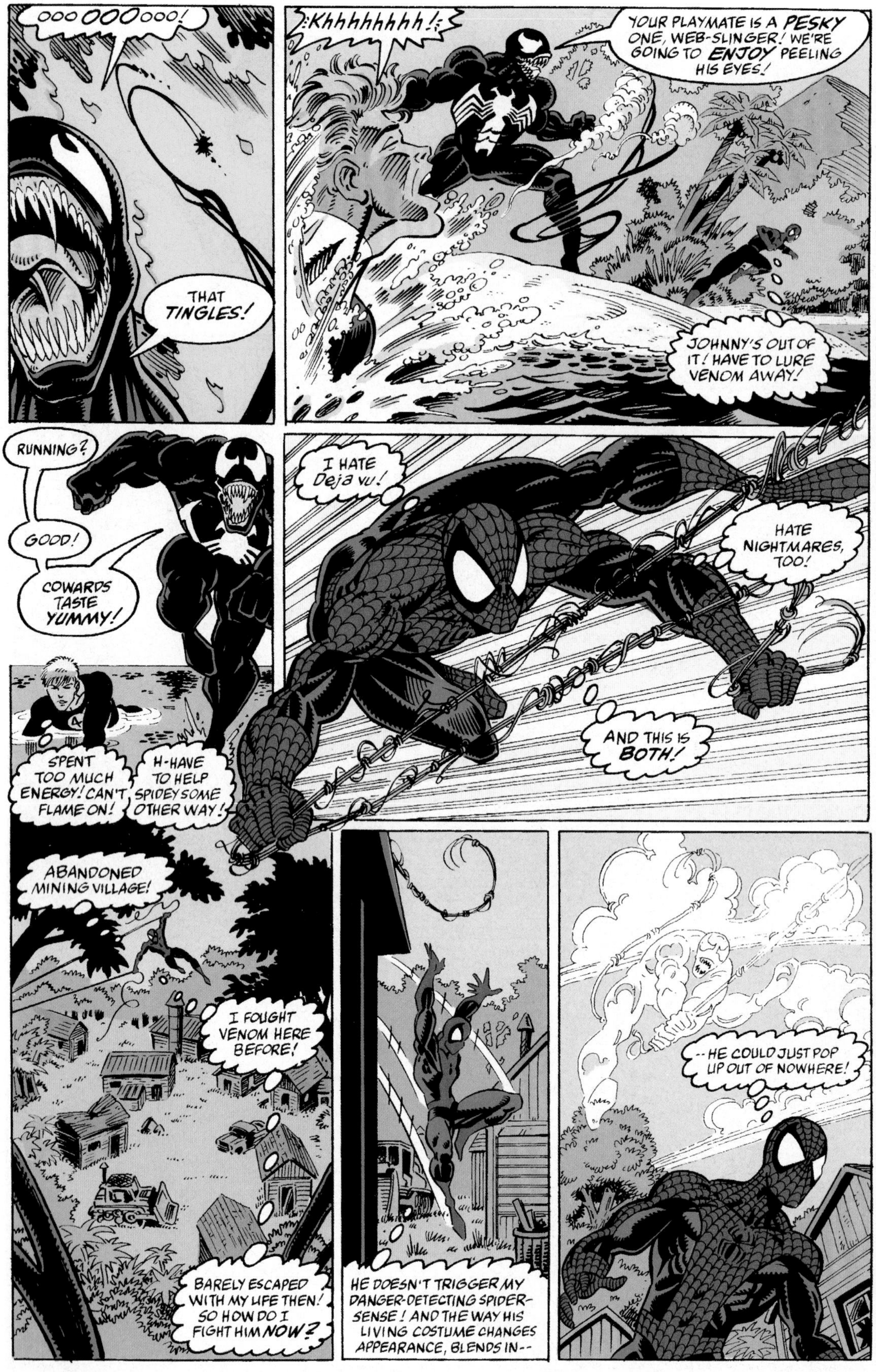
OOO OOO OOO!
THAT TINGLES!
:Khhhhhhhh!:
YOUR PLAYMATE IS A PESKY ONE, WEB-SLINGER! WE'RE GOING TO ENJOY PEELING HIS EYES!
JOHNNY'S OUT OF IT! HAVE TO LURE VENOM AWAY!
RUNNING?
GOOD!
COWARDS TASTE YUMMY!
I HATE Deja vu!
HATE NIGHTMARES, TOO!
AND THIS IS BOTH!
SPENT TOO MUCH ENERGY! CAN'T FLAME ON!
H-HAVE TO HELP SPIDEY SOME OTHER WAY!
ABANDONED MINING VILLAGE!
I FOUGHT VENOM HERE BEFORE!
BARELY ESCAPED WITH MY LIFE THEN! SO HOW DO I FIGHT HIM NOW?
HE DOESN'T TRIGGER MY DANGER-DETECTING SPIDER-SENSE! AND THE WAY HIS LIVING COSTUME CHANGES APPEARANCE, BLENDS IN--
--HE COULD JUST POP UP OUT OF NOWHERE!

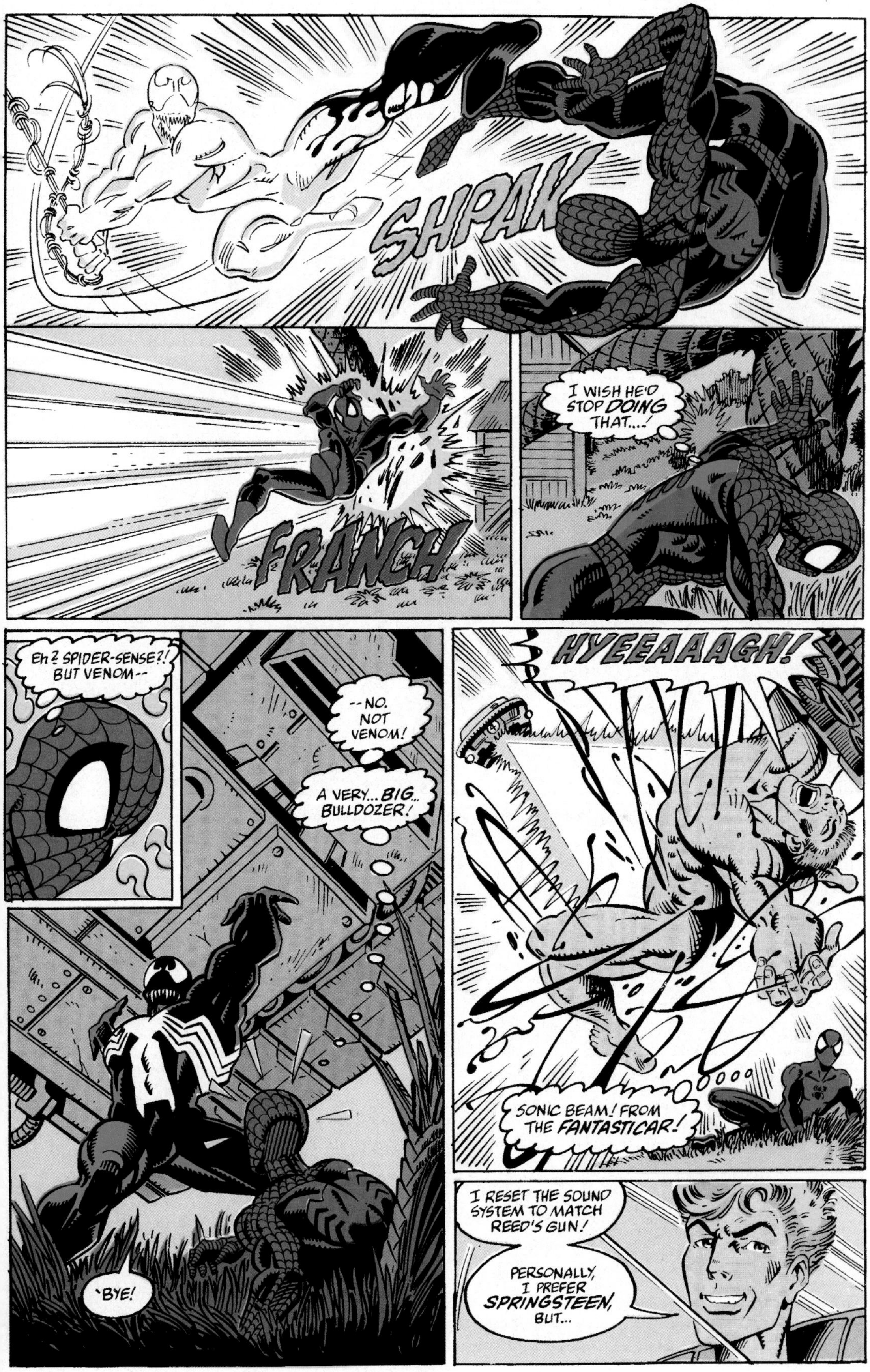
SHPAK
FRANCH
I WISH HE'D STOP DOING THAT...!
Eh? SPIDER-SENSE?! BUT VENOM--
--NO. NOT VENOM!
A VERY... BIG... BULLDOZER!
'BYE!
HYEEAAAAGH!
SONIC BEAM! FROM THE FANTASTICAR!
I RESET THE SOUND SYSTEM TO MATCH REED'S GUN!
PERSONALLY, I PREFER SPRINGSTEEN, BUT...

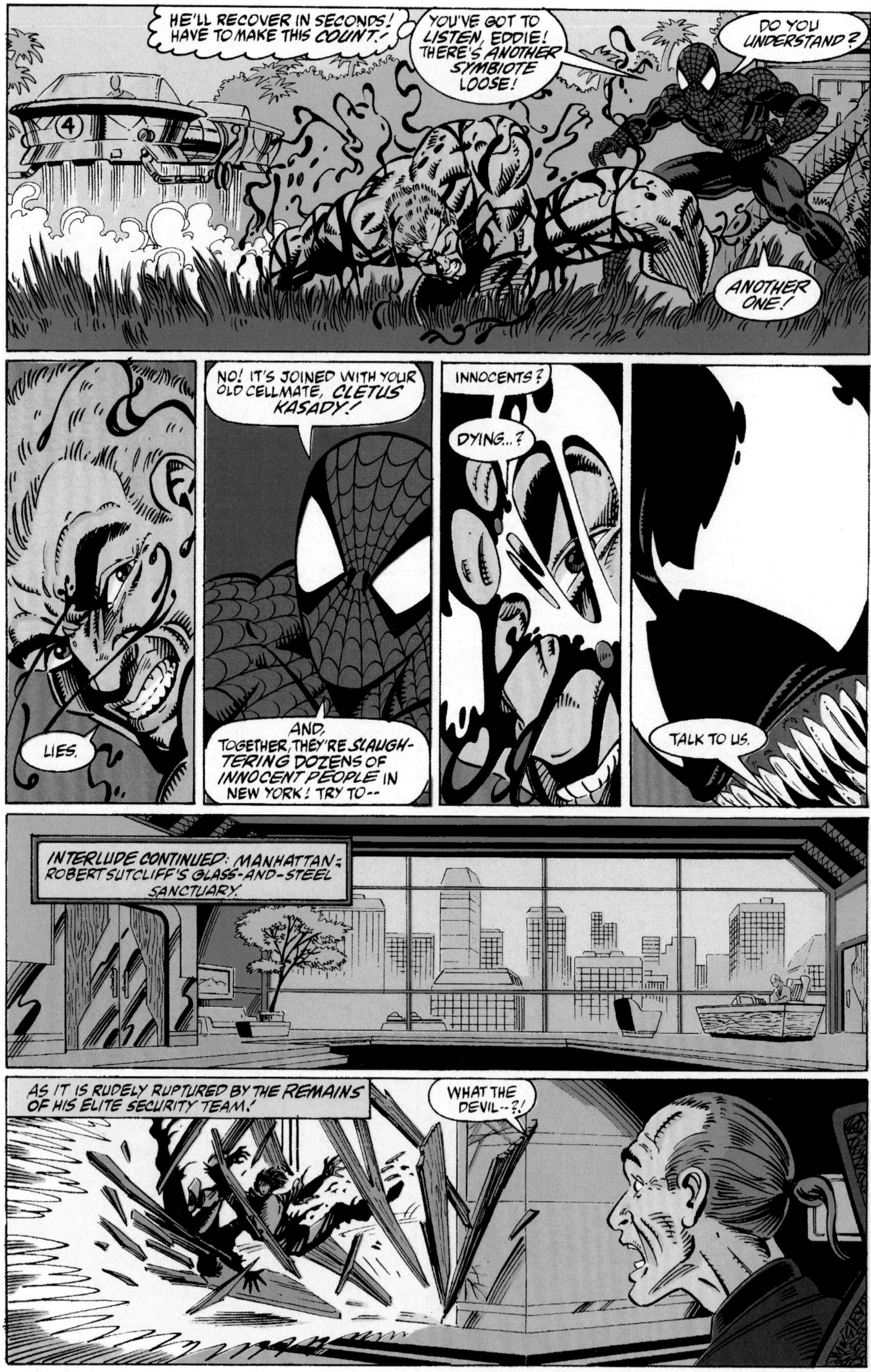
HE'LL RECOVER IN SECONDS! HAVE TO MAKE THIS COUNT!
YOU'VE GOT TO LISTEN, EDDIE! THERE'S ANOTHER SYMBIOTE LOOSE!
DO YOU UNDERSTAND?
ANOTHER ONE!
LIES.
NO! IT'S JOINED WITH YOUR OLD CELLMATE, CLETUS KASADY!
AND, TOGETHER, THEY'RE SLAUGHTERING DOZENS OF INNOCENT PEOPLE IN NEW YORK! TRY TO--
INNOCENTS?
DYING...?
TALK TO US.
INTERLUDE CONTINUED: MANHATTAN: ROBERT SUTCLIFF'S GLASS-AND-STEEL SANCTUARY.
AS IT IS RUDELY RUPTURED BY THE REMAINS OF HIS ELITE SECURITY TEAM!
WHAT THE DEVIL--?!

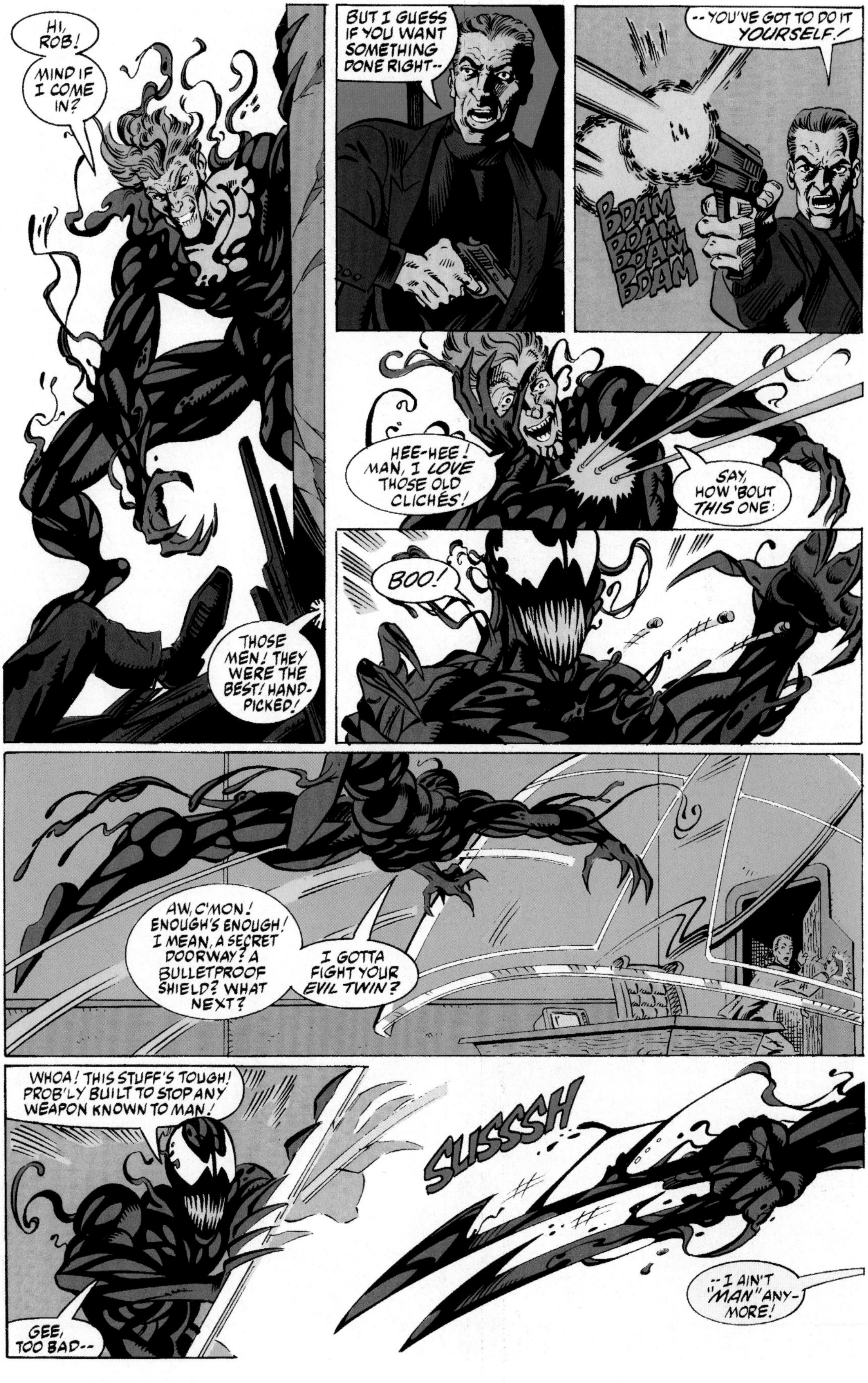

HI, ROB!
MIND IF I COME IN?
BUT I GUESS IF YOU WANT SOMETHING DONE RIGHT--
--YOU'VE GOT TO DO IT YOURSELF!
BDAM BDAM BDAM BDAM
HEE-HEE! MAN, I LOVE THOSE OLD CLICHÉS!
SAY, HOW 'BOUT THIS ONE:
THOSE MEN! THEY WERE THE BEST! HAND-PICKED!
BOO!
AW, C'MON! ENOUGH'S ENOUGH! I MEAN, A SECRET DOORWAY? A BULLETPROOF SHIELD? WHAT NEXT?
I GOTTA FIGHT YOUR EVIL TWIN?
WHOA! THIS STUFF'S TOUGH! PROB'LY BUILT TO STOP ANY WEAPON KNOWN TO MAN!
SLISSSH
GEE, TOO BAD--
--I AIN'T "MAN" ANY-MORE!

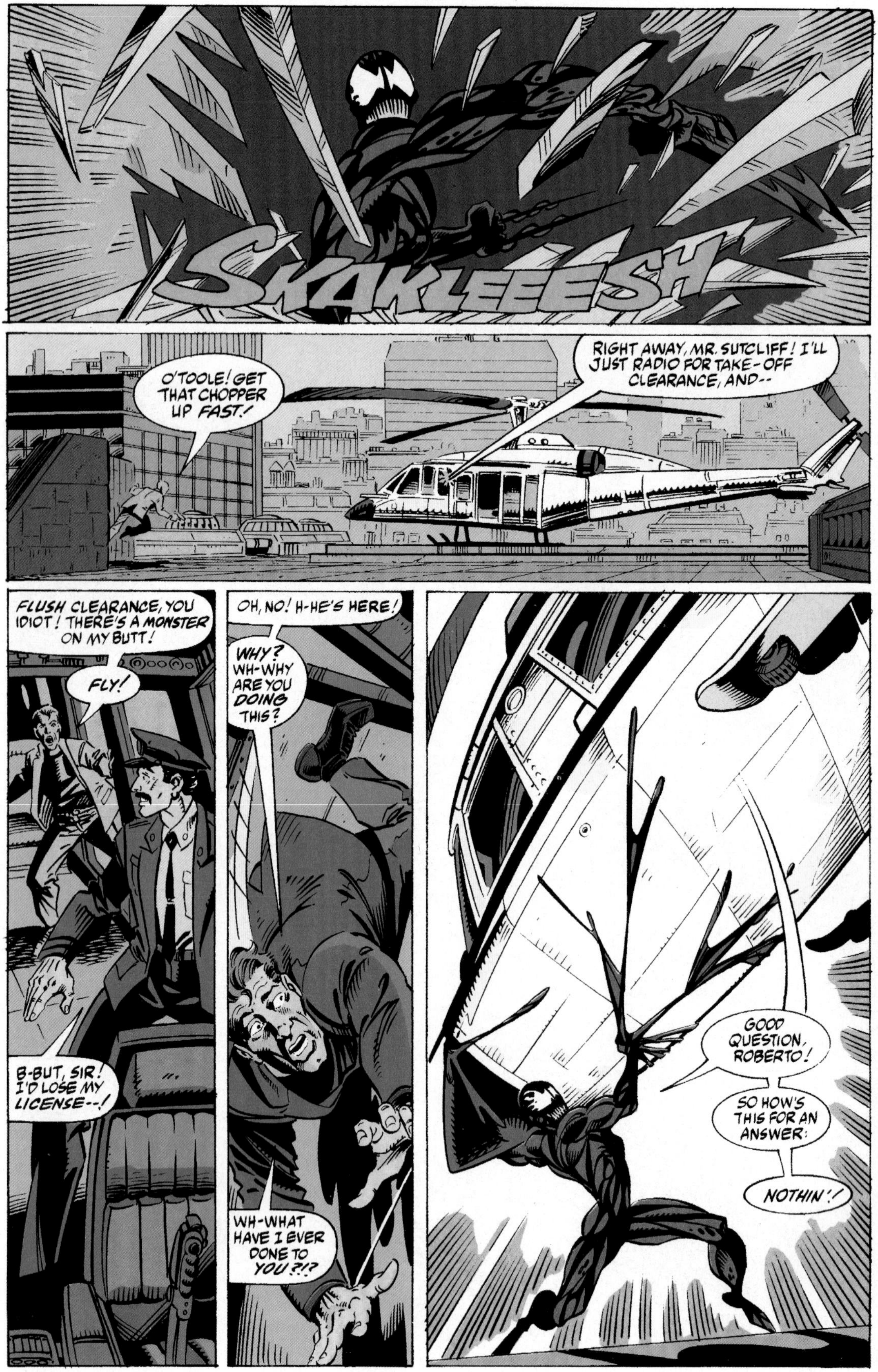
SKAKLEEESH
O'TOOLE! GET THAT CHOPPER UP FAST!
RIGHT AWAY, MR. SUTCLIFF! I'LL JUST RADIO FOR TAKE-OFF CLEARANCE, AND--
FLUSH CLEARANCE, YOU IDIOT! THERE'S A MONSTER ON MY BUTT!
FLY!
B-BUT, SIR! I'D LOSE MY LICENSE--!
OH, NO! H-HE'S HERE!
WHY? WH-WHY ARE YOU DOING THIS?
WH-WHAT HAVE I EVER DONE TO YOU?!?
GOOD QUESTION, ROBERTO!
SO HOW'S THIS FOR AN ANSWER:
NOTHIN'!

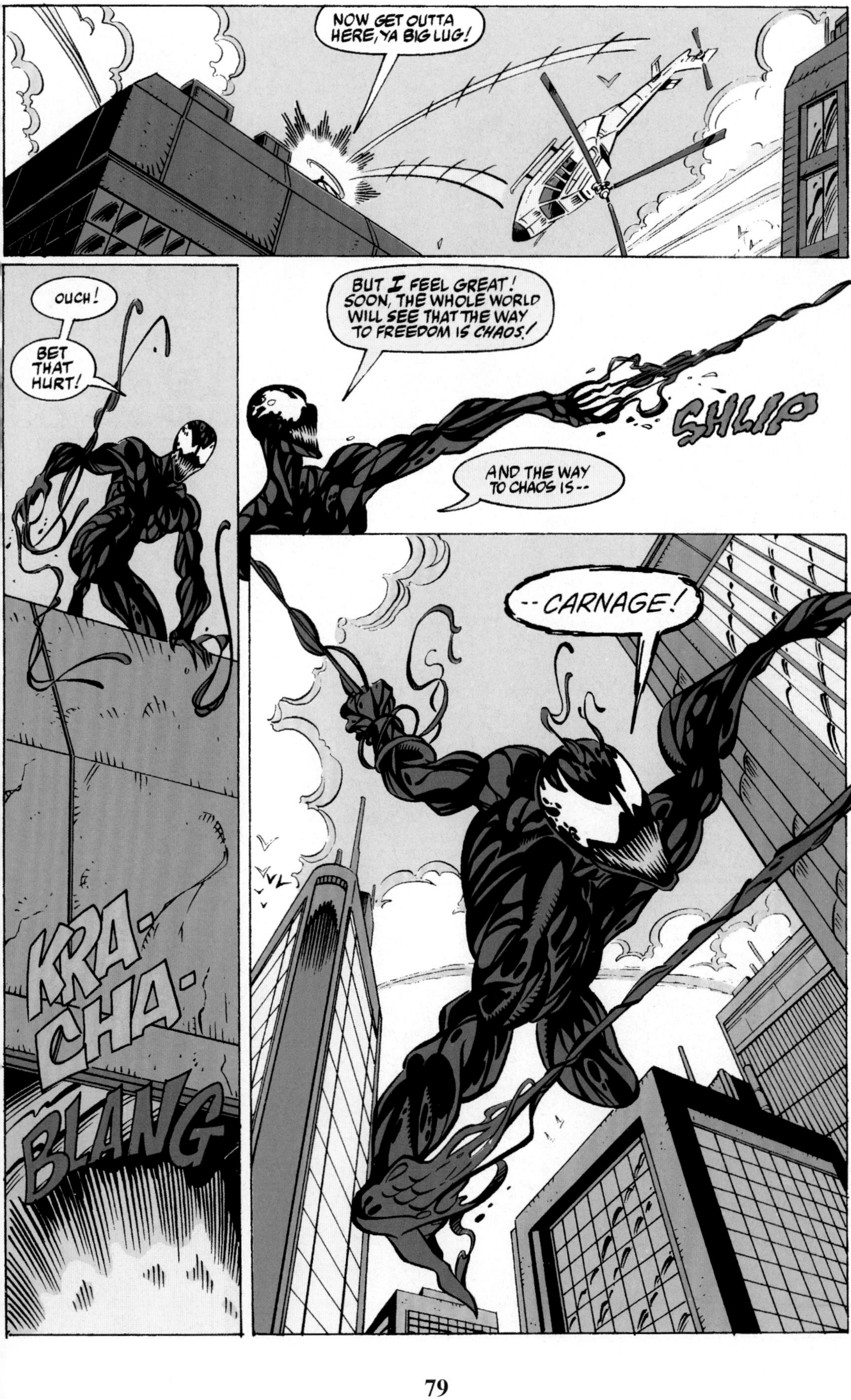
NOW GET OUTTA HERE, YA BIG LUG!
OUCH!
BET THAT HURT!
BUT I FEEL GREAT! SOON, THE WHOLE WORLD WILL SEE THAT THE WAY TO FREEDOM IS CHAOS!
SHLIP
AND THE WAY TO CHAOS IS--
--CARNAGE!
KRA-CHA-BLANG

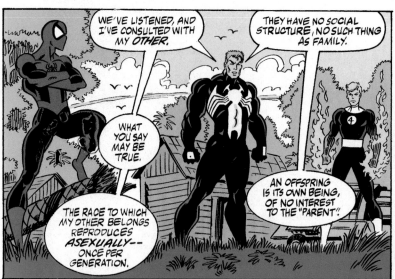

WE'VE LISTENED, AND I'VE CONSULTED WITH MY *OTHER.*

THEY HAVE NO SOCIAL STRUCTURE, NO SUCH THING AS FAMILY.

WHAT YOU SAY MAY BE TRUE.

THE RACE TO WHICH MY OTHER BELONGS REPRODUCES *ASEXUALLY*-- ONCE PER GENERATION.

AN OFFSPRING IS ITS OWN BEING, OF NO INTEREST TO THE "PARENT".

THUS, MY OTHER SAW LITTLE REASON TO TELL ME IT HAD "*GIVEN BIRTH*" DURING OUR ESCAPE FROM RYKER'S ISLAND!

APPARENTLY, GESTATING IN AN ALIEN ENVIRONMENT-- *EARTH*-- CAUSED THAT SYMBIOTE TO DEVELOP UNIQUE POWERS.

THIS IS DISTURBING.

BUT EVEN MORE SO IS ITS MERGER WITH A CONSCIENCELESS SOCIOPATH LIKE *KASADY!*

WE WERE INNOCENT ONCE. BEFORE *YOU*, SPIDER-MAN RUINED US!

AND WE STILL REGARD INNOCENCE AS A PRECIOUS COMMODITY.

WE'LL HELP. BUT WHEN IT'S OVER--

--WE GO *FREE!*

NOT THAT BROCK KNOWS I'M ALIVE, HE WON'T REST TILL I'M *DEAD.*

BUT IF I REFUSE, EVERY DEATH AT CARNAGE'S HANDS WILL BE ON *MY* SHOULDERS!

SPIDEY! YOU *CAN'T--!*

BELIEVE ME, JOHNNY, I *KNOW* I CAN'T.

JUST LIKE I KNOW--

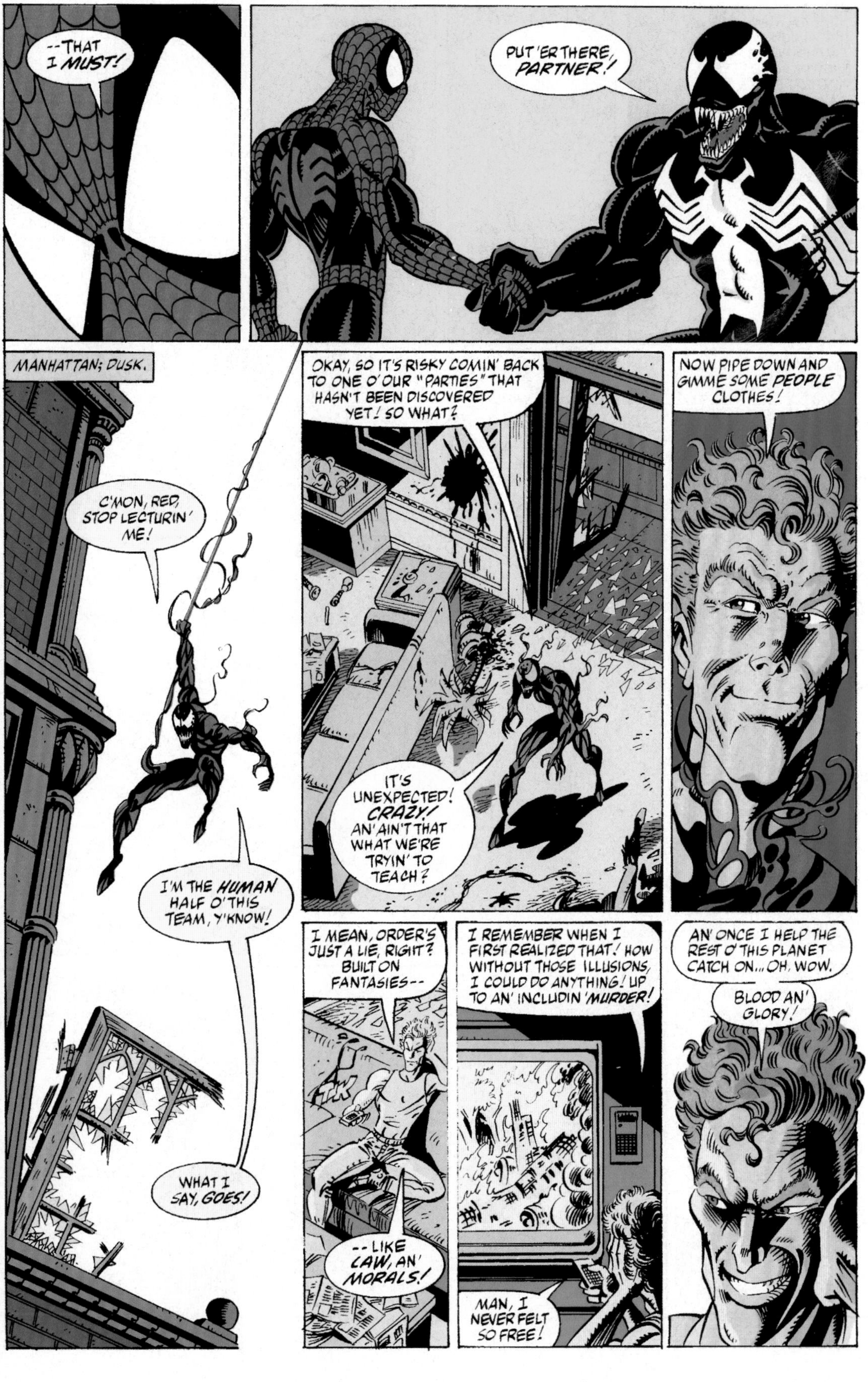
--THAT I MUST!
PUT 'ER THERE, PARTNER!
MANHATTAN; DUSK.
C'MON, RED, STOP LECTURIN' ME!
I'M THE HUMAN HALF O' THIS TEAM, Y'KNOW!
WHAT I SAY, GOES!
OKAY, SO IT'S RISKY COMIN' BACK TO ONE O' OUR "PARTIES" THAT HASN'T BEEN DISCOVERED YET! SO WHAT?
IT'S UNEXPECTED! CRAZY! AN' AIN'T THAT WHAT WE'RE TRYIN' TO TEACH?
NOW PIPE DOWN AND GIMME SOME PEOPLE CLOTHES!
I MEAN, ORDER'S JUST A LIE, RIGHT? BUILT ON FANTASIES--
--LIKE LAW, AN' MORALS!
I REMEMBER WHEN I FIRST REALIZED THAT! HOW WITHOUT THOSE ILLUSIONS, I COULD DO ANYTHING! UP TO AN' INCLUDIN 'MURDER!
MAN, I NEVER FELT SO FREE!
AN' ONCE I HELP THE REST O' THIS PLANET CATCH ON... OH, WOW.
BLOOD AN' GLORY!

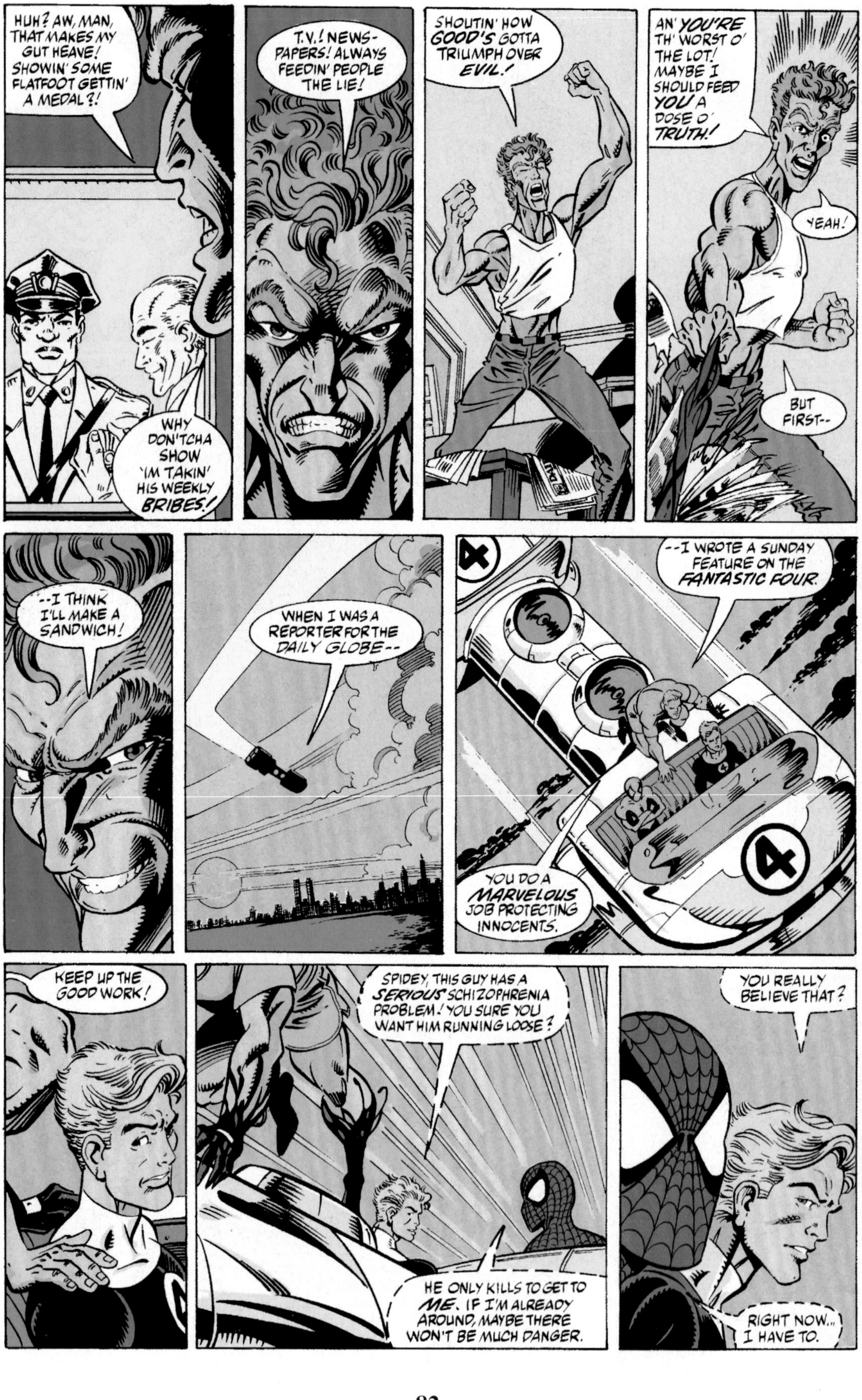
HUH? AW, MAN, THAT MAKES MY GUT HEAVE! SHOWIN' SOME FLATFOOT GETTIN' A MEDAL?!
WHY DON'TCHA SHOW 'IM TAKIN' HIS WEEKLY BRIBES!
T.V.! NEWS-PAPERS! ALWAYS FEEDIN' PEOPLE THE LIE!
SHOUTIN' HOW GOOD'S GOTTA TRIUMPH OVER EVIL!
AN' YOU'RE TH' WORST O' THE LOT! MAYBE I SHOULD FEED YOU A DOSE O' TRUTH!
YEAH!
BUT FIRST--
--I THINK I'LL MAKE A SANDWICH!
WHEN I WAS A REPORTER FOR THE DAILY GLOBE--
--I WROTE A SUNDAY FEATURE ON THE FANTASTIC FOUR.
YOU DO A MARVELOUS JOB PROTECTING INNOCENTS.
KEEP UP THE GOOD WORK!
SPIDEY, THIS GUY HAS A SERIOUS SCHIZOPHRENIA PROBLEM! YOU SURE YOU WANT HIM RUNNING LOOSE?
HE ONLY KILLS TO GET TO ME. IF I'M ALREADY AROUND, MAYBE THERE WON'T BE MUCH DANGER.
YOU REALLY BELIEVE THAT?
RIGHT NOW... I HAVE TO.

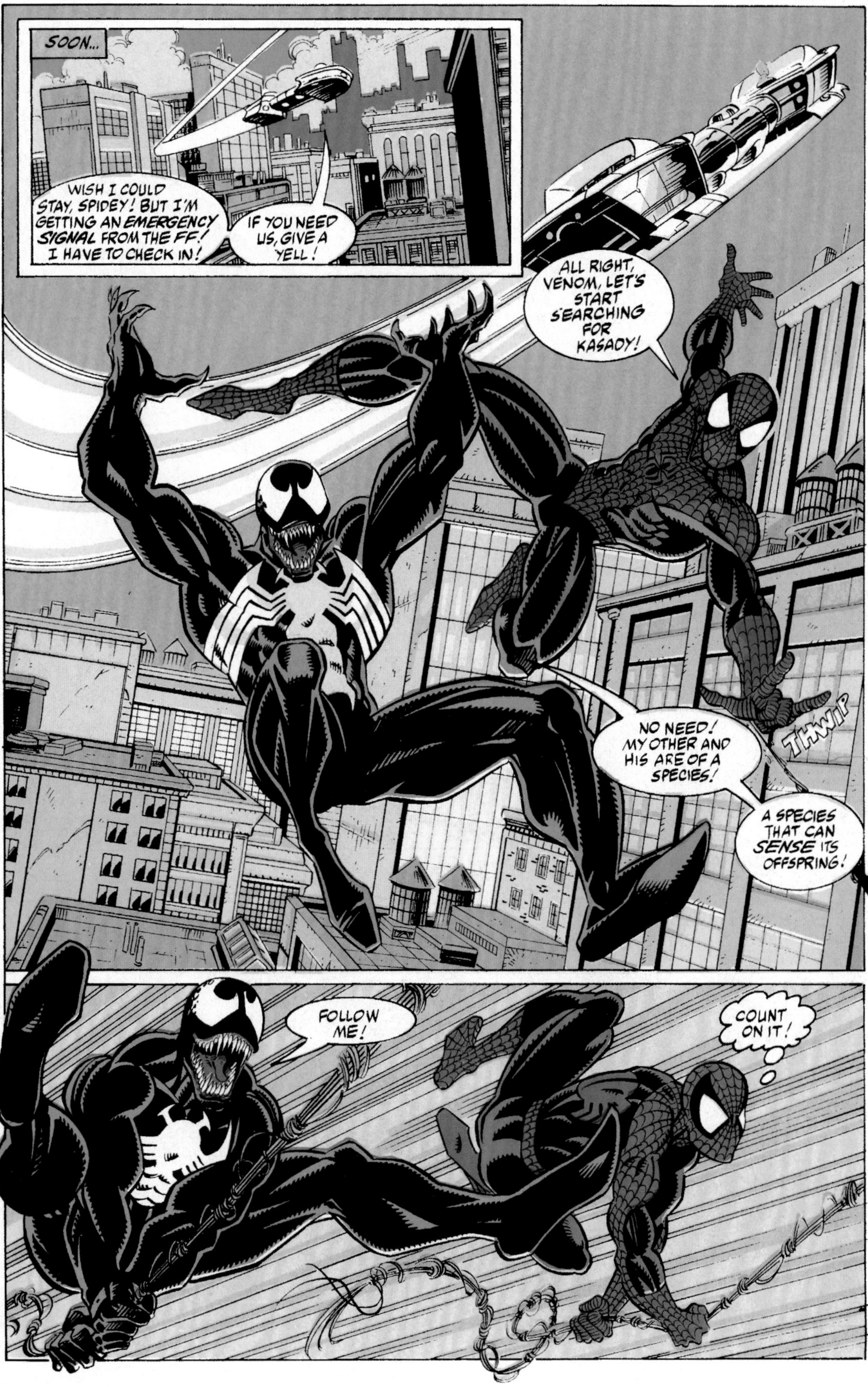
SOON...
WISH I COULD STAY, SPIDEY! BUT I'M GETTING AN EMERGENCY SIGNAL FROM THE FF! I HAVE TO CHECK IN!
IF YOU NEED US, GIVE A YELL!
ALL RIGHT, VENOM, LET'S START SEARCHING FOR KASADY!
NO NEED! MY OTHER AND HIS ARE OF A SPECIES!
THWIP
A SPECIES THAT CAN SENSE ITS OFFSPRING!
FOLLOW ME!
COUNT ON IT!

WHAT? NO GREY POUPON?!

KASADY!

WELL, WELL.

DAD!

THIS IS WEIRD, SEEING THEM TOGETHER!

WE WERE GIVEN POWER FROM THE STARS! IT'S OBSCENE TO USE IT FOR SENSELESS SLAUGHTER!

GET REAL, BROCK! IN OUR CELL, ALL YOU COULD TALK ABOUT WAS FILLETIN' THE SPIDER-DUDE!

SO LET'S DO 'IM.

I'LL HELP.

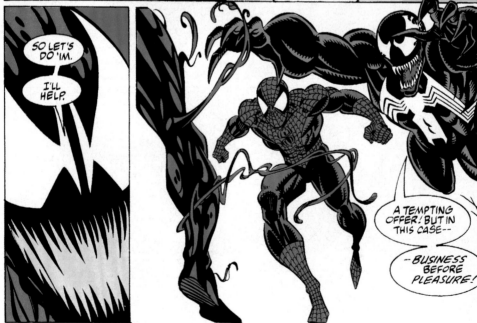

A TEMPTING OFFER! BUT IN THIS CASE--

--BUSINESS BEFORE PLEASURE!

84

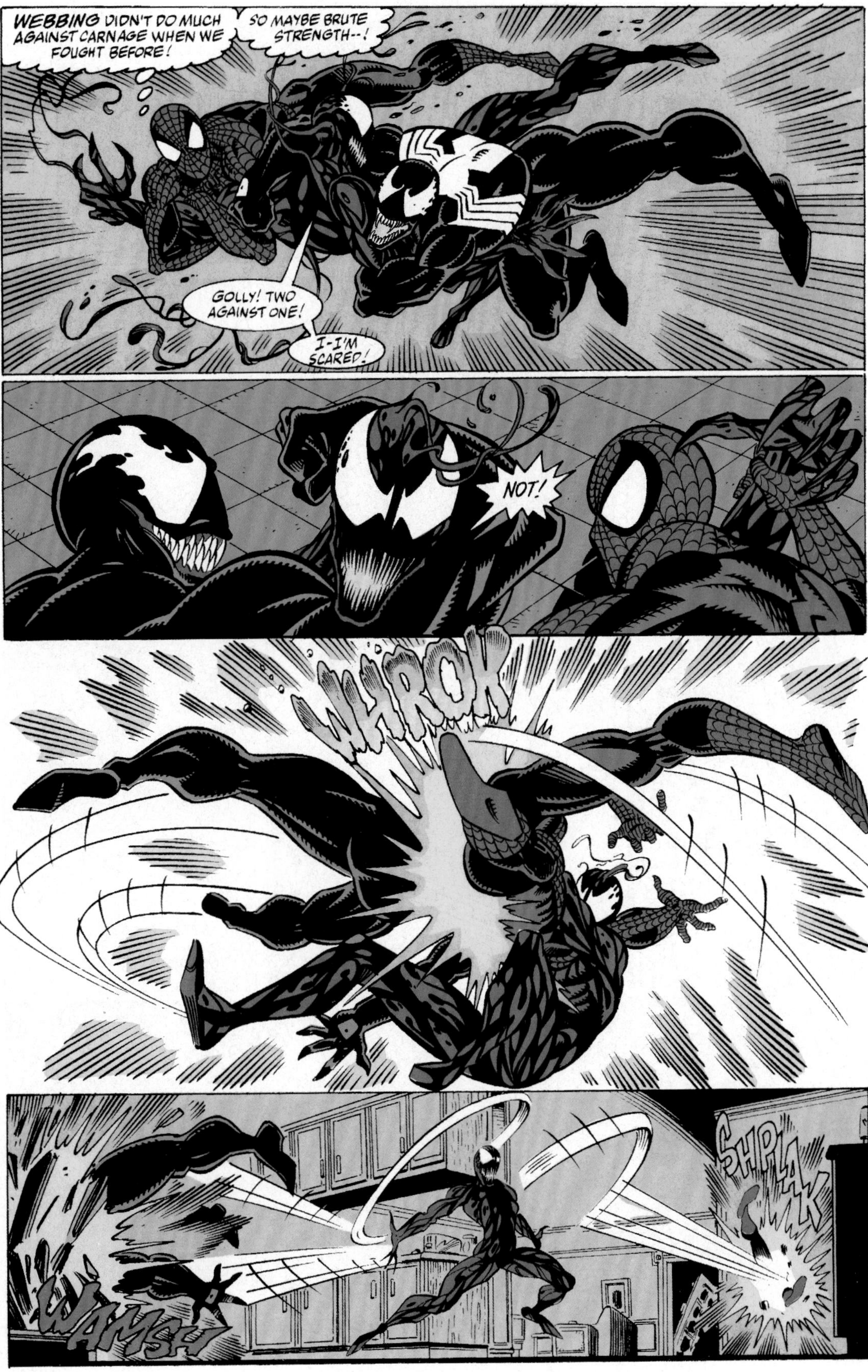

WEBBING DIDN'T DO MUCH AGAINST CARNAGE WHEN WE FOUGHT BEFORE!
SO MAYBE BRUTE STRENGTH--!
GOLLY! TWO AGAINST ONE!
I-I'M SCARED!
NOT!
WHROK
SHPLAK
WAMSH

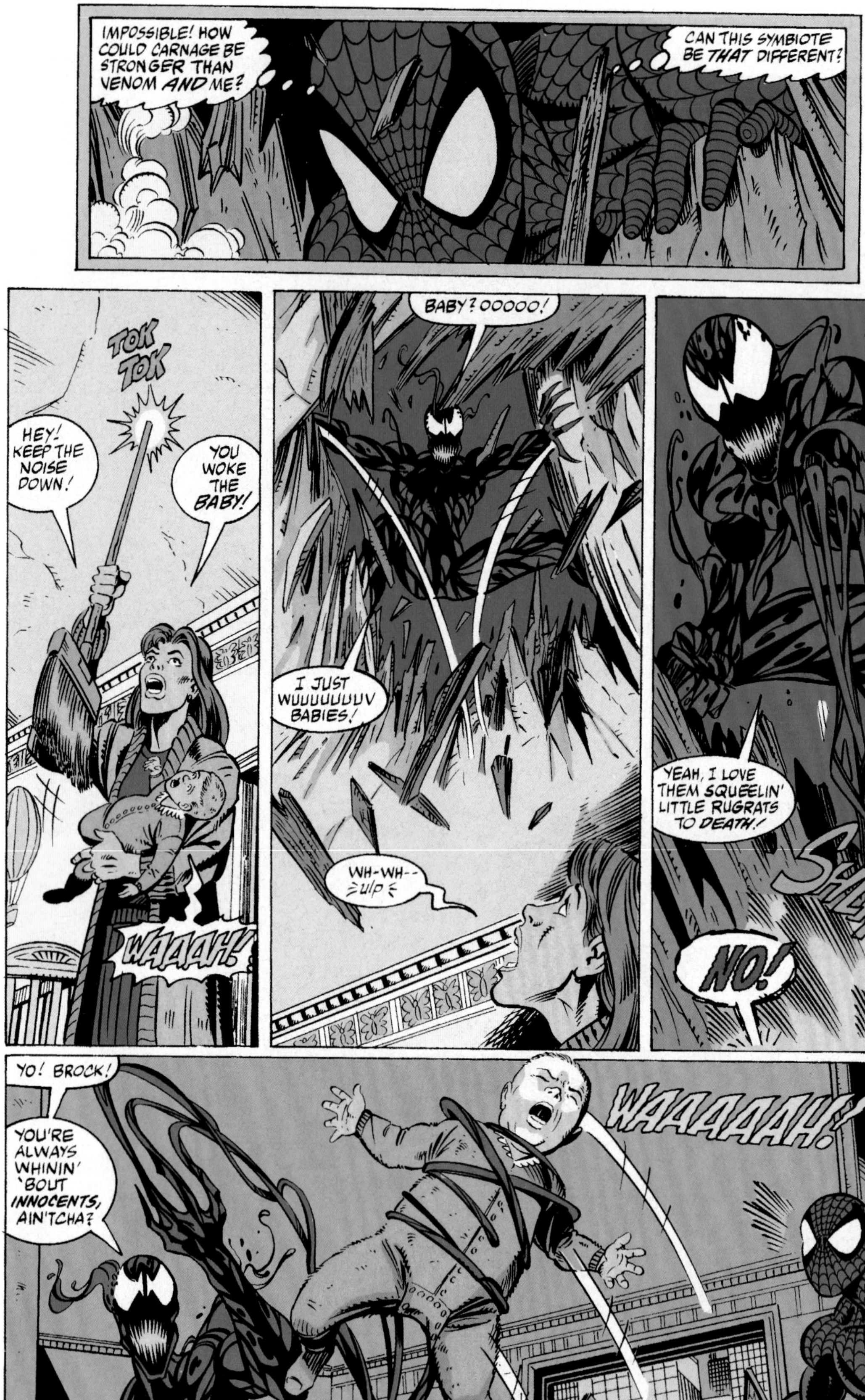
IMPOSSIBLE! HOW COULD CARNAGE BE STRONGER THAN VENOM AND ME?
CAN THIS SYMBIOTE BE THAT DIFFERENT?
TOK TOK
HEY! KEEP THE NOISE DOWN!
YOU WOKE THE BABY!
WAAAH!
BABY? OOOOO!
I JUST WUUUUUUUV BABIES!
WH-WH-- gulp
YEAH, I LOVE THEM SQUEELIN' LITTLE RUGRATS TO DEATH!
SHLIP
NO!
YO! BROCK!
YOU'RE ALWAYS WHININ' 'BOUT INNOCENTS, AIN'TCHA?
WAAAAAH!

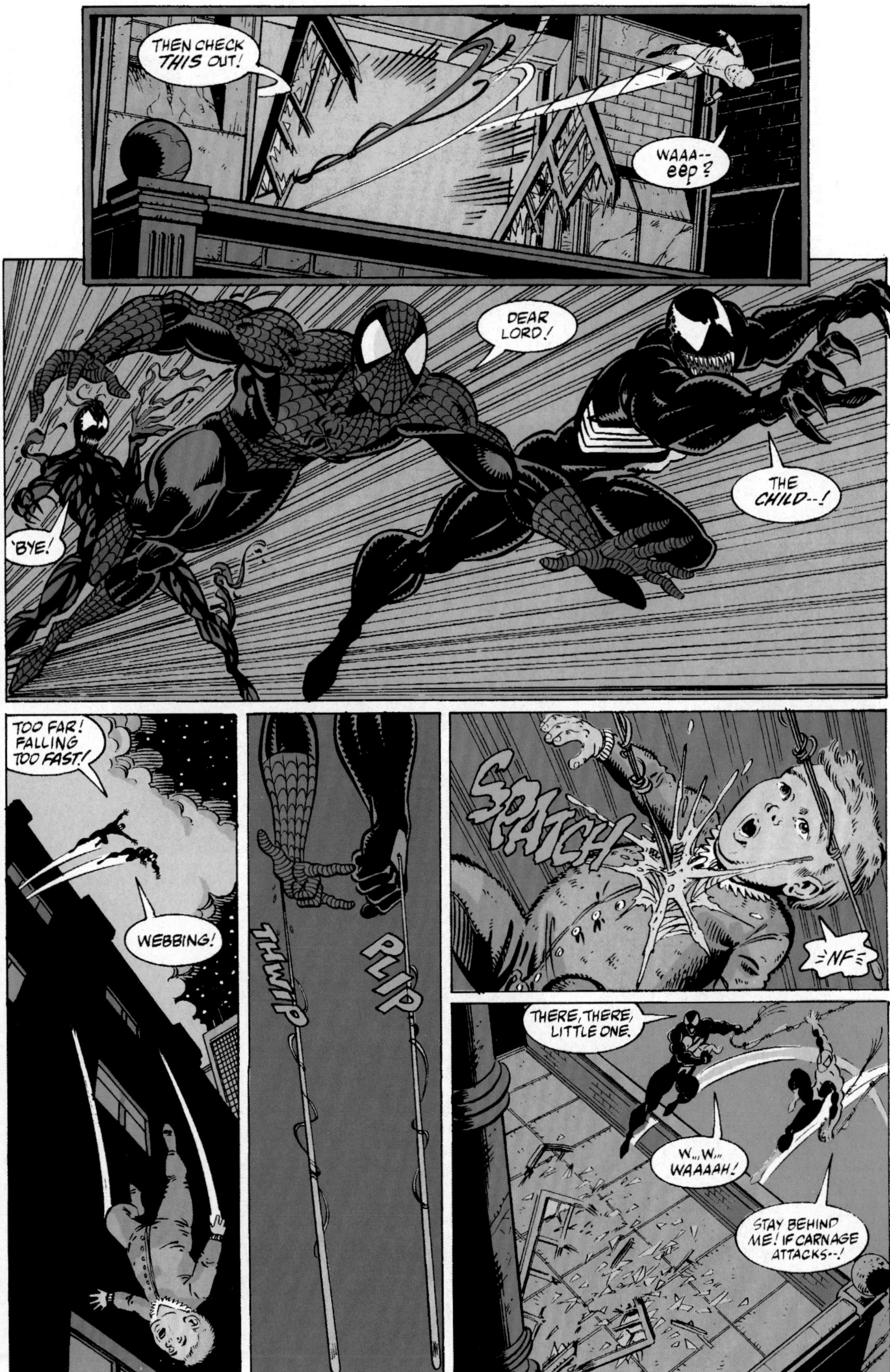
THEN CHECK THIS OUT!
WAAA-- eep?
DEAR LORD!
THE CHILD--!
'BYE!
TOO FAR! FALLING TOO FAST!
WEBBING!
THWIP
PLIP
SPLATCH
NF
THERE, THERE, LITTLE ONE.
W...W... WAAAAH!
STAY BEHIND ME! IF CARNAGE ATTACKS--!

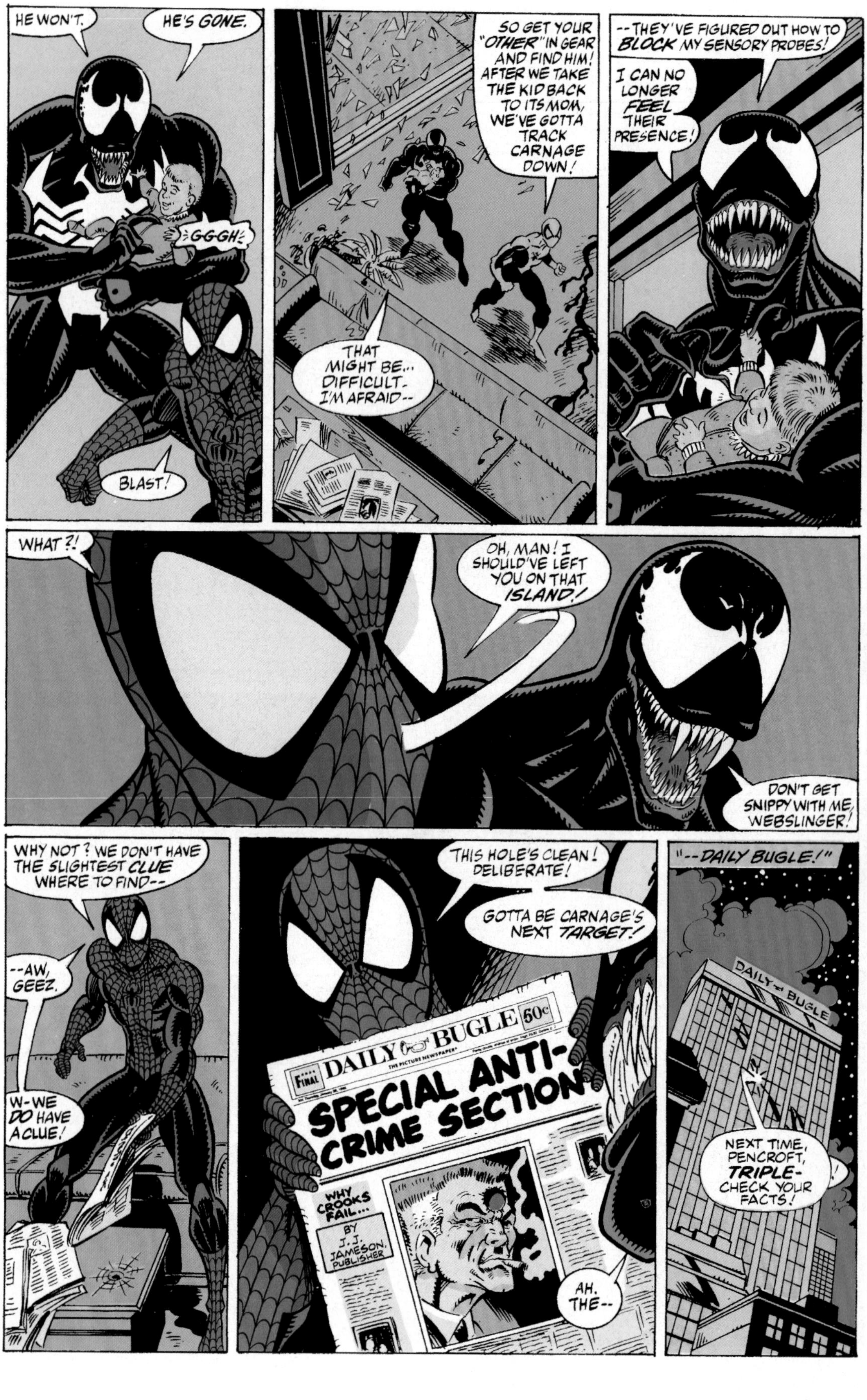
HE WON'T.
HE'S GONE.
GGGH!
BLAST!
SO GET YOUR "OTHER" IN GEAR AND FIND HIM! AFTER WE TAKE THE KID BACK TO ITS MOM, WE'VE GOTTA TRACK CARNAGE DOWN!
THAT MIGHT BE... DIFFICULT. I'M AFRAID--
--THEY'VE FIGURED OUT HOW TO BLOCK MY SENSORY PROBES!
I CAN NO LONGER FEEL THEIR PRESENCE!
WHAT?!
OH, MAN! I SHOULD'VE LEFT YOU ON THAT ISLAND!
DON'T GET SNIPPY WITH ME, WEBSLINGER!
WHY NOT? WE DON'T HAVE THE SLIGHTEST CLUE WHERE TO FIND--
--AW, GEEZ.
W-WE DO HAVE A CLUE!
THIS HOLE'S CLEAN! DELIBERATE!
GOTTA BE CARNAGE'S NEXT TARGET!
DAILY BUGLE 50¢
FINAL
THE PICTURE NEWSPAPER
SPECIAL ANTI-CRIME SECTION
WHY CROOKS FAIL...
BY J. J. JAMESON, PUBLISHER
AH. THE--
"--DAILY BUGLE!"
DAILY BUGLE
NEXT TIME, PENCROFT, TRIPLE-CHECK YOUR FACTS!

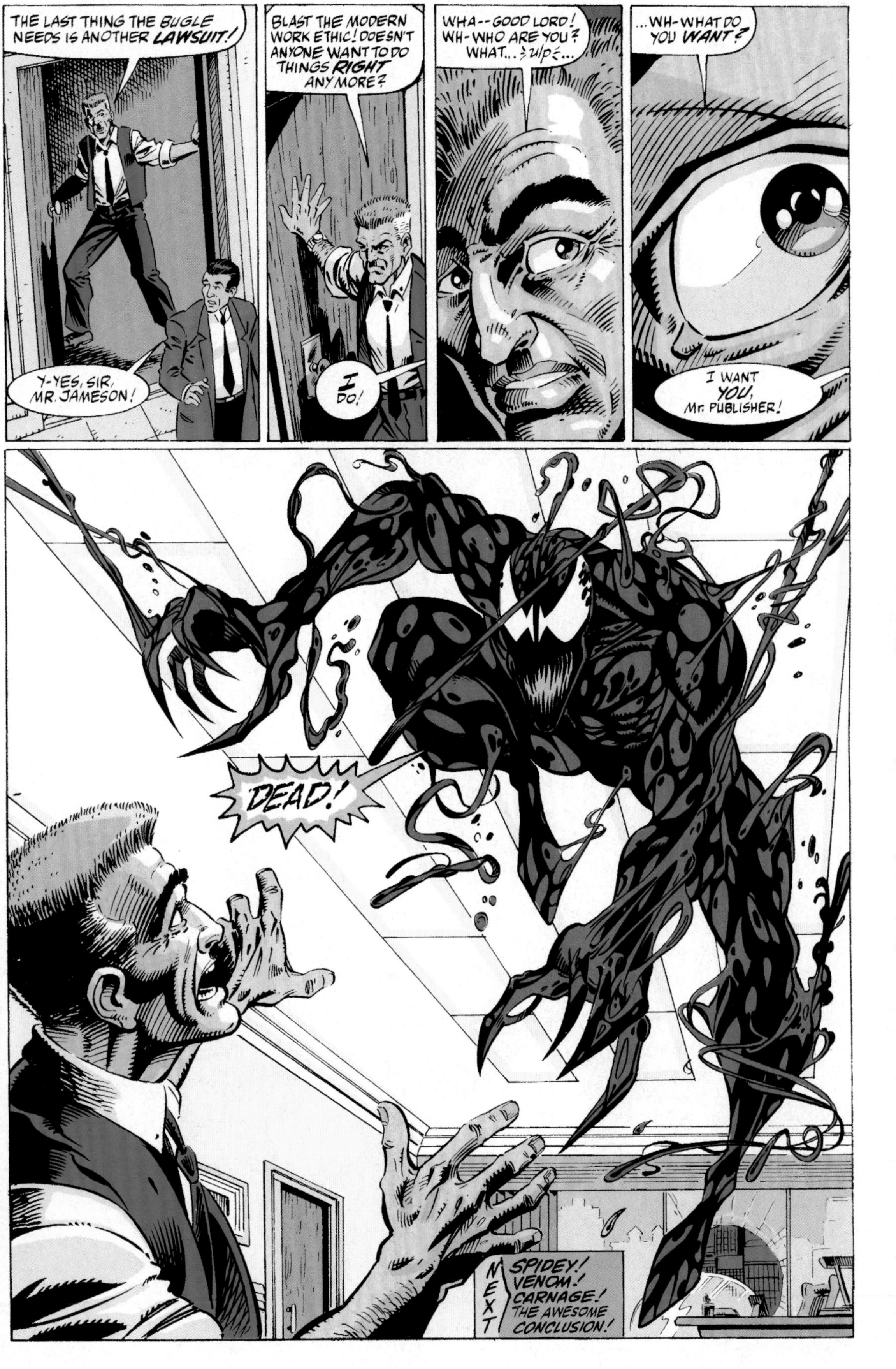
THE LAST THING THE BUGLE NEEDS IS ANOTHER LAWSUIT!
Y-YES, SIR, MR. JAMESON!
BLAST THE MODERN WORK ETHIC! DOESN'T ANYONE WANT TO DO THINGS RIGHT ANY MORE?
I DO!
WHA--GOOD LORD! WH-WHO ARE YOU? WHAT... ≷ulp≶...
...WH-WHAT DO YOU WANT?
I WANT YOU, Mr. PUBLISHER!
DEAD!
NEXT SPIDEY! VENOM! CARNAGE! THE AWESOME CONCLUSION!

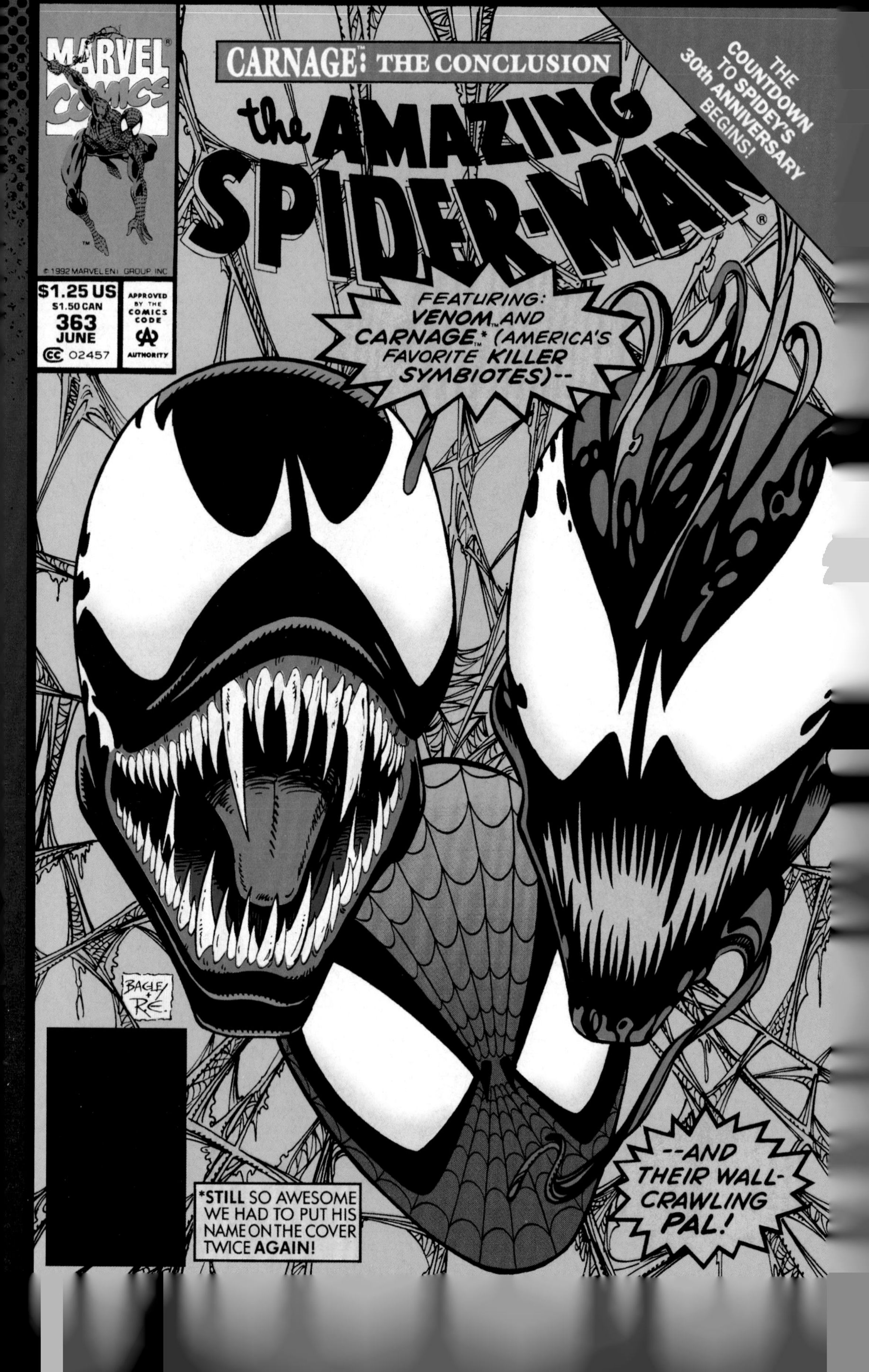

MARVEL COMICS
CARNAGE: THE CONCLUSION
the AMAZING SPIDER-MAN
THE COUNTDOWN TO SPIDEY'S 30th ANNIVERSARY BEGINS!
© 1992 MARVEL ENT. GROUP, INC.
$1.25 US $1.50 CAN 363 JUNE
02457
APPROVED BY THE COMICS CODE AUTHORITY
FEATURING: VENOM AND CARNAGE* (AMERICA'S FAVORITE KILLER SYMBIOTES)--
BAGLEY + RE.
--AND THEIR WALL-CRAWLING PAL!
*STILL SO AWESOME WE HAD TO PUT HIS NAME ON THE COVER TWICE AGAIN!

BITTEN BY A RADIOACTIVE SPIDER, STUDENT **PETER PARKER** GAINED THE PROPORTIONATE STRENGTH AND AGILITY OF AN ARACHNID! ARMED WITH HIS WONDROUS WEB-SHOOTERS, THE RELUCTANT SUPER HERO STRUGGLES WITH SINISTER SUPER-VILLAINS, MAKING ENDS MEET, AND MAINTAINING SOME SEMBLANCE OF A NORMAL LIFE!

Stan Lee PRESENTS: **THE AMAZING SPIDER-MAN®**

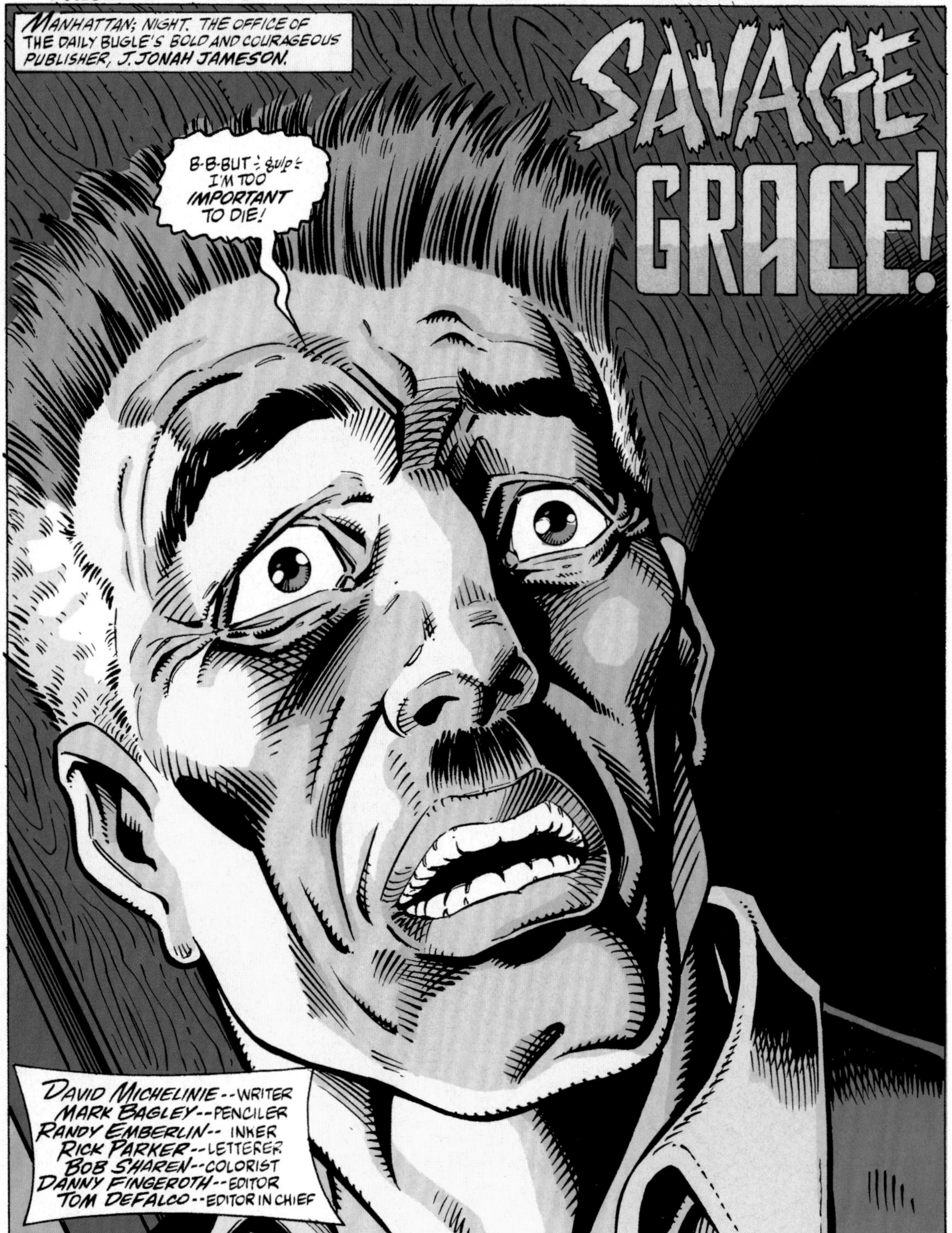
MANHATTAN; NIGHT. THE OFFICE OF THE DAILY BUGLE'S BOLD AND COURAGEOUS PUBLISHER, J. JONAH JAMESON.
SAVAGE GRACE!
B-B-BUT -gulp- I'M TOO IMPORTANT TO DIE!
DAVID MICHELINIE--WRITER
MARK BAGLEY--PENCILER
RANDY EMBERLIN--INKER
RICK PARKER--LETTERER
BOB SHAREN--COLORIST
DANNY FINGEROTH--EDITOR
TOM DEFALCO--EDITOR IN CHIEF

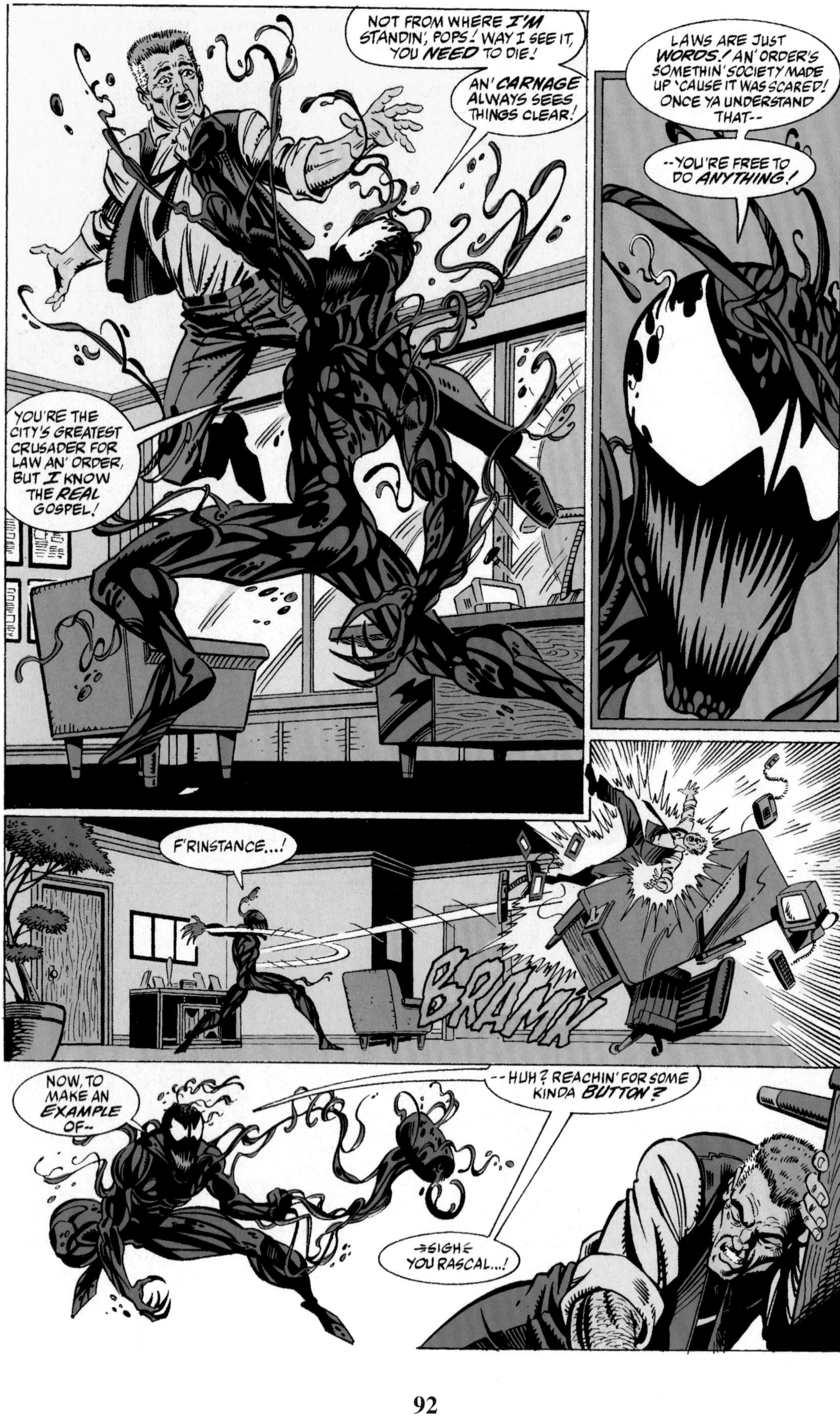
NOT FROM WHERE I'M STANDIN', POPS! WAY I SEE IT, YOU NEED TO DIE!
AN' CARNAGE ALWAYS SEES THINGS CLEAR!
YOU'RE THE CITY'S GREATEST CRUSADER FOR LAW AN' ORDER, BUT I KNOW THE REAL GOSPEL!
LAWS ARE JUST WORDS! AN' ORDER'S SOMETHIN' SOCIETY MADE UP 'CAUSE IT WAS SCARED! ONCE YA UNDERSTAND THAT--
--YOU'RE FREE TO DO ANYTHING!
F'RINSTANCE...!
BRAMK
NOW, TO MAKE AN EXAMPLE OF--
--HUH? REACHIN' FOR SOME KINDA BUTTON?
SIGH YOU RASCAL...!

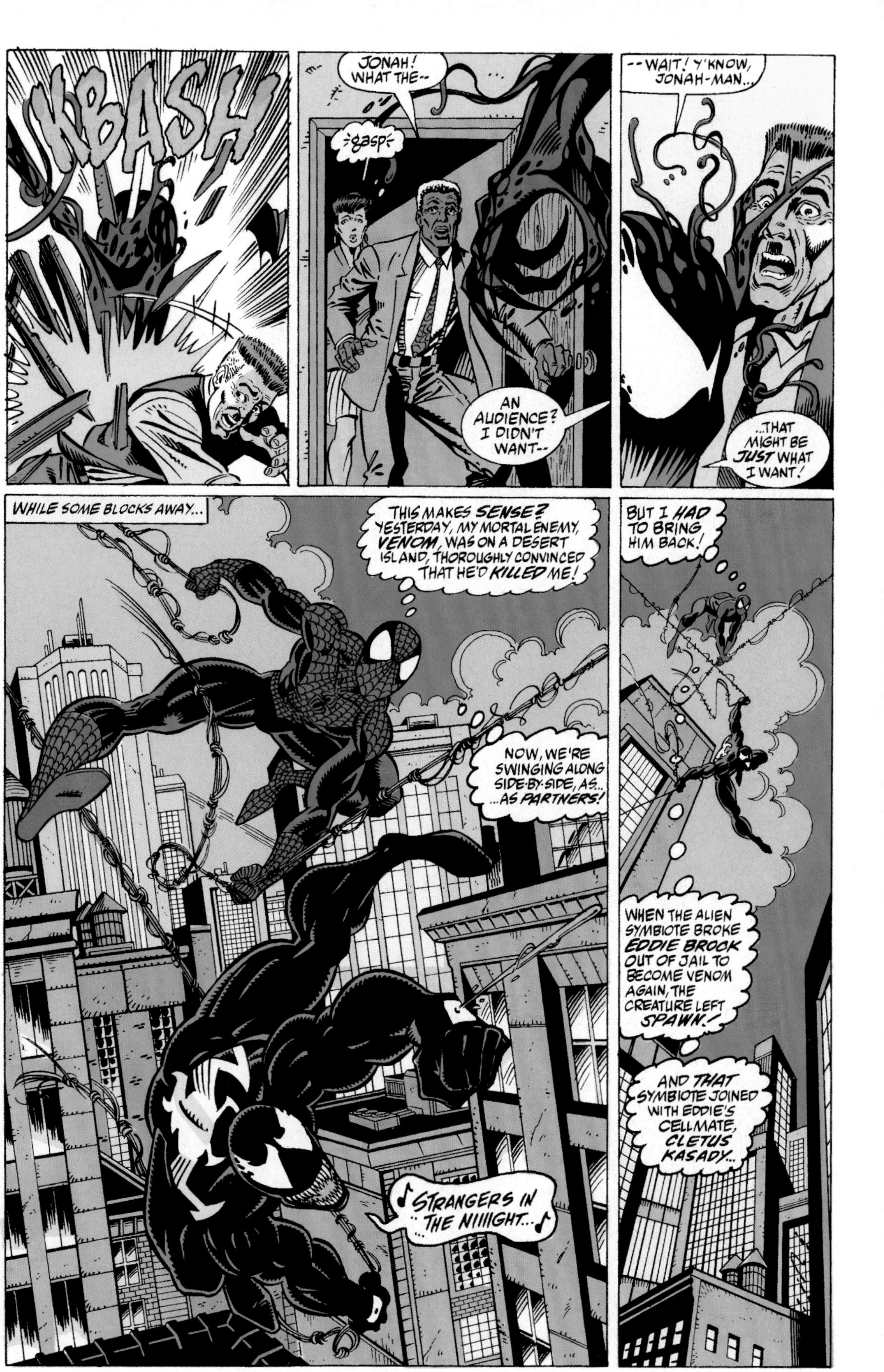
KBASH
JONAH! WHAT THE--
-gasp-
AN AUDIENCE? I DIDN'T WANT--
--WAIT! Y'KNOW, JONAH-MAN...
...THAT MIGHT BE JUST WHAT I WANT!
WHILE SOME BLOCKS AWAY...
THIS MAKES SENSE? YESTERDAY, MY MORTAL ENEMY, VENOM, WAS ON A DESERT ISLAND, THOROUGHLY CONVINCED THAT HE'D KILLED ME!
NOW, WE'RE SWINGING ALONG SIDE-BY-SIDE, AS... ...AS PARTNERS!
STRANGERS IN THE NIIIIGHT...
BUT I HAD TO BRING HIM BACK!
WHEN THE ALIEN SYMBIOTE BROKE EDDIE BROCK OUT OF JAIL TO BECOME VENOM AGAIN, THE CREATURE LEFT SPAWN!
AND THAT SYMBIOTE JOINED WITH EDDIE'S CELLMATE, CLETUS KASADY...

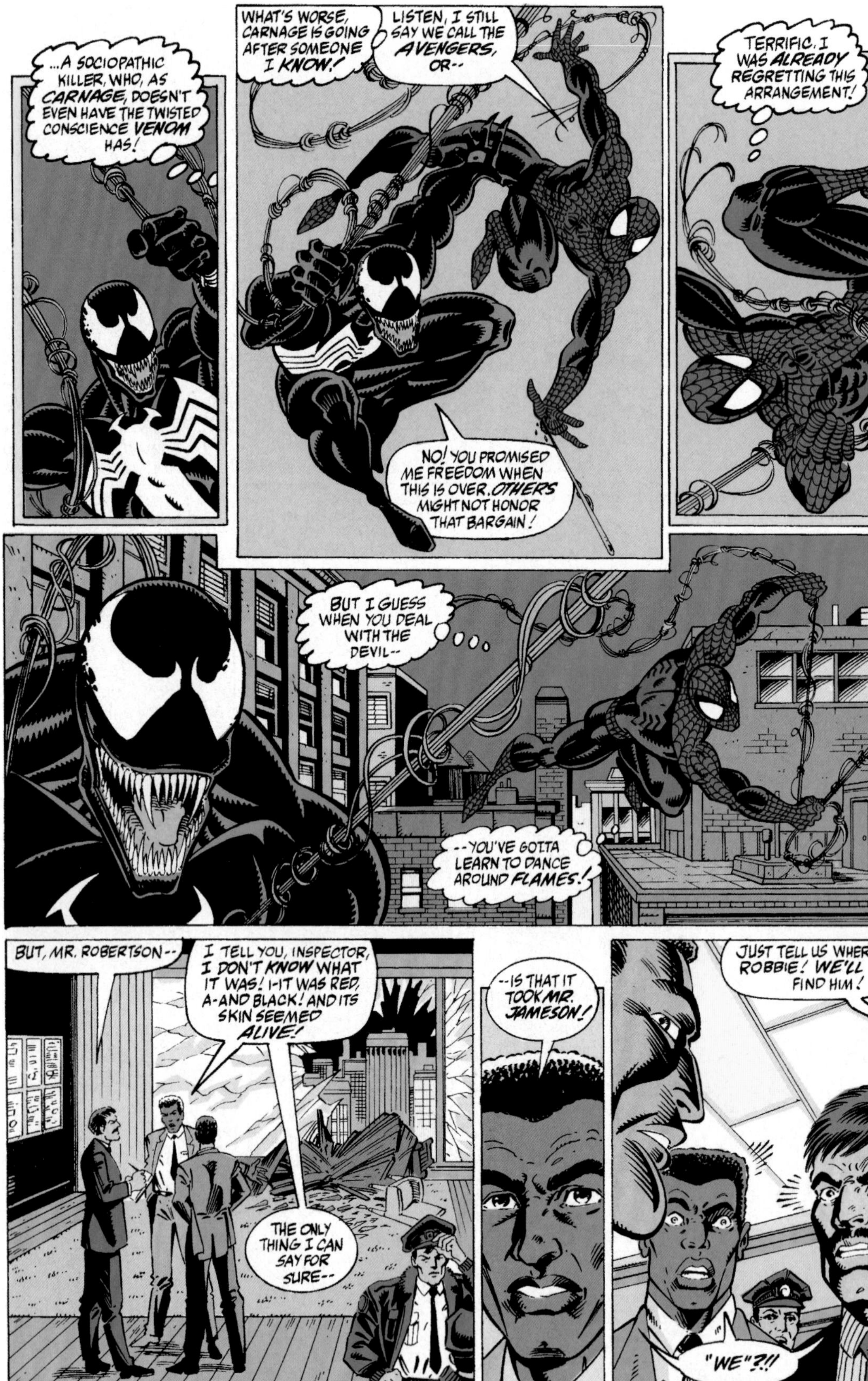
...A SOCIOPATHIC KILLER, WHO, AS CARNAGE, DOESN'T EVEN HAVE THE TWISTED CONSCIENCE VENOM HAS!
WHAT'S WORSE, CARNAGE IS GOING AFTER SOMEONE I KNOW!
LISTEN, I STILL SAY WE CALL THE AVENGERS, OR--
NO! YOU PROMISED ME FREEDOM WHEN THIS IS OVER. OTHERS MIGHT NOT HONOR THAT BARGAIN!
TERRIFIC. I WAS ALREADY REGRETTING THIS ARRANGEMENT!
BUT I GUESS WHEN YOU DEAL WITH THE DEVIL--
--YOU'VE GOTTA LEARN TO DANCE AROUND FLAMES!
BUT, MR. ROBERTSON--
I TELL YOU, INSPECTOR, I DON'T KNOW WHAT IT WAS! I-IT WAS RED, A-AND BLACK! AND ITS SKIN SEEMED ALIVE!
THE ONLY THING I CAN SAY FOR SURE--
--IS THAT IT TOOK MR. JAMESON!
JUST TELL US WHERE, ROBBIE! WE'LL FIND HIM!
"WE"?!!

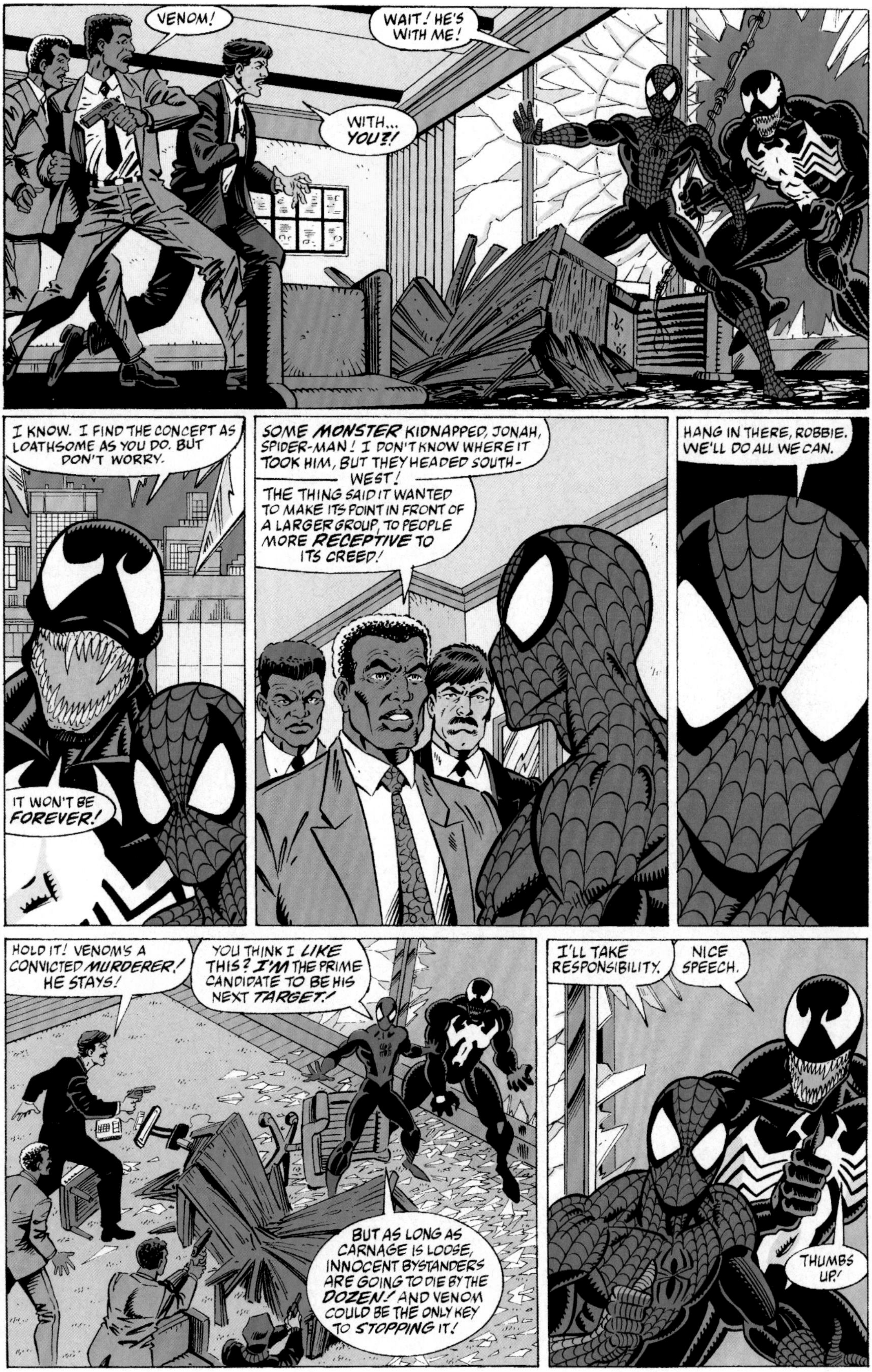
VENOM!
WAIT! HE'S WITH ME!
WITH... YOU?!
I KNOW. I FIND THE CONCEPT AS LOATHSOME AS YOU DO. BUT DON'T WORRY.
IT WON'T BE FOREVER!
SOME MONSTER KIDNAPPED, JONAH, SPIDER-MAN! I DON'T KNOW WHERE IT TOOK HIM, BUT THEY HEADED SOUTH-WEST!
THE THING SAID IT WANTED TO MAKE ITS POINT IN FRONT OF A LARGER GROUP, TO PEOPLE MORE RECEPTIVE TO ITS CREED!
HANG IN THERE, ROBBIE. WE'LL DO ALL WE CAN.
HOLD IT! VENOM'S A CONVICTED MURDERER! HE STAYS!
YOU THINK I LIKE THIS? I'M THE PRIME CANDIDATE TO BE HIS NEXT TARGET!
BUT AS LONG AS CARNAGE IS LOOSE, INNOCENT BYSTANDERS ARE GOING TO DIE BY THE DOZEN! AND VENOM COULD BE THE ONLY KEY TO STOPPING IT!
I'LL TAKE RESPONSIBILITY.
NICE SPEECH.
THUMBS UP!

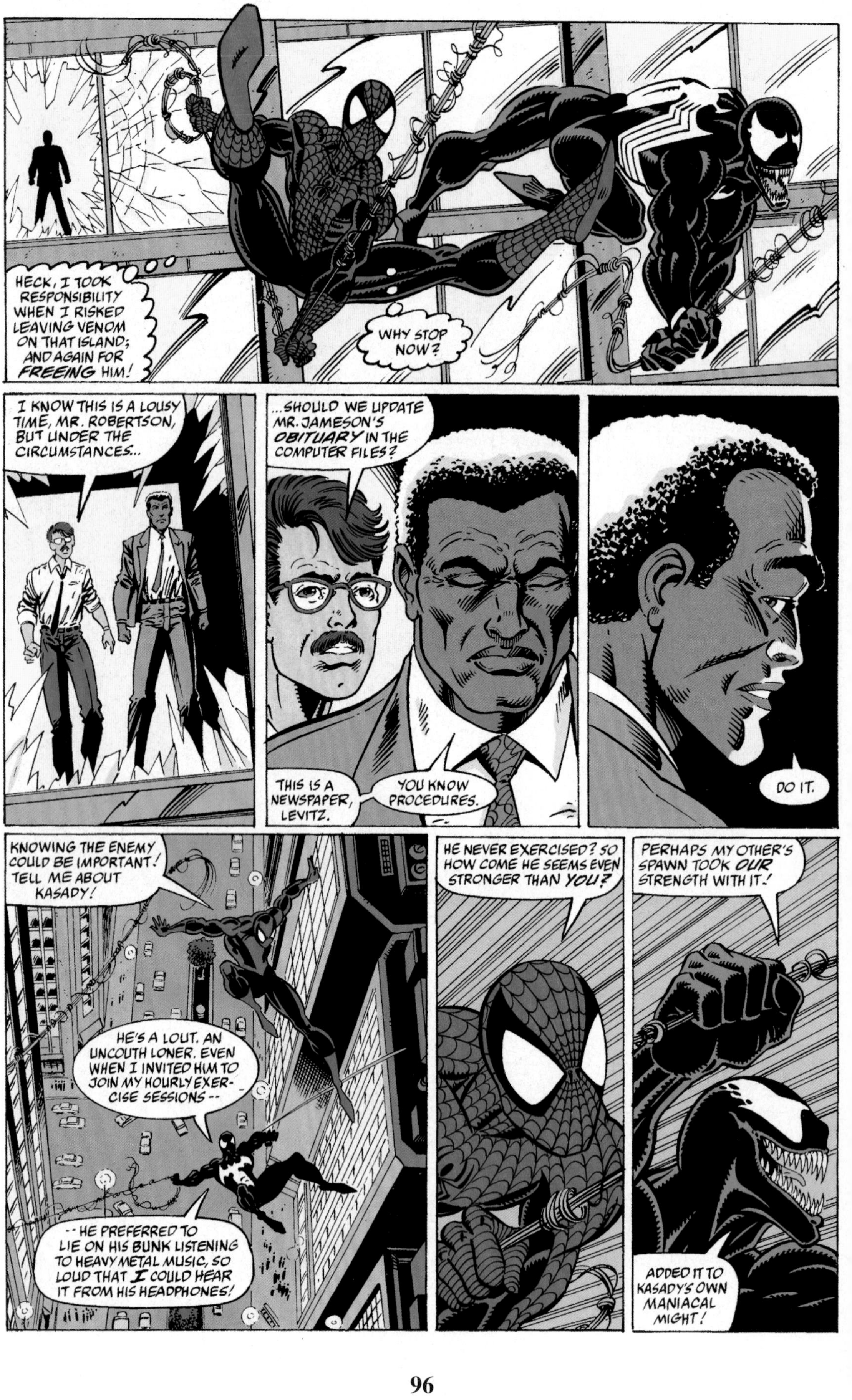

HECK, I TOOK RESPONSIBILITY WHEN I RISKED LEAVING VENOM ON THAT ISLAND; AND AGAIN FOR FREEING HIM!
WHY STOP NOW?
I KNOW THIS IS A LOUSY TIME, MR. ROBERTSON, BUT UNDER THE CIRCUMSTANCES...
...SHOULD WE UPDATE MR. JAMESON'S OBITUARY IN THE COMPUTER FILES?
THIS IS A NEWSPAPER, LEVITZ.
YOU KNOW PROCEDURES.
DO IT.
KNOWING THE ENEMY COULD BE IMPORTANT! TELL ME ABOUT KASADY!
HE'S A LOUT. AN UNCOUTH LONER. EVEN WHEN I INVITED HIM TO JOIN MY HOURLY EXER-CISE SESSIONS --
-- HE PREFERRED TO LIE ON HIS BUNK LISTENING TO HEAVY METAL MUSIC, SO LOUD THAT I COULD HEAR IT FROM HIS HEADPHONES!
HE NEVER EXERCISED? SO HOW COME HE SEEMS EVEN STRONGER THAN YOU?
PERHAPS MY OTHER'S SPAWN TOOK OUR STRENGTH WITH IT!
ADDED IT TO KASADY'S OWN MANIACAL MIGHT!

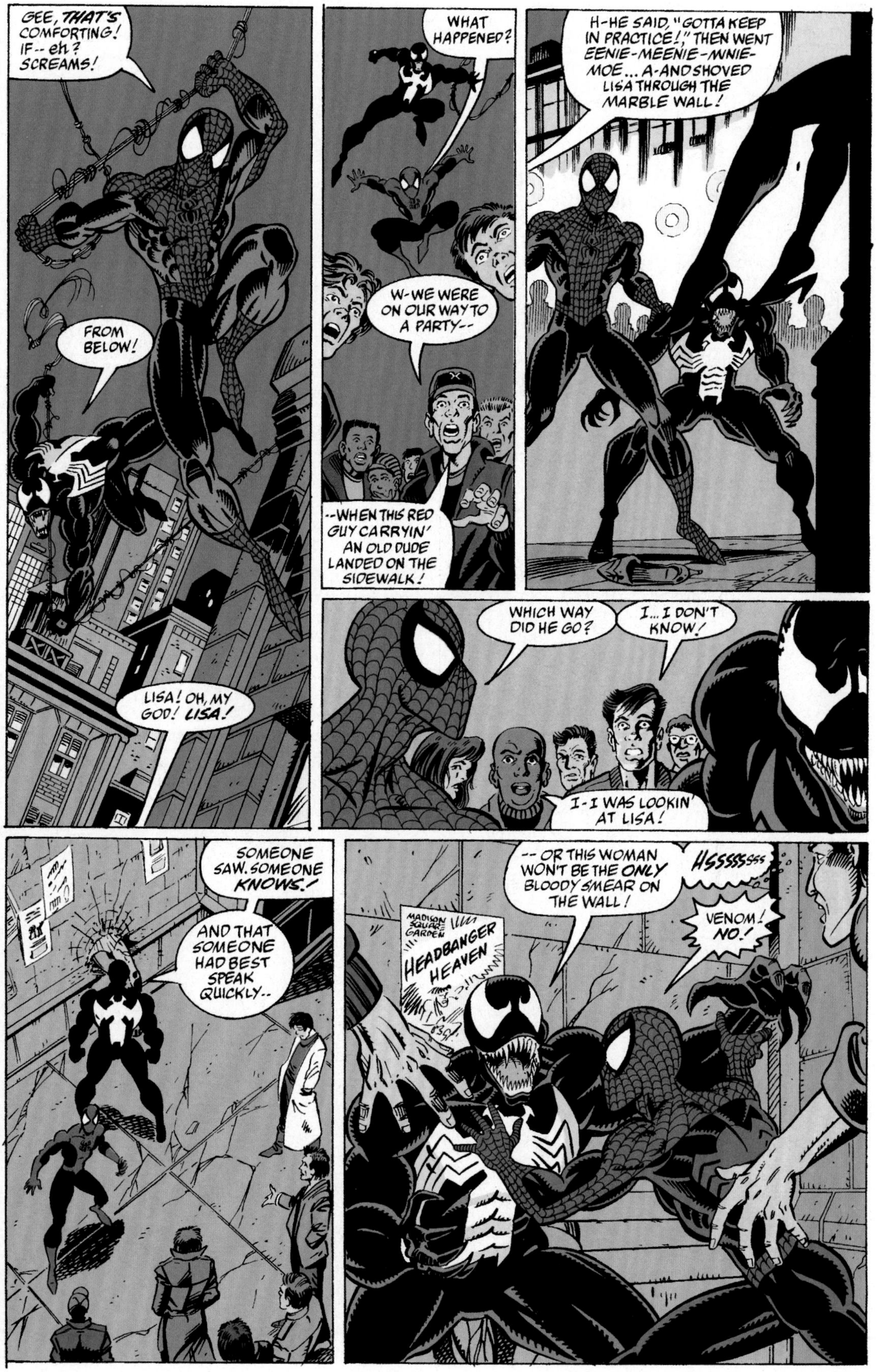
GEE, THAT'S COMFORTING! IF-- eh? SCREAMS!
FROM BELOW!
LISA! OH, MY GOD! LISA!
WHAT HAPPENED?
W-WE WERE ON OUR WAY TO A PARTY--
--WHEN THIS RED GUY CARRYIN' AN OLD DUDE LANDED ON THE SIDEWALK!
H-HE SAID, "GOTTA KEEP IN PRACTICE!," THEN WENT EENIE-MEENIE-MINIE-MOE... A-AND SHOVED LISA THROUGH THE MARBLE WALL!
WHICH WAY DID HE GO?
I... I DON'T KNOW!
I-I WAS LOOKIN' AT LISA!
SOMEONE SAW. SOMEONE KNOWS!
AND THAT SOMEONE HAD BEST SPEAK QUICKLY..
-- OR THIS WOMAN WON'T BE THE ONLY BLOODY SMEAR ON THE WALL!
MADISON SQUARE GARDEN
HEADBANGER HEAVEN
HSSSSSSSS
VENOM! NO!

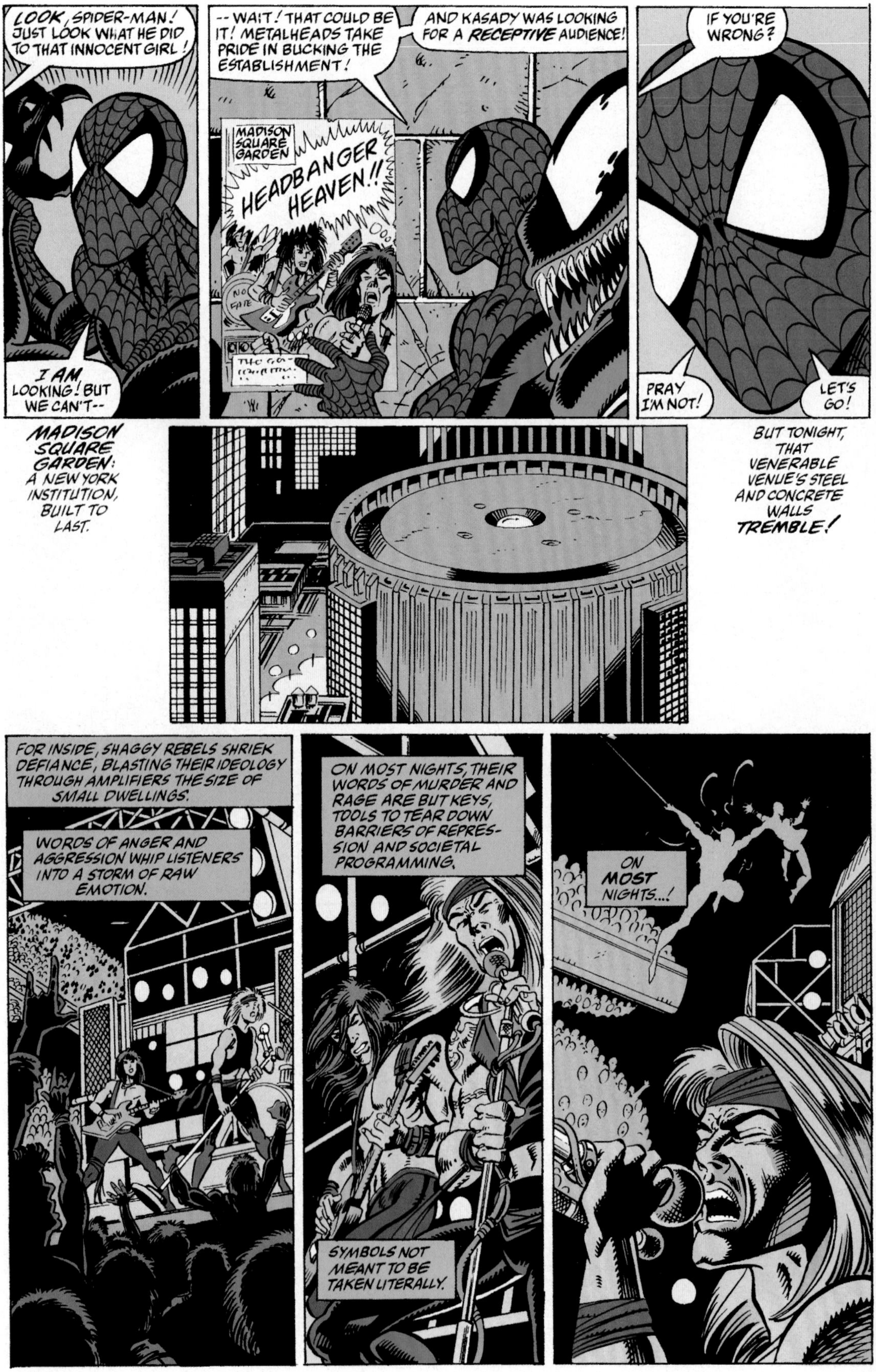

LOOK, SPIDER-MAN! JUST LOOK WHAT HE DID TO THAT INNOCENT GIRL!
I AM LOOKING! BUT WE CAN'T--
-- WAIT! THAT COULD BE IT! METALHEADS TAKE PRIDE IN BUCKING THE ESTABLISHMENT!
MADISON SQUARE GARDEN
HEADBANGER HEAVEN!!
AND KASADY WAS LOOKING FOR A RECEPTIVE AUDIENCE!
IF YOU'RE WRONG?
PRAY I'M NOT!
LET'S GO!
MADISON SQUARE GARDEN: A NEW YORK INSTITUTION, BUILT TO LAST.
BUT TONIGHT, THAT VENERABLE VENUE'S STEEL AND CONCRETE WALLS TREMBLE!
FOR INSIDE, SHAGGY REBELS SHRIEK DEFIANCE, BLASTING THEIR IDEOLOGY THROUGH AMPLIFIERS THE SIZE OF SMALL DWELLINGS.
WORDS OF ANGER AND AGGRESSION WHIP LISTENERS INTO A STORM OF RAW EMOTION.
ON MOST NIGHTS, THEIR WORDS OF MURDER AND RAGE ARE BUT KEYS, TOOLS TO TEAR DOWN BARRIERS OF REPRES-SION AND SOCIETAL PROGRAMMING.
SYMBOLS NOT MEANT TO BE TAKEN LITERALLY.
ON MOST NIGHTS...!

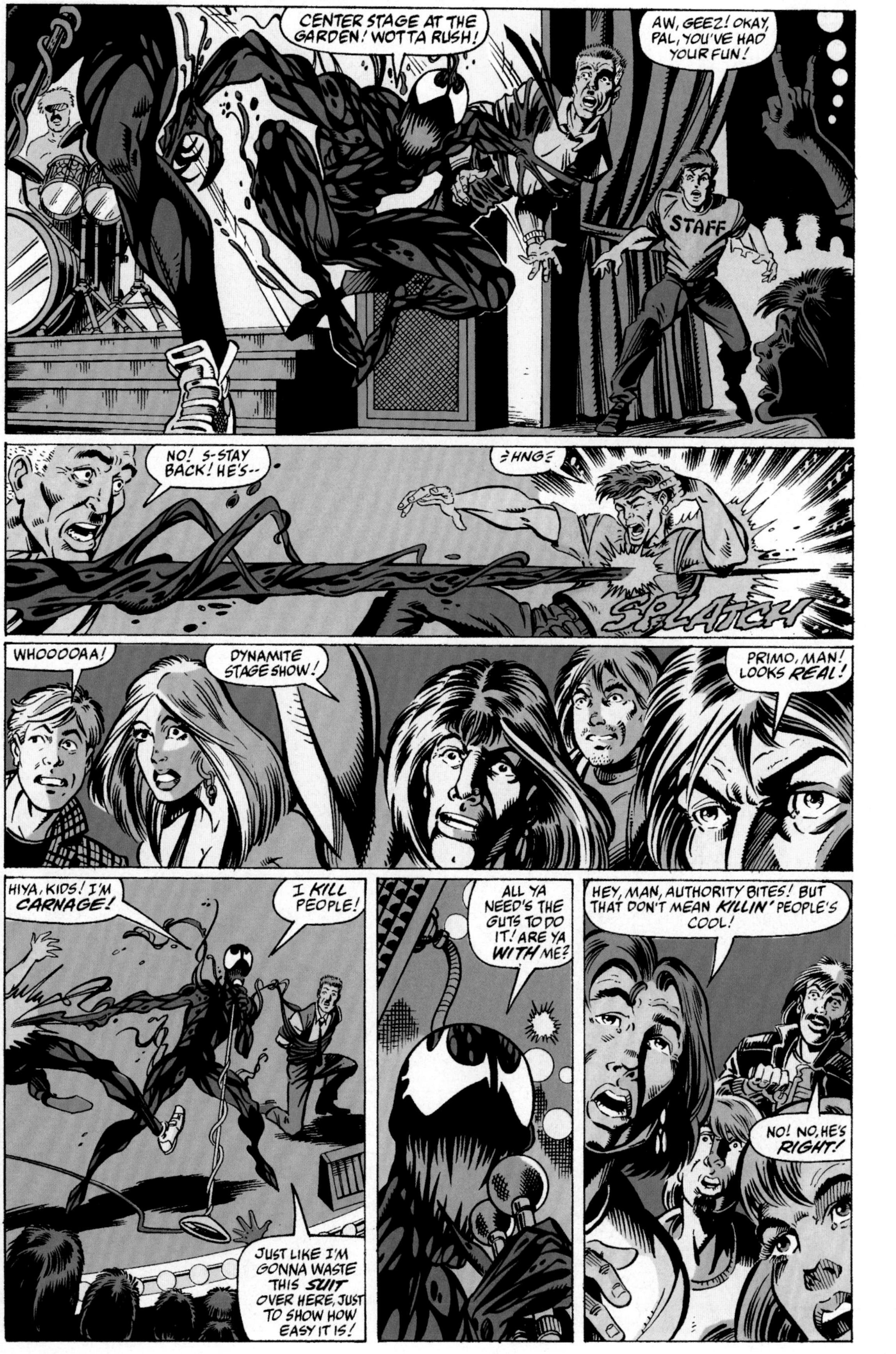
CENTER STAGE AT THE GARDEN! WOTTA RUSH!
AW, GEEZ! OKAY, PAL, YOU'VE HAD YOUR FUN!
STAFF
NO! S-STAY BACK! HE'S--
HNG
SPLATCH
WHOOOOAA!
DYNAMITE STAGE SHOW!
PRIMO, MAN! LOOKS REAL!
HIYA, KIDS! I'M CARNAGE!
I KILL PEOPLE!
JUST LIKE I'M GONNA WASTE THIS SUIT OVER HERE, JUST TO SHOW HOW EASY IT IS!
ALL YA NEED'S THE GUTS TO DO IT! ARE YA WITH ME?
HEY, MAN, AUTHORITY BITES! BUT THAT DON'T MEAN KILLIN' PEOPLE'S COOL!
NO! NO, HE'S RIGHT!

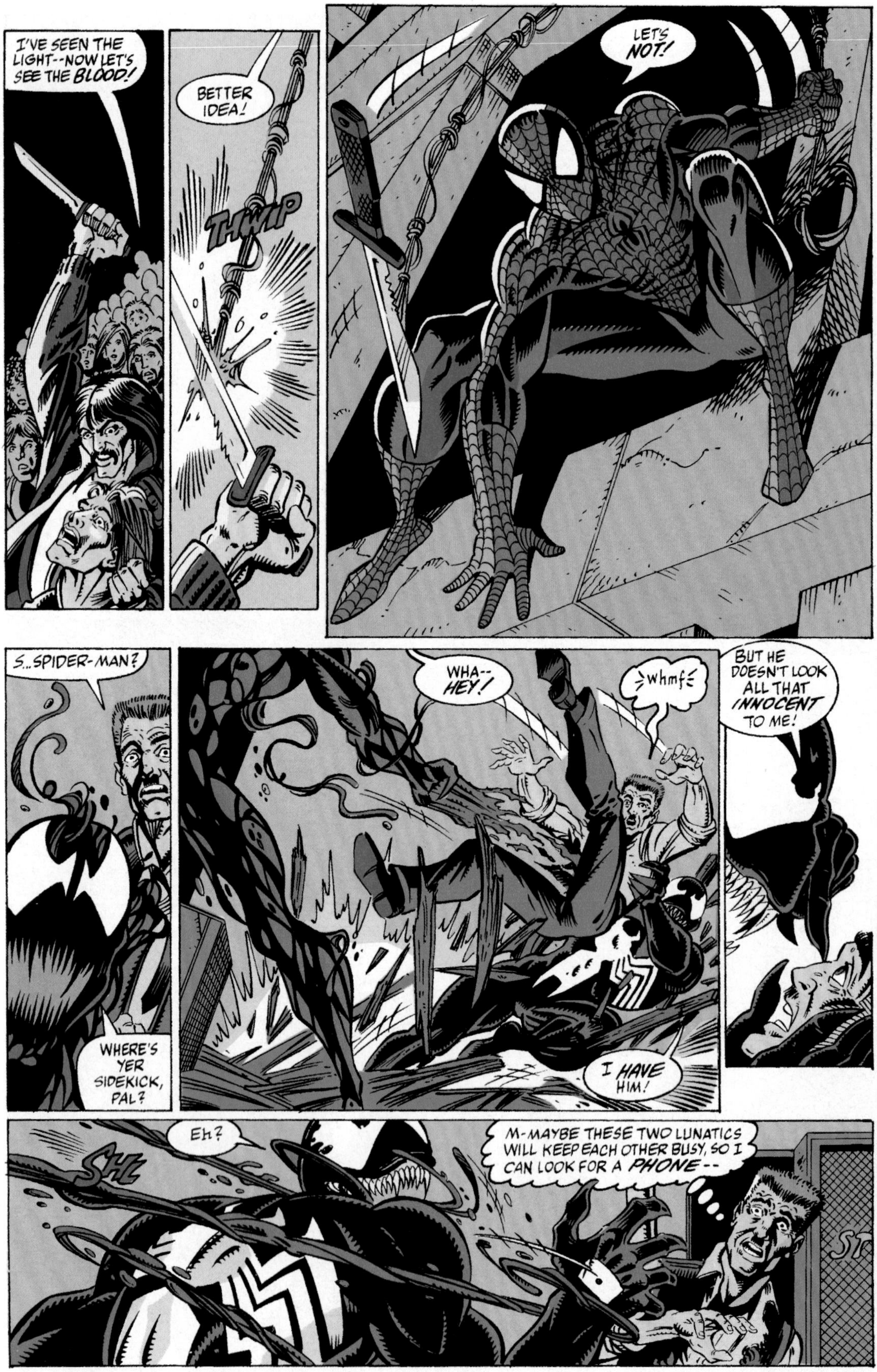

I'VE SEEN THE LIGHT--NOW LET'S SEE THE BLOOD!
BETTER IDEA!
THWIP
LET'S NOT!
S...SPIDER-MAN?
WHERE'S YER SIDEKICK, PAL?
WHA-- HEY!
whmf
I HAVE HIM!
BUT HE DOESN'T LOOK ALL THAT INNOCENT TO ME!
Eh?
SHL
M-MAYBE THESE TWO LUNATICS WILL KEEP EACH OTHER BUSY, SO I CAN LOOK FOR A PHONE--

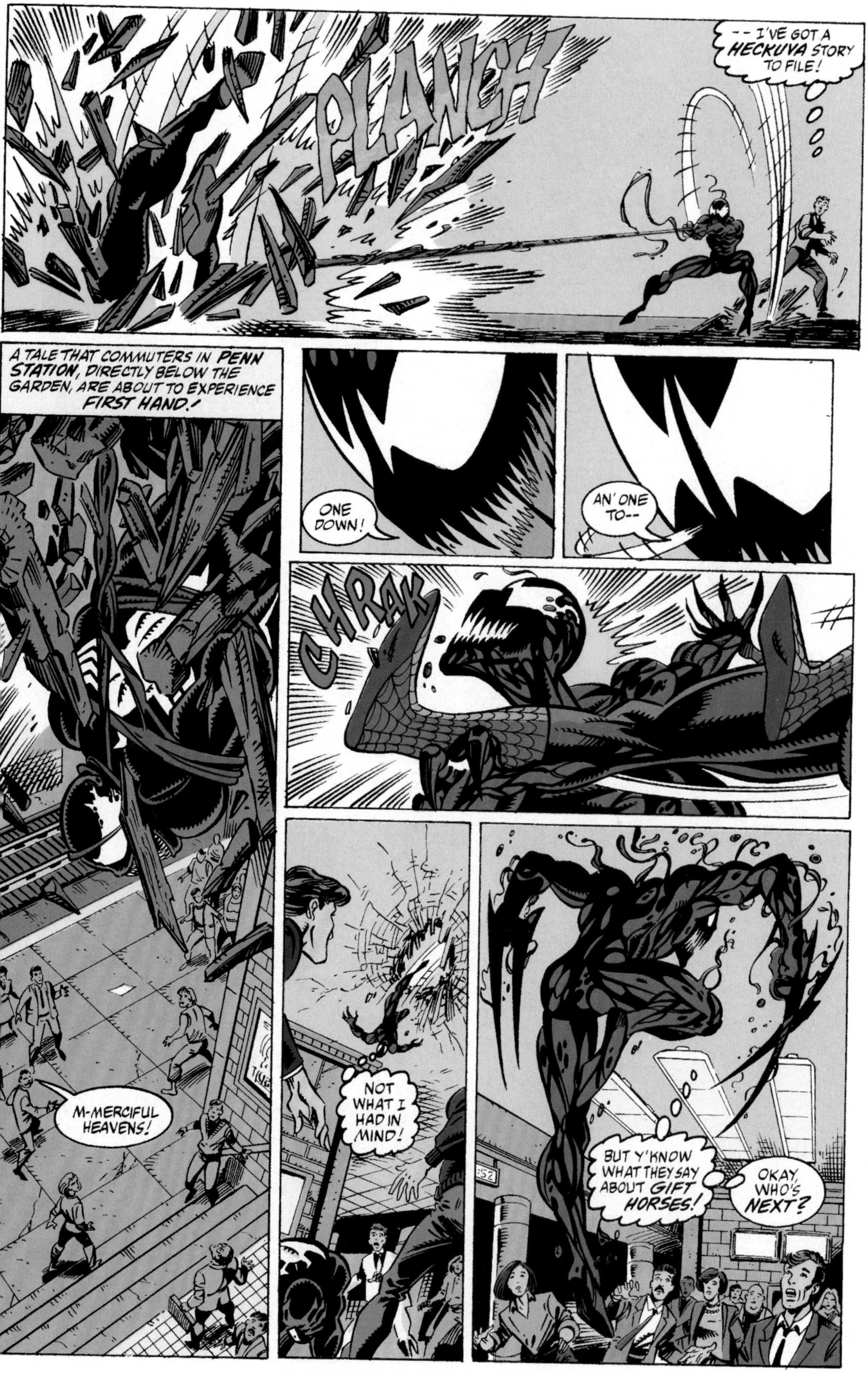

-- I'VE GOT A HECKUVA STORY TO FILE!
PLANCH
A TALE THAT COMMUTERS IN PENN STATION, DIRECTLY BELOW THE GARDEN, ARE ABOUT TO EXPERIENCE FIRST HAND!
ONE DOWN!
AN' ONE TO--
CHRAK
M-MERCIFUL HEAVENS!
NOT WHAT I HAD IN MIND!
BUT Y'KNOW WHAT THEY SAY ABOUT GIFT HORSES!
OKAY, WHO'S NEXT?

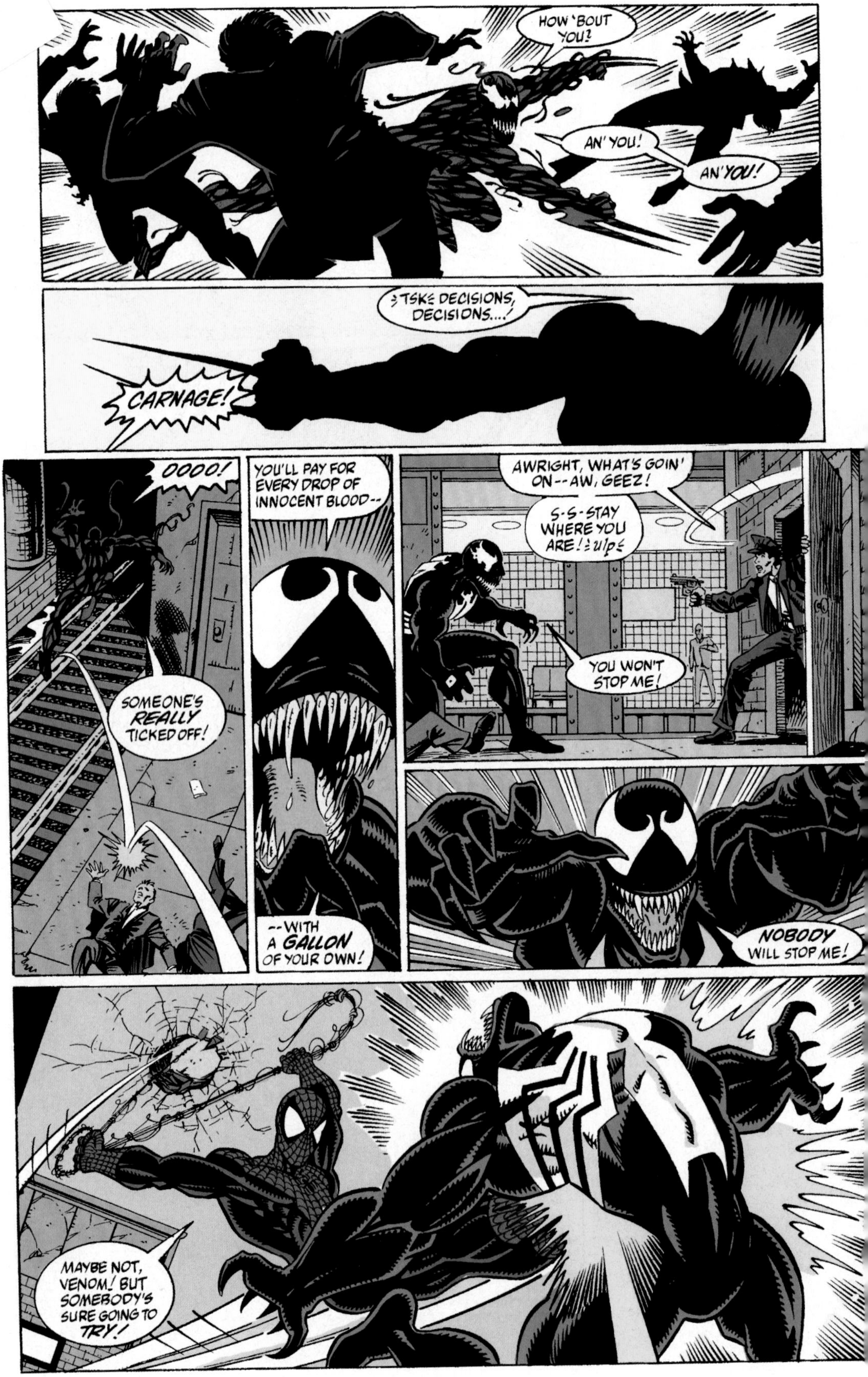
HOW 'BOUT YOU?
AN' YOU!
AN' YOU!
TSK DECISIONS, DECISIONS...!
CARNAGE!
OOOO!
SOMEONE'S REALLY TICKED OFF!
YOU'LL PAY FOR EVERY DROP OF INNOCENT BLOOD--
--WITH A GALLON OF YOUR OWN!
AWRIGHT, WHAT'S GOIN' ON--AW, GEEZ!
S-S-STAY WHERE YOU ARE! ulp
YOU WON'T STOP ME!
NOBODY WILL STOP ME!
MAYBE NOT, VENOM! BUT SOMEBODY'S SURE GOING TO TRY!

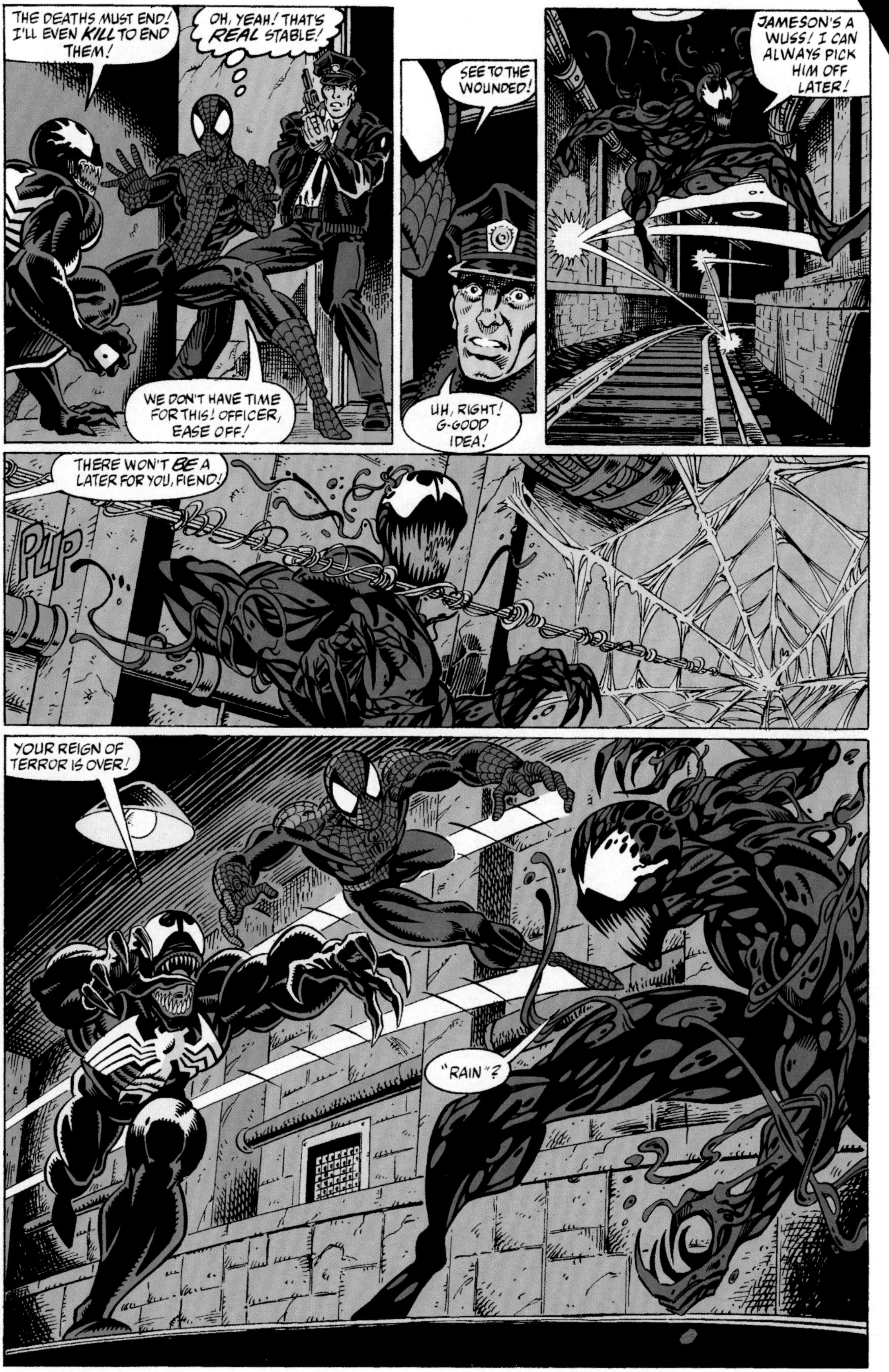
THE DEATHS MUST END! I'LL EVEN KILL TO END THEM!
OH, YEAH! THAT'S REAL STABLE!
WE DON'T HAVE TIME FOR THIS! OFFICER, EASE OFF!
SEE TO THE WOUNDED!
UH, RIGHT! G-GOOD IDEA!
JAMESON'S A WUSS! I CAN ALWAYS PICK HIM OFF LATER!
THERE WON'T BE A LATER FOR YOU, FIEND!
PLIP
YOUR REIGN OF TERROR IS OVER!
"RAIN"?

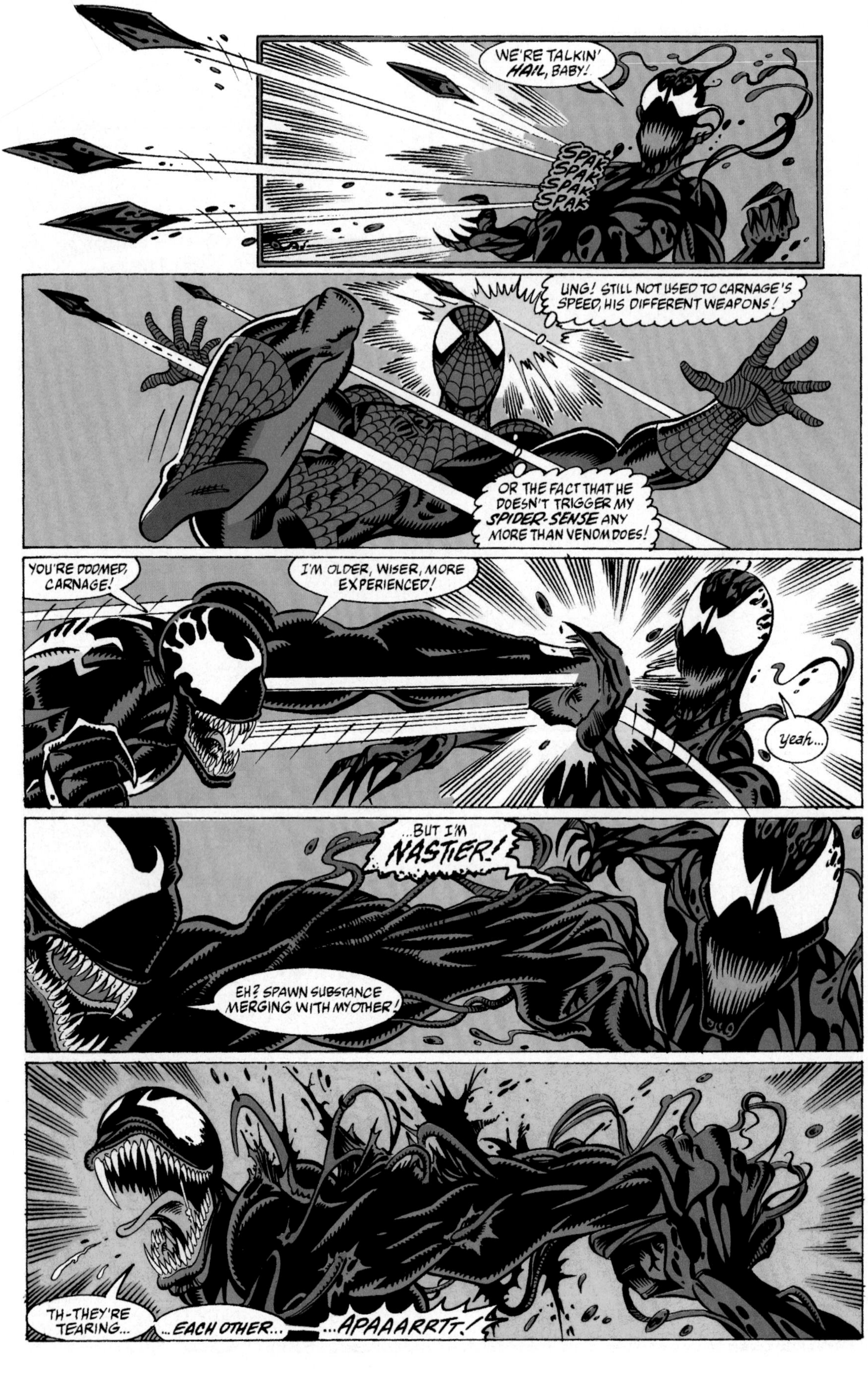
WE'RE TALKIN' HAIL, BABY!
SPAK SPAK SPAK SPAK
UNG! STILL NOT USED TO CARNAGE'S SPEED, HIS DIFFERENT WEAPONS!
OR THE FACT THAT HE DOESN'T TRIGGER MY SPIDER-SENSE ANY MORE THAN VENOM DOES!
YOU'RE DOOMED, CARNAGE!
I'M OLDER, WISER, MORE EXPERIENCED!
yeah...
...BUT I'M NASTIER!
EH? SPAWN SUBSTANCE MERGING WITH MY OTHER!
TH-THEY'RE TEARING...
...EACH OTHER...
...APAAARRTT!

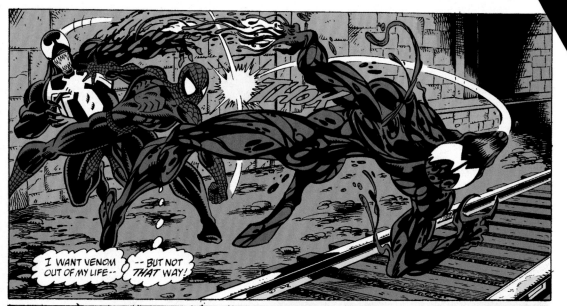

I WANT VENOM OUT OF MY LIFE-- --BUT NOT *THAT* WAY!

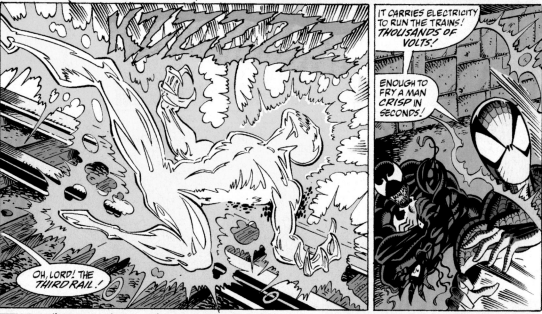

OH, LORD! THE *THIRD RAIL!*

IT CARRIES ELECTRICITY TO RUN THE TRAINS! *THOUSANDS OF VOLTS!*

ENOUGH TO FRY A MAN *CRISP* IN SECONDS!

THWOOM

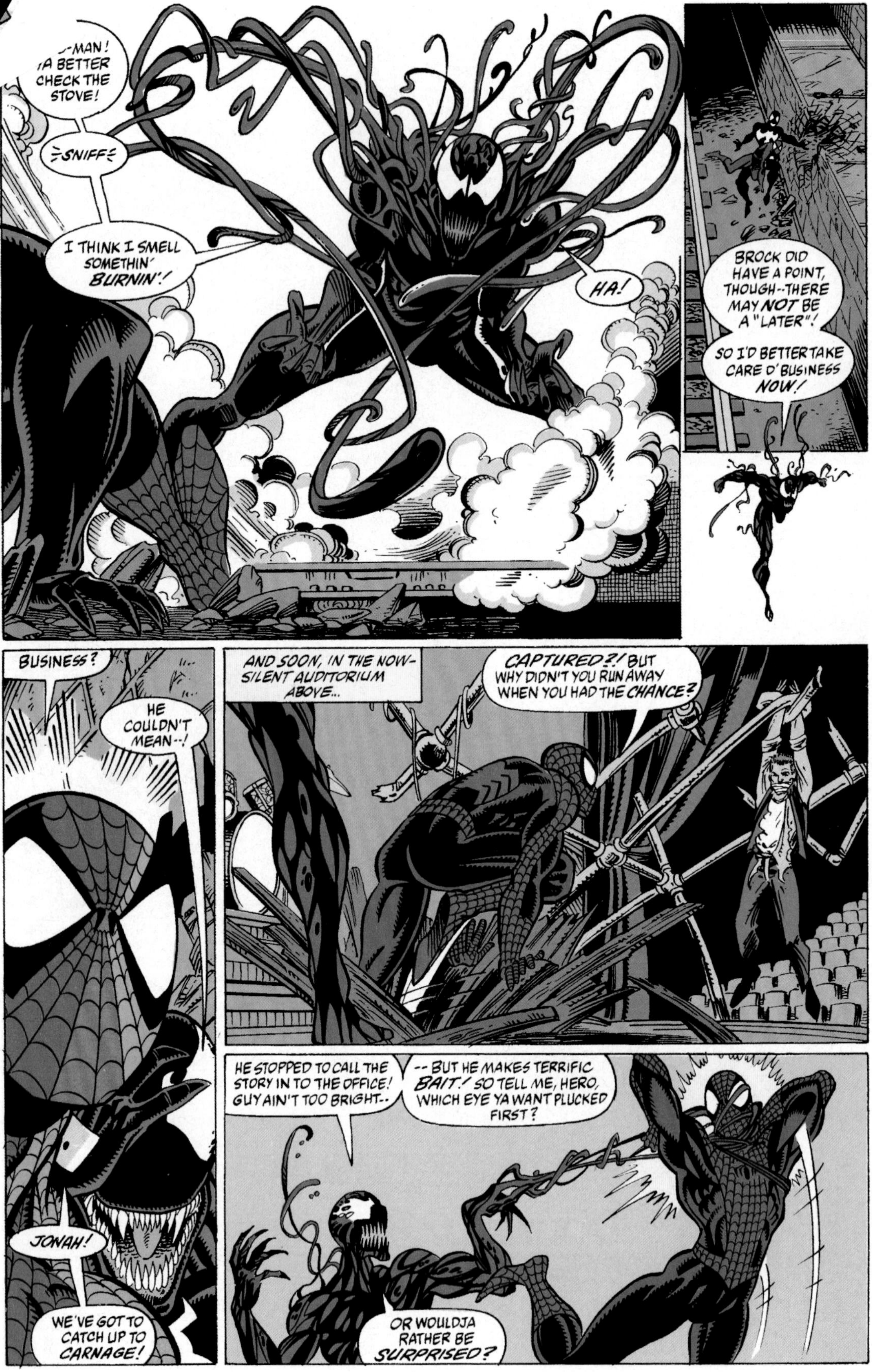
-MAN! YA BETTER CHECK THE STOVE!
=SNIFF=
I THINK I SMELL SOMETHIN' BURNIN'!
HA!
BROCK DID HAVE A POINT, THOUGH--THERE MAY NOT BE A "LATER"!
SO I'D BETTER TAKE CARE O' BUSINESS NOW!
BUSINESS?
HE COULDN'T MEAN--!
JONAH!
WE'VE GOT TO CATCH UP TO CARNAGE!
AND SOON, IN THE NOW-SILENT AUDITORIUM ABOVE...
CAPTURED?! BUT WHY DIDN'T YOU RUN AWAY WHEN YOU HAD THE CHANCE?
HE STOPPED TO CALL THE STORY IN TO THE OFFICE! GUY AIN'T TOO BRIGHT--
-- BUT HE MAKES TERRIFIC BAIT! SO TELL ME, HERO, WHICH EYE YA WANT PLUCKED FIRST?
OR WOULDJA RATHER BE SURPRISED?

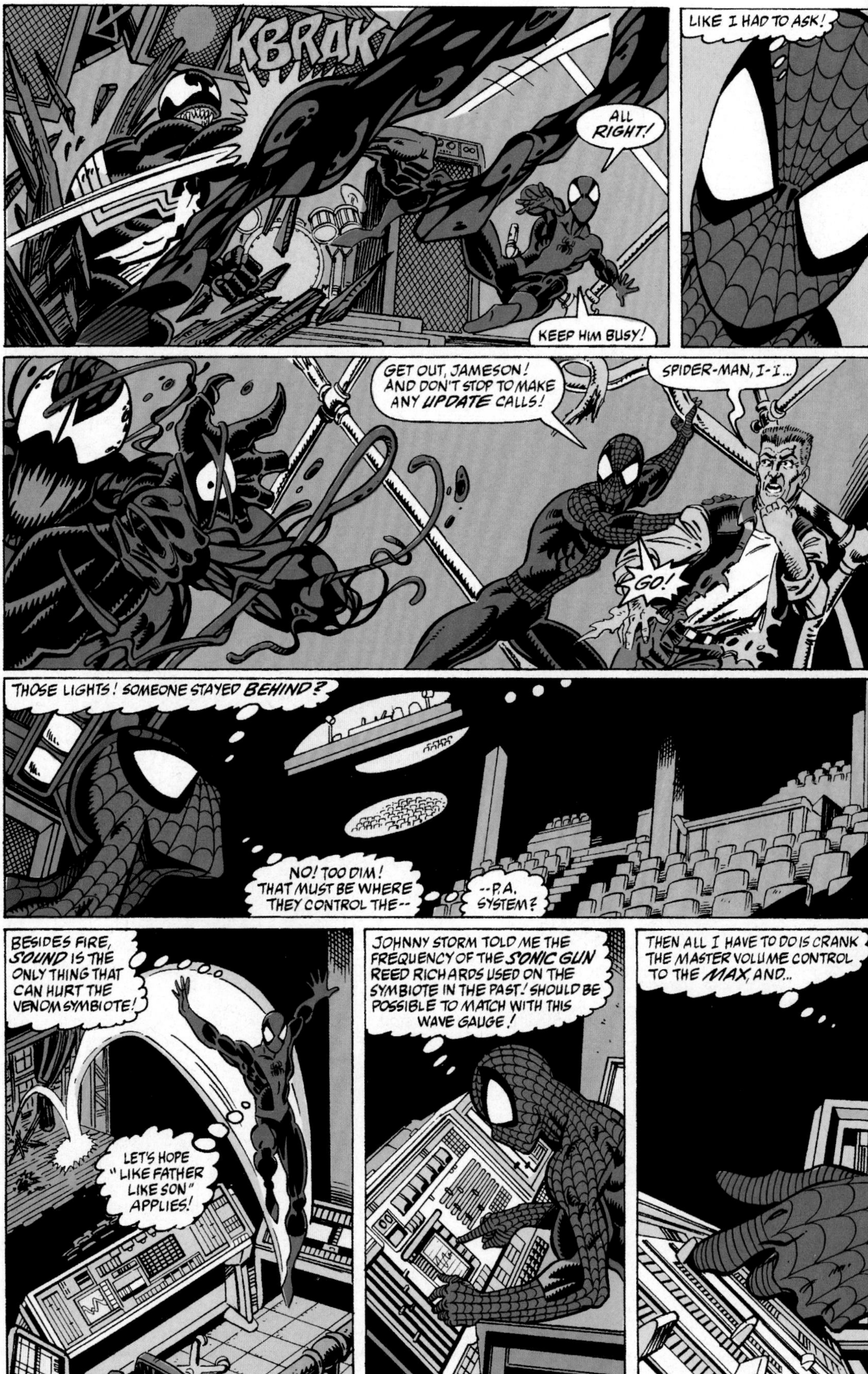

KBRAK
ALL RIGHT!
KEEP HIM BUSY!
LIKE I HAD TO ASK!
GET OUT, JAMESON! AND DON'T STOP TO MAKE ANY UPDATE CALLS!
SPIDER-MAN, I-I...
GO!
THOSE LIGHTS! SOMEONE STAYED BEHIND?
NO! TOO DIM! THAT MUST BE WHERE THEY CONTROL THE--
--P.A. SYSTEM?
BESIDES FIRE, SOUND IS THE ONLY THING THAT CAN HURT THE VENOM SYMBIOTE!
LET'S HOPE "LIKE FATHER LIKE SON" APPLIES!
JOHNNY STORM TOLD ME THE FREQUENCY OF THE SONIC GUN REED RICHARDS USED ON THE SYMBIOTE IN THE PAST! SHOULD BE POSSIBLE TO MATCH WITH THIS WAVE GAUGE!
THEN ALL I HAVE TO DO IS CRANK THE MASTER VOLUME CONTROL TO THE MAX, AND...

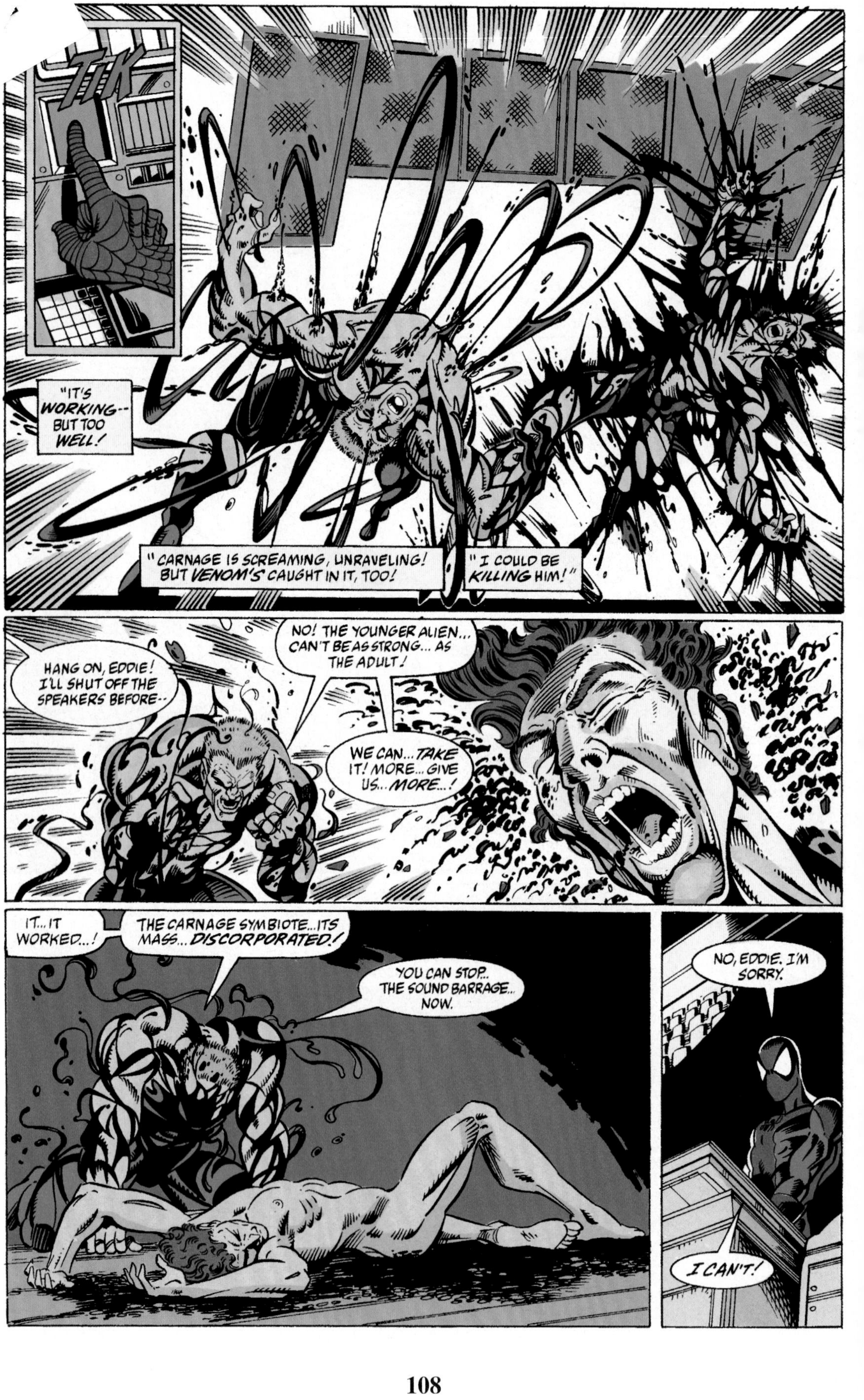

TIK
"IT'S WORKING-- BUT TOO WELL!
"CARNAGE IS SCREAMING, UNRAVELING! BUT VENOM'S CAUGHT IN IT, TOO!
"I COULD BE KILLING HIM!"
HANG ON, EDDIE! I'LL SHUT OFF THE SPEAKERS BEFORE--
NO! THE YOUNGER ALIEN... CAN'T BE AS STRONG... AS THE ADULT!
WE CAN... TAKE IT! MORE... GIVE US... MORE...!
IT... IT WORKED...!
THE CARNAGE SYMBIOTE... ITS MASS... DISCORPORATED!
YOU CAN STOP... THE SOUND BARRAGE... NOW.
NO, EDDIE. I'M SORRY.
I CAN'T!

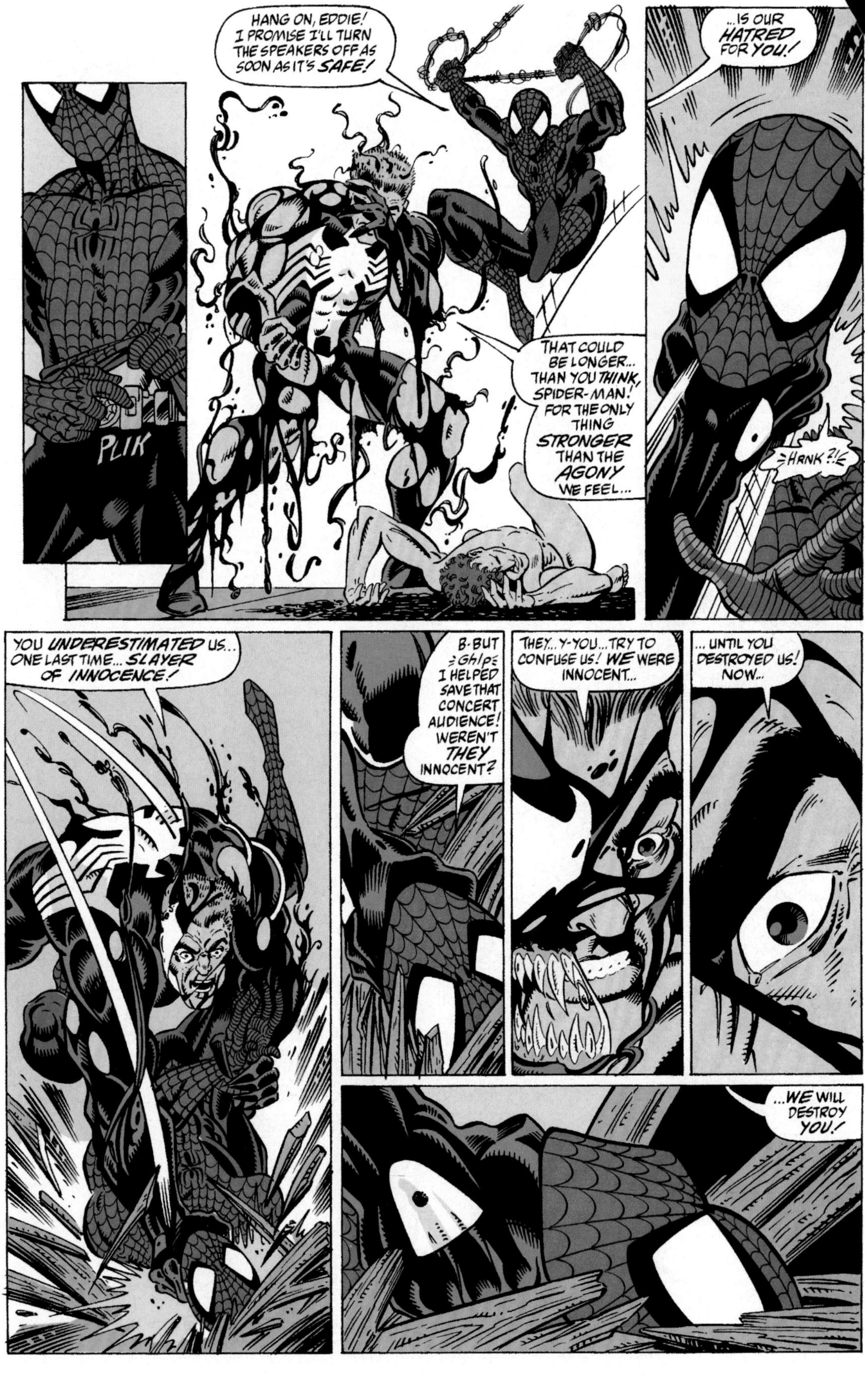
HANG ON, EDDIE! I PROMISE I'LL TURN THE SPEAKERS OFF AS SOON AS IT'S SAFE!
PLIK
THAT COULD BE LONGER... THAN YOU THINK, SPIDER-MAN! FOR THE ONLY THING STRONGER THAN THE AGONY WE FEEL...
...IS OUR HATRED FOR YOU!
HRNK?!
YOU UNDERESTIMATED US... ONE LAST TIME... SLAYER OF INNOCENCE!
B-BUT Ghlp I HELPED SAVE THAT CONCERT AUDIENCE! WEREN'T THEY INNOCENT?
THEY... Y-YOU... TRY TO CONFUSE US! WE WERE INNOCENT...
...UNTIL YOU DESTROYED US! NOW...
...WE WILL DESTROY YOU!

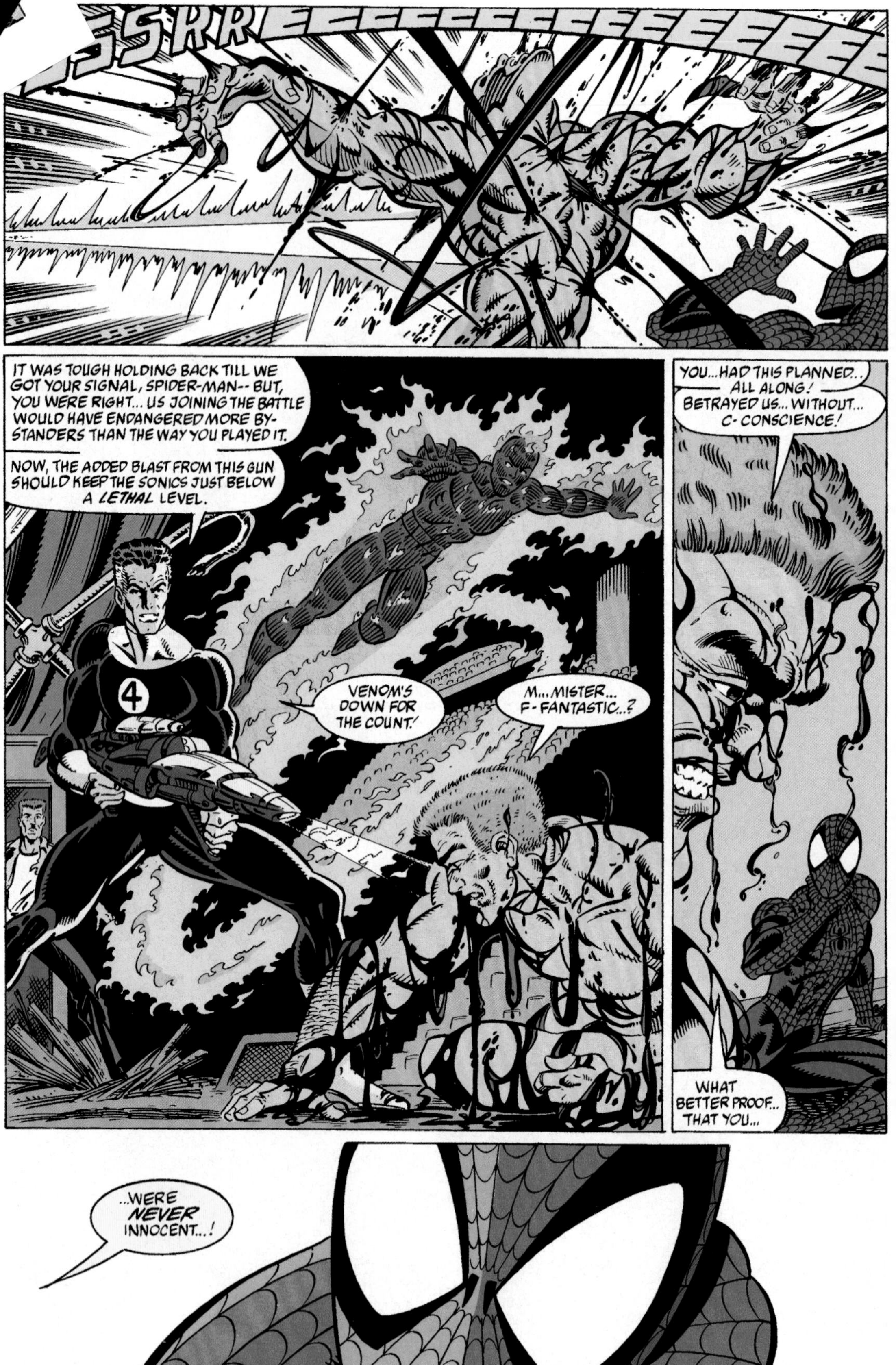
SSRREEEEEEEEEEEEEEEEEE
IT WAS TOUGH HOLDING BACK TILL WE GOT YOUR SIGNAL, SPIDER-MAN-- BUT, YOU WERE RIGHT... US JOINING THE BATTLE WOULD HAVE ENDANGERED MORE BYSTANDERS THAN THE WAY YOU PLAYED IT.
NOW, THE ADDED BLAST FROM THIS GUN SHOULD KEEP THE SONICS JUST BELOW A LETHAL LEVEL.
VENOM'S DOWN FOR THE COUNT!
M... MISTER... F-FANTASTIC...?
YOU... HAD THIS PLANNED... ALL ALONG! BETRAYED US... WITHOUT... C-CONSCIENCE!
WHAT BETTER PROOF... THAT YOU...
...WERE NEVER INNOCENT...!

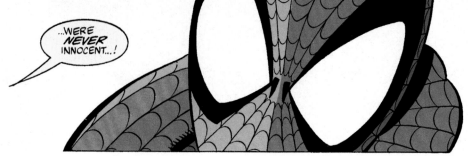

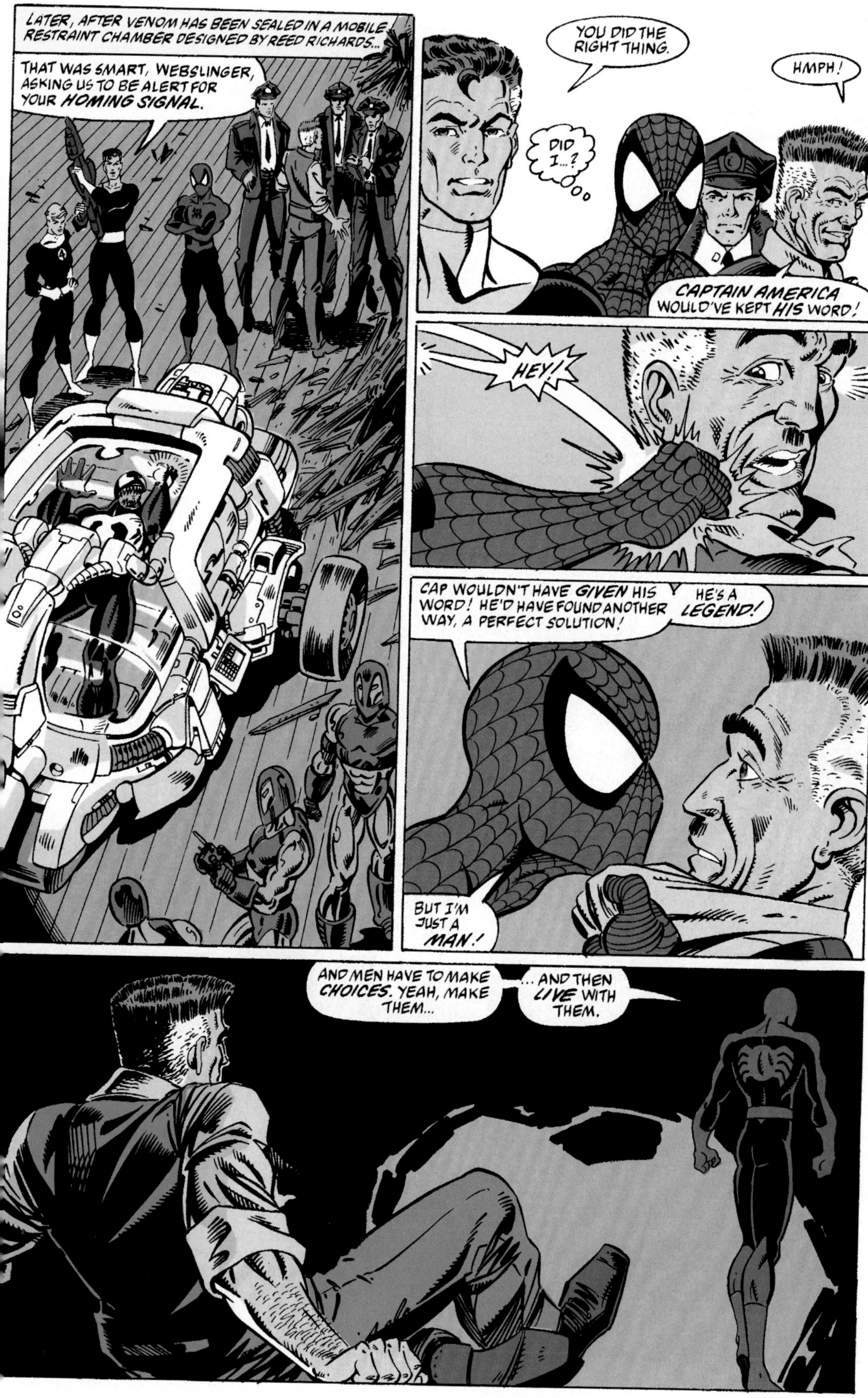
LATER, AFTER VENOM HAS BEEN SEALED IN A MOBILE RESTRAINT CHAMBER DESIGNED BY REED RICHARDS...
THAT WAS SMART, WEBSLINGER, ASKING US TO BE ALERT FOR YOUR HOMING SIGNAL.
YOU DID THE RIGHT THING.
DID I...?
HMPH!
CAPTAIN AMERICA WOULD'VE KEPT HIS WORD!
HEY!
CAP WOULDN'T HAVE GIVEN HIS WORD! HE'D HAVE FOUND ANOTHER WAY, A PERFECT SOLUTION!
HE'S A LEGEND!
BUT I'M JUST A MAN!
AND MEN HAVE TO MAKE CHOICES. YEAH, MAKE THEM...
...AND THEN LIVE WITH THEM.

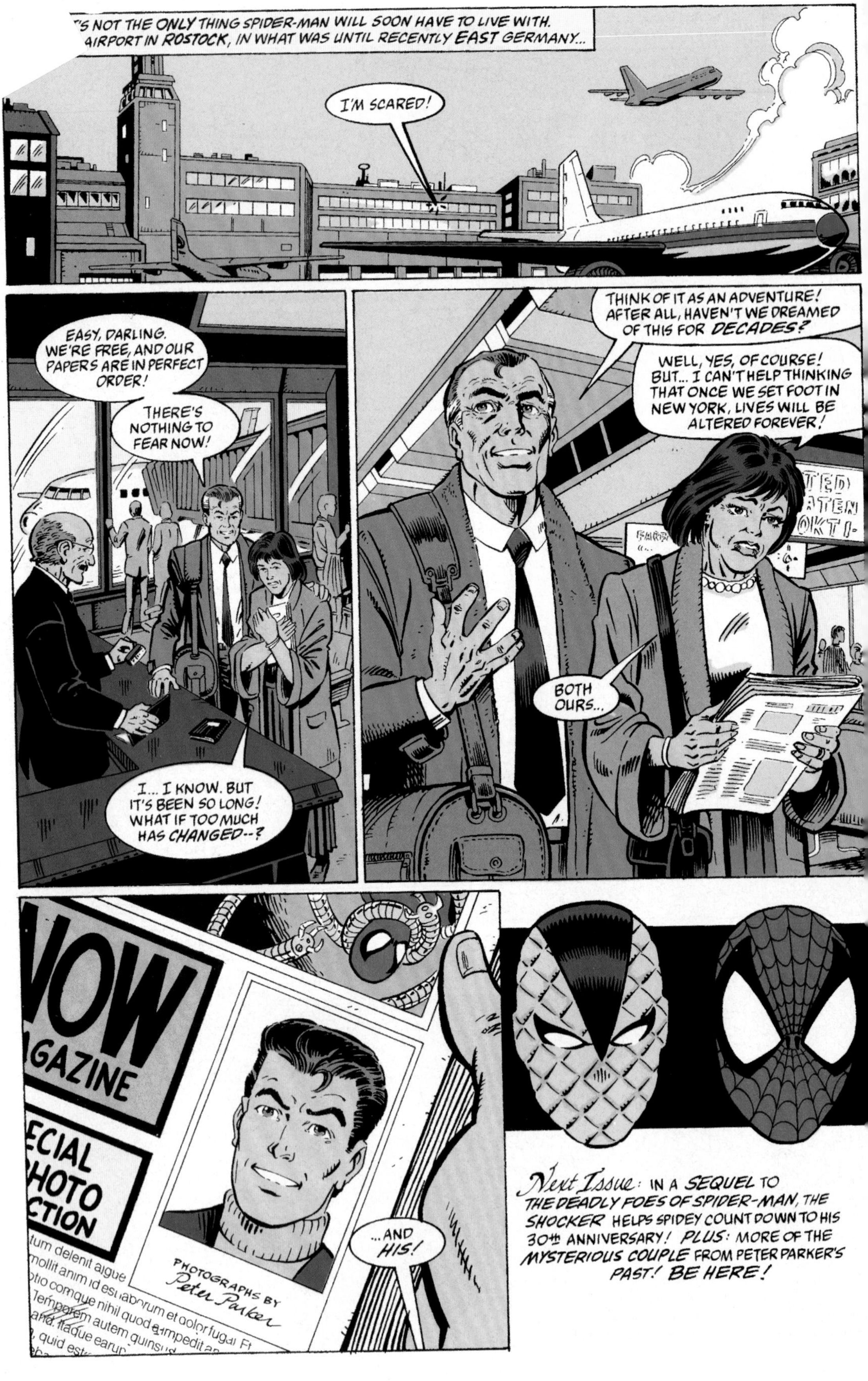
'S NOT THE ONLY THING SPIDER-MAN WILL SOON HAVE TO LIVE WITH. AIRPORT IN ROSTOCK, IN WHAT WAS UNTIL RECENTLY EAST GERMANY...
I'M SCARED!
EASY, DARLING. WE'RE FREE, AND OUR PAPERS ARE IN PERFECT ORDER!
THERE'S NOTHING TO FEAR NOW!
I... I KNOW. BUT IT'S BEEN SO LONG! WHAT IF TOO MUCH HAS CHANGED--?
THINK OF IT AS AN ADVENTURE! AFTER ALL, HAVEN'T WE DREAMED OF THIS FOR DECADES?
WELL, YES, OF COURSE! BUT... I CAN'T HELP THINKING THAT ONCE WE SET FOOT IN NEW YORK, LIVES WILL BE ALTERED FOREVER!
BOTH OURS...
NOW
GAZINE
ECIAL
HOTO
CTION
PHOTOGRAPHS BY
Peter Parker
...AND HIS!
Next Issue: IN A SEQUEL TO THE DEADLY FOES OF SPIDER-MAN, THE SHOCKER HELPS SPIDEY COUNT DOWN TO HIS 30th ANNIVERSARY! PLUS: MORE OF THE MYSTERIOUS COUPLE FROM PETER PARKER'S PAST! BE HERE!

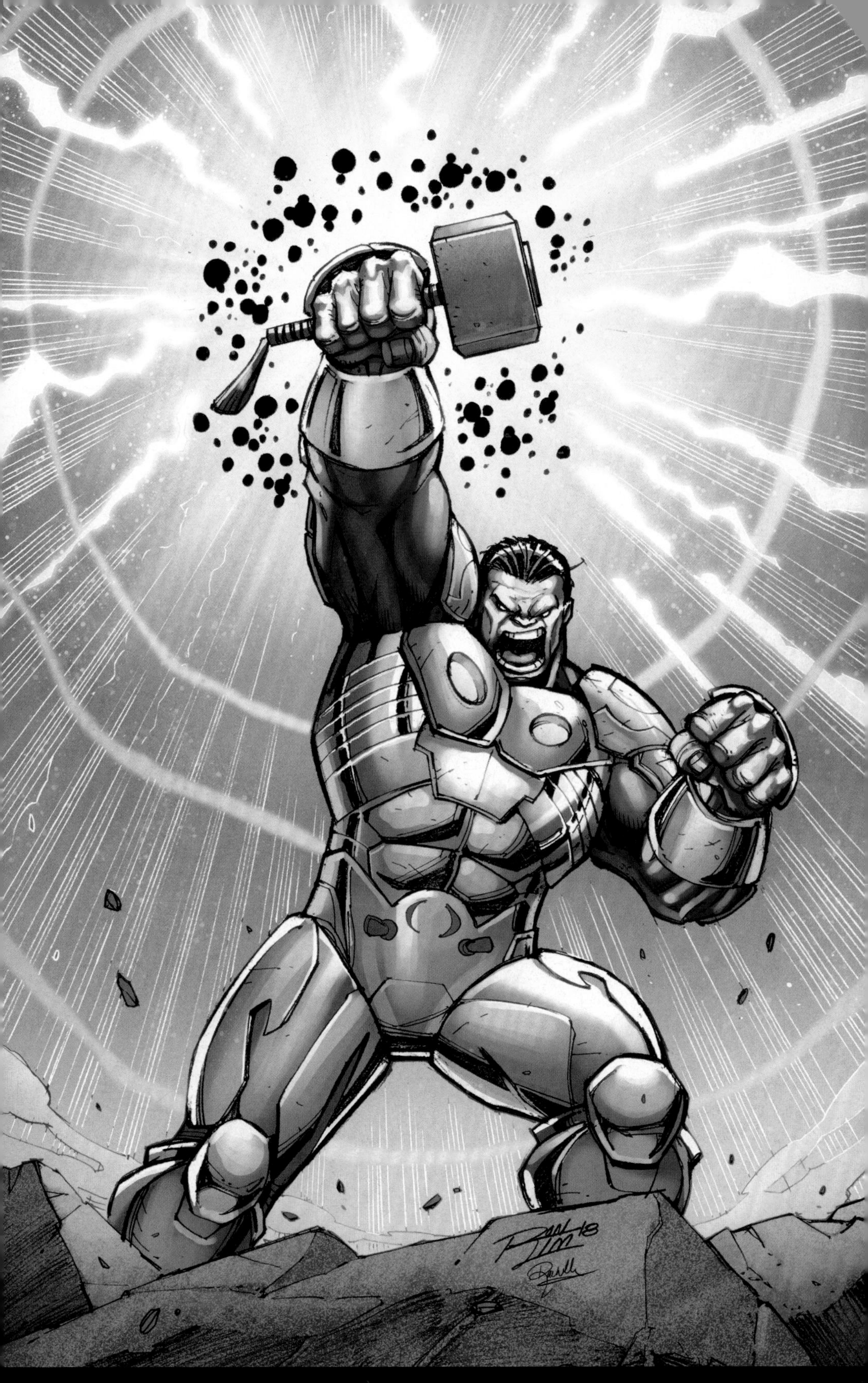

#161 HULK VARIANT BY

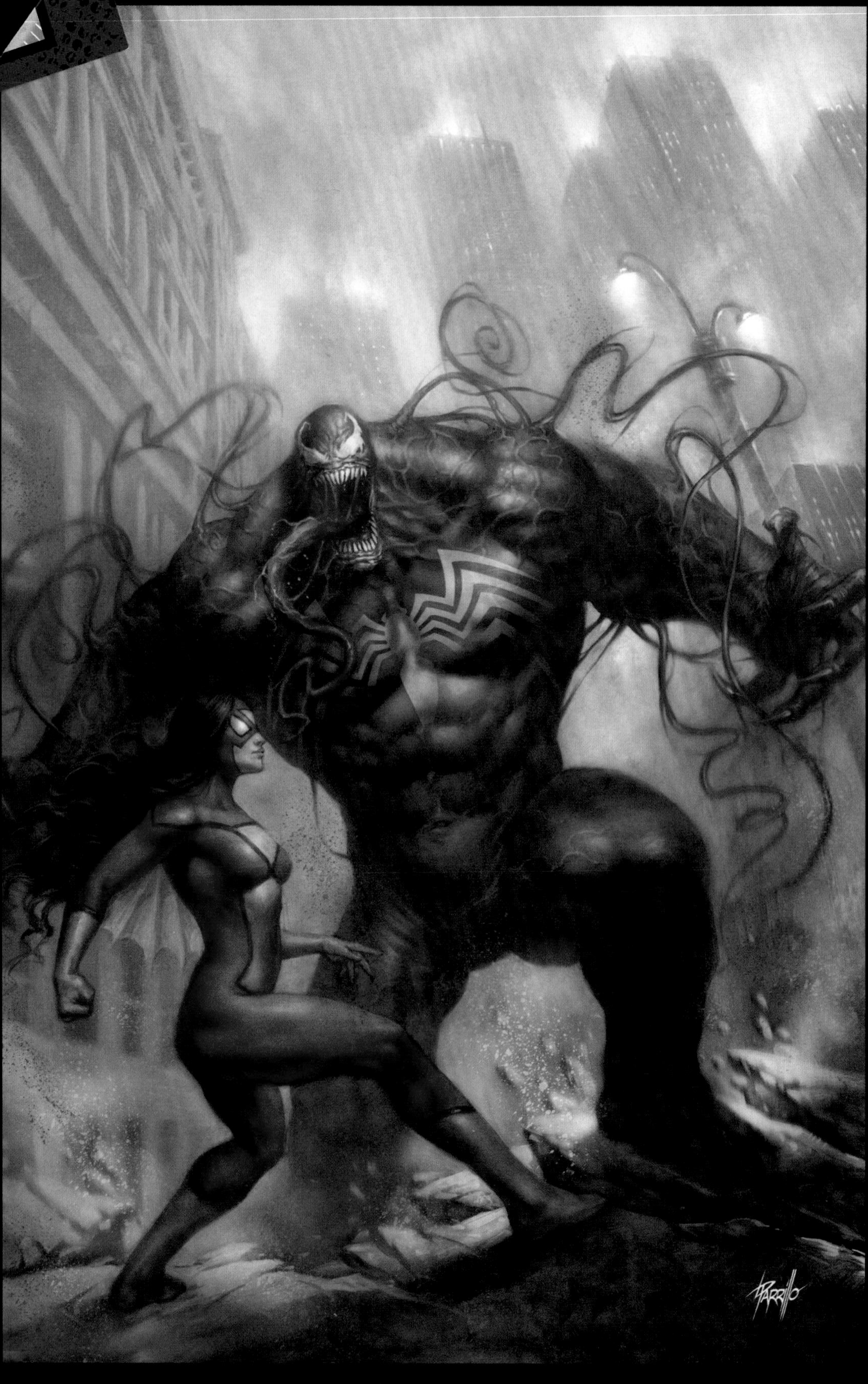

#161 VARIANT BY
LUCIO PARRILLO

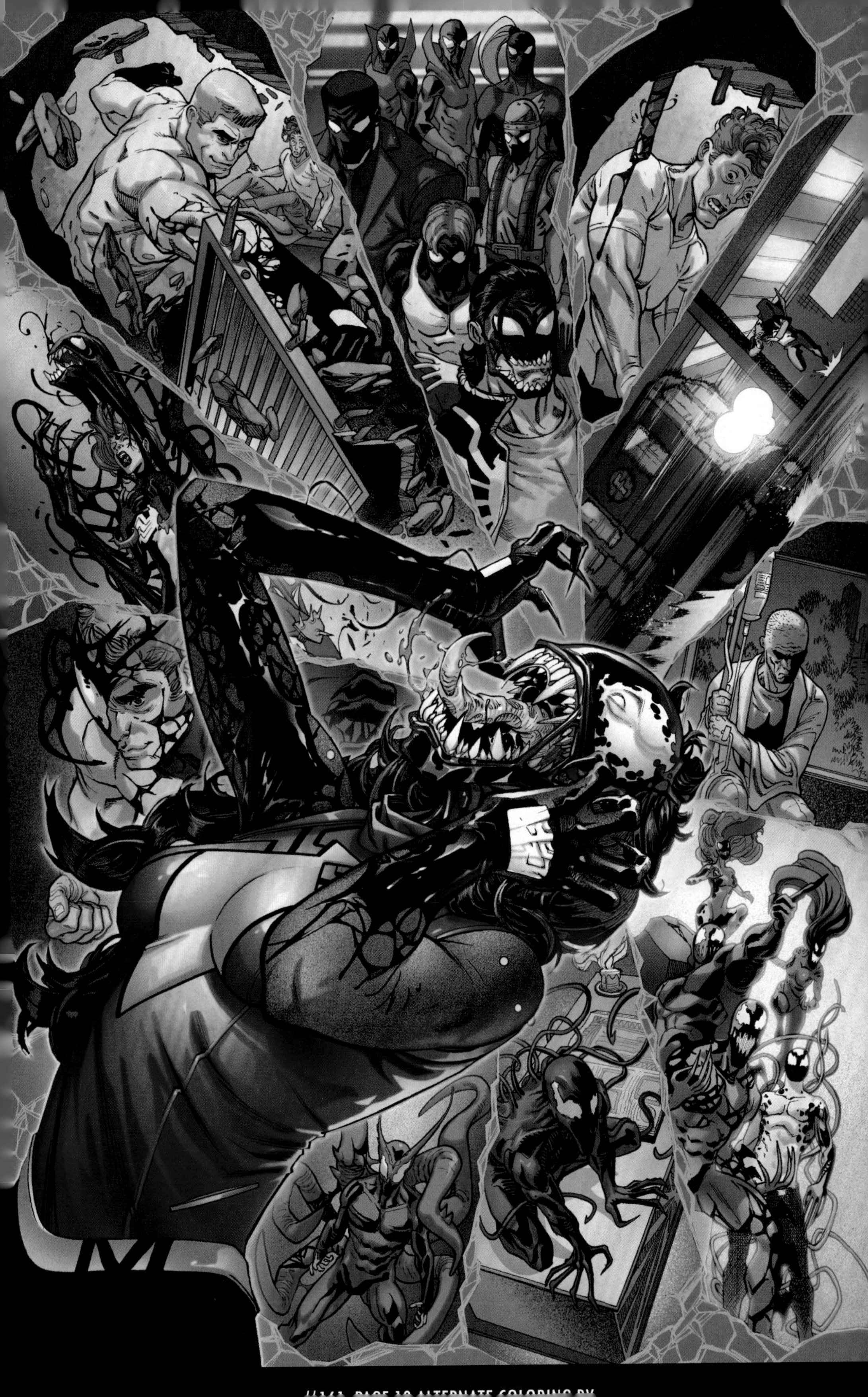

#161, PAGE 19 ALTERNATE COLORING BY

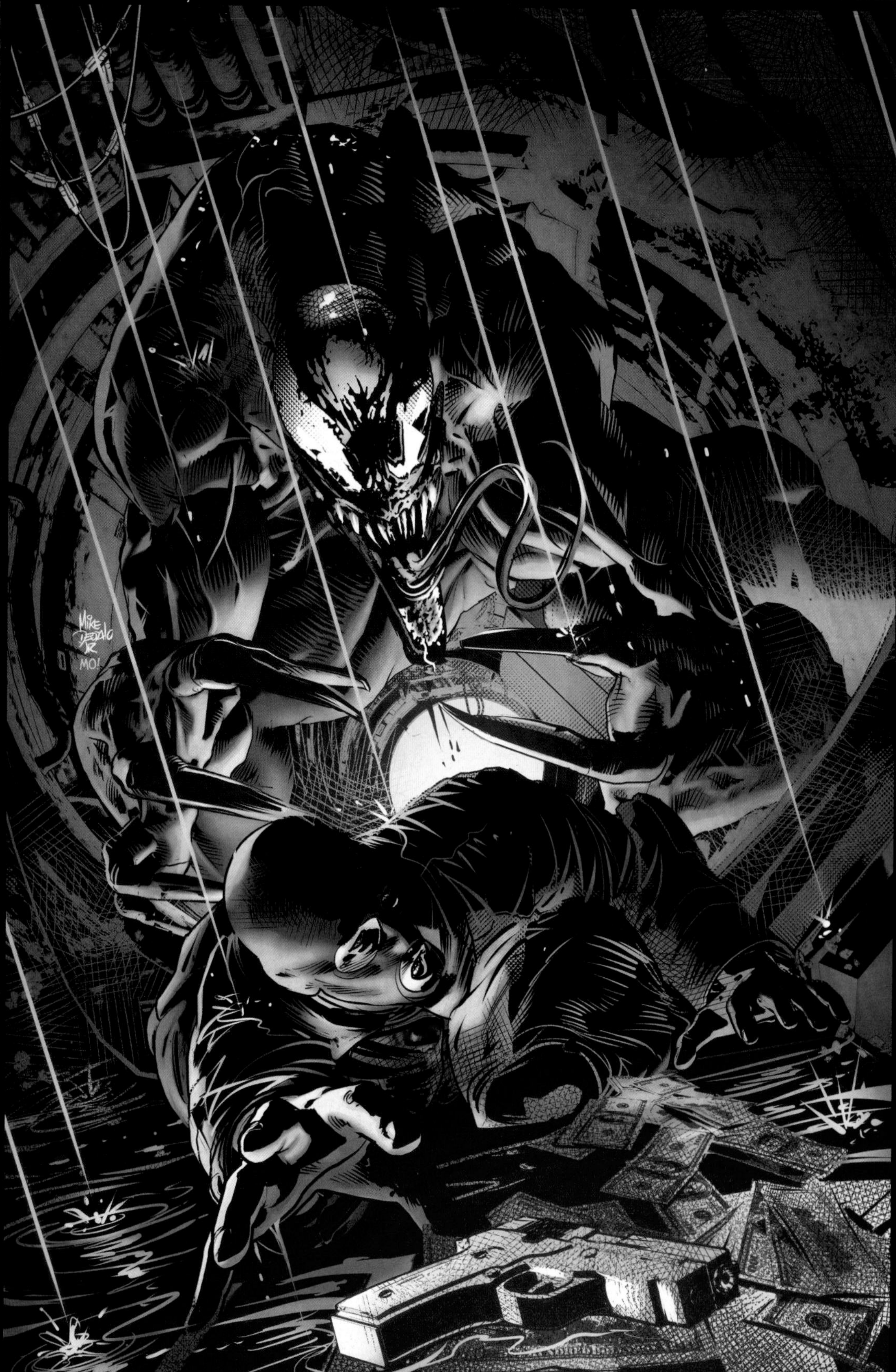

#165 VARIANT BY
MIKE DEODATO JR. & MORRY HOLLOWELL

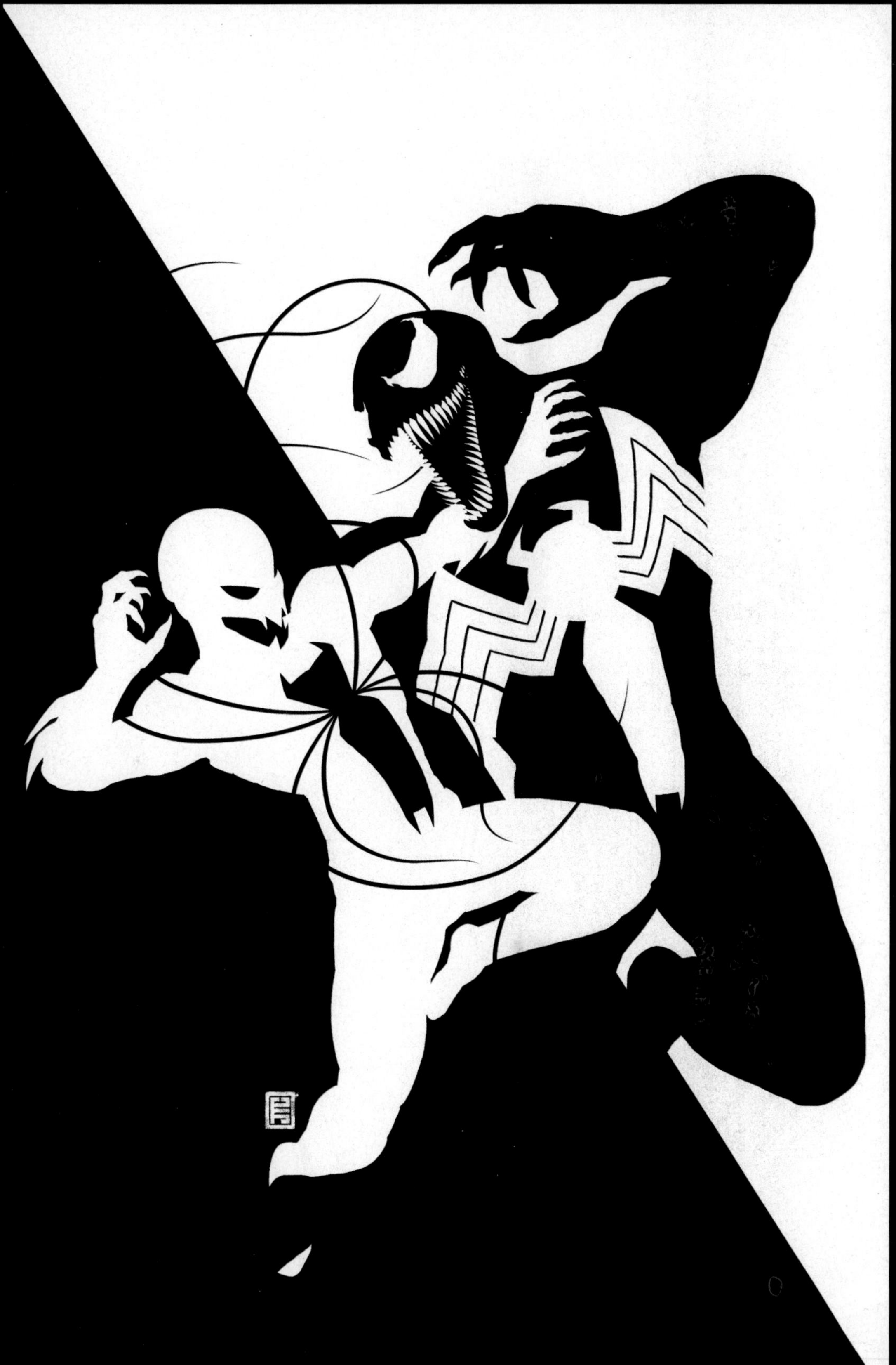

VENOM #164 BY
JOHN TYLER CHRISTOPHER

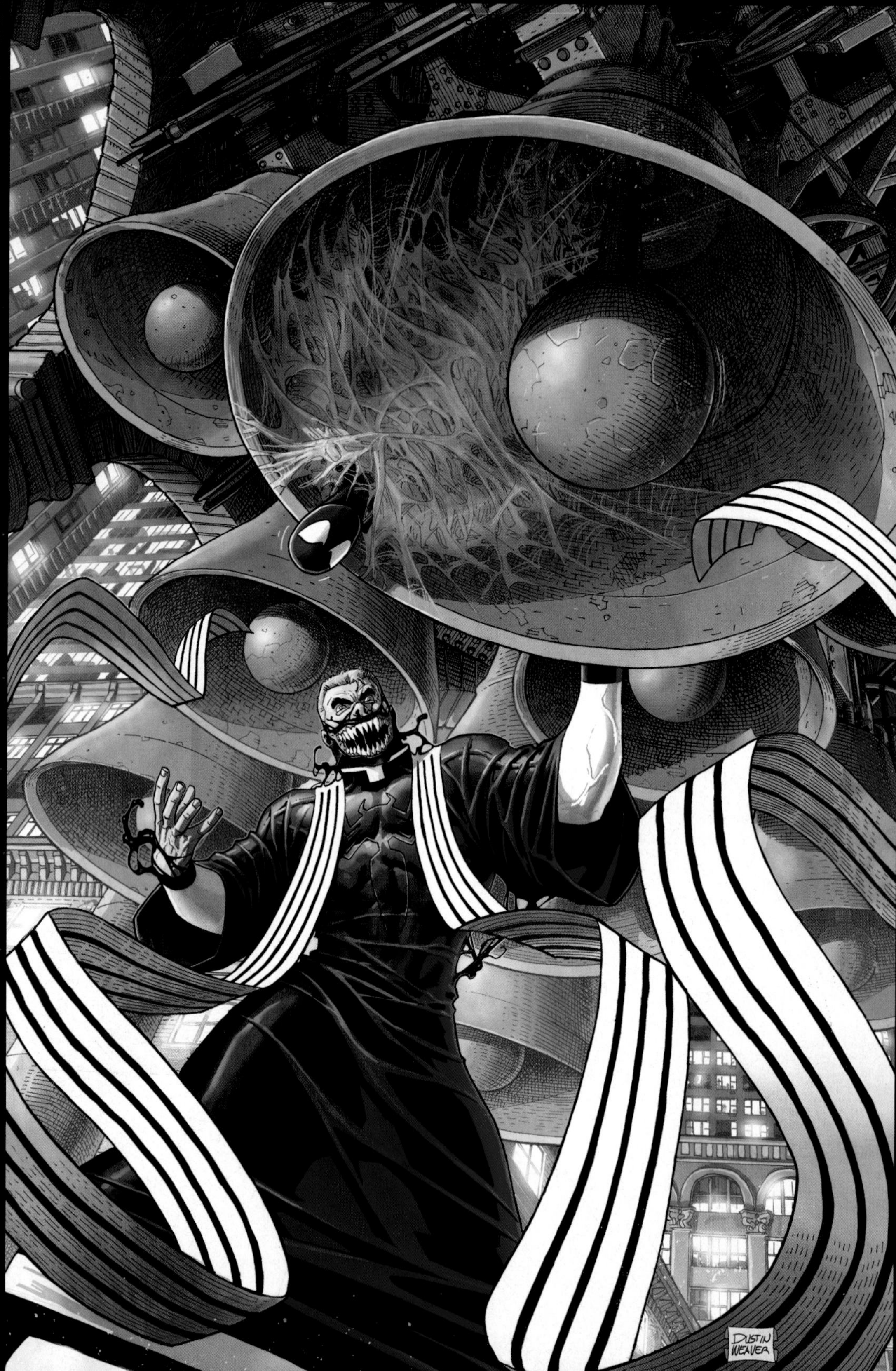
DUSTIN WEAVER

ALL-NEW WOLVERINE #33 BY
DUSTIN WEAVER

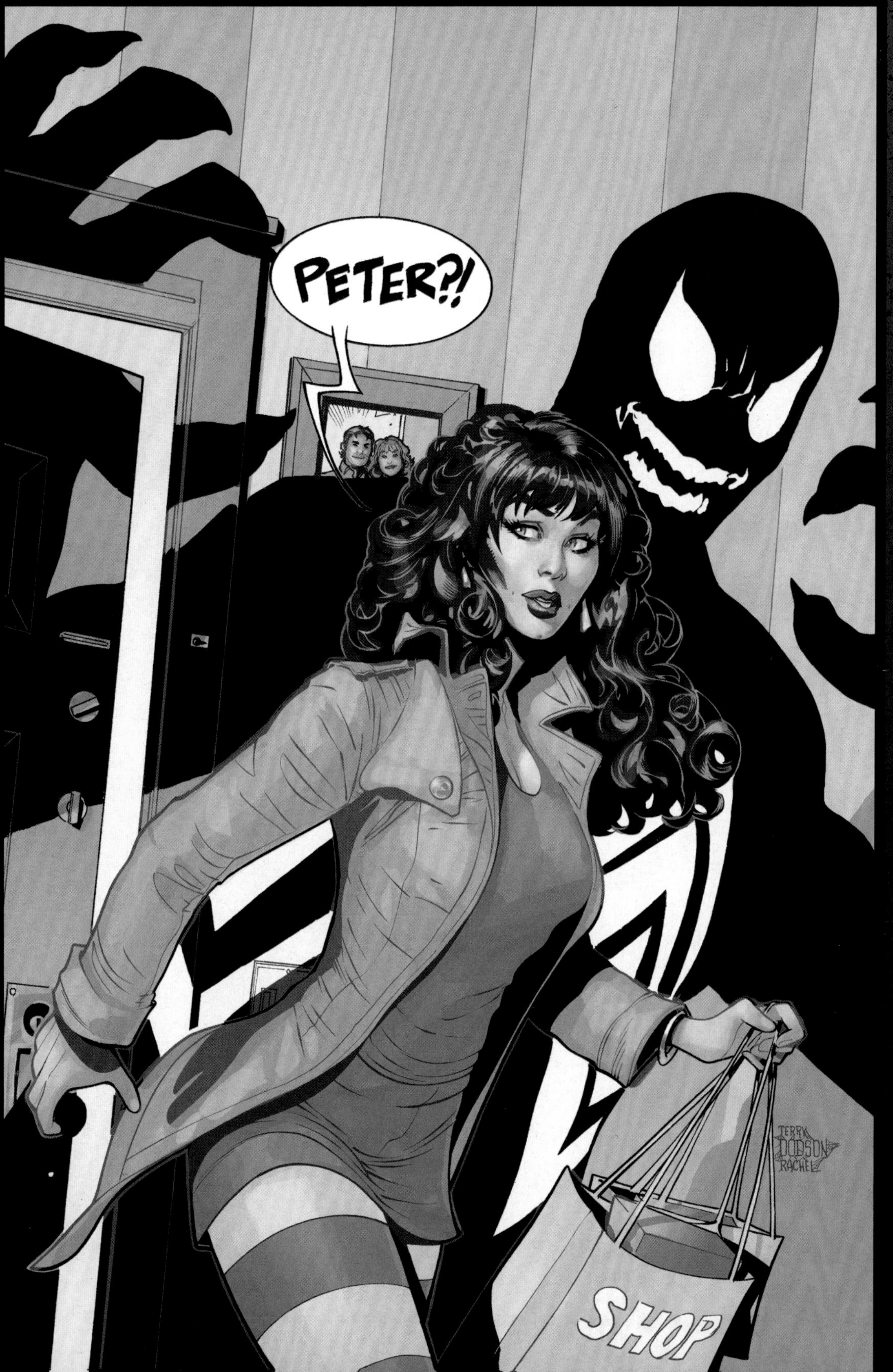
PETER?!
SHOP
TERRY DODSON RACHEL

AMAZING SPIDER-MAN #798 BY
TERRY DODSON & RACHEL DODSON

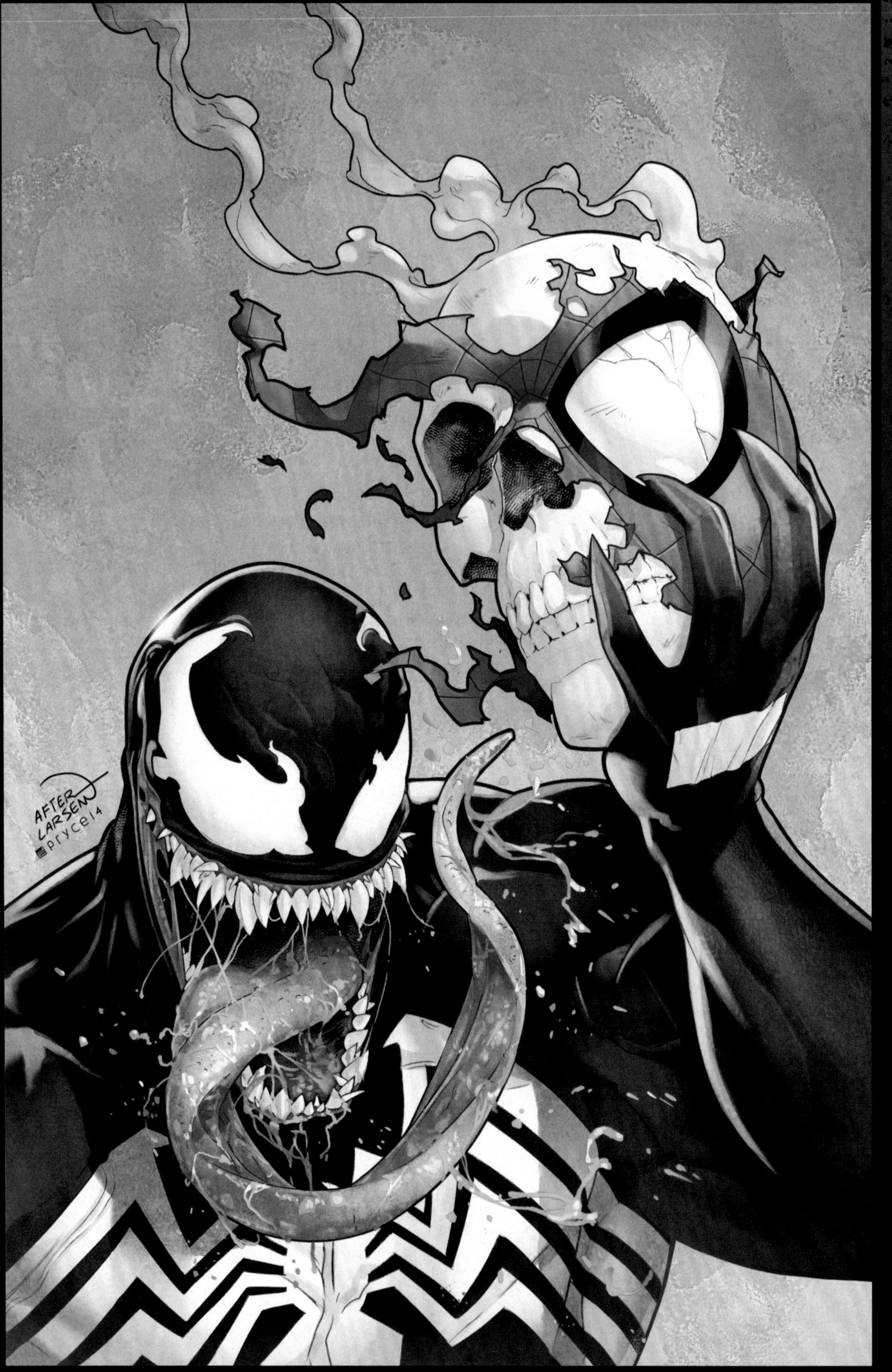
AFTER
LARSEN
pryce14

AVENGERS #687 BY
JAMAL CAMPBELL

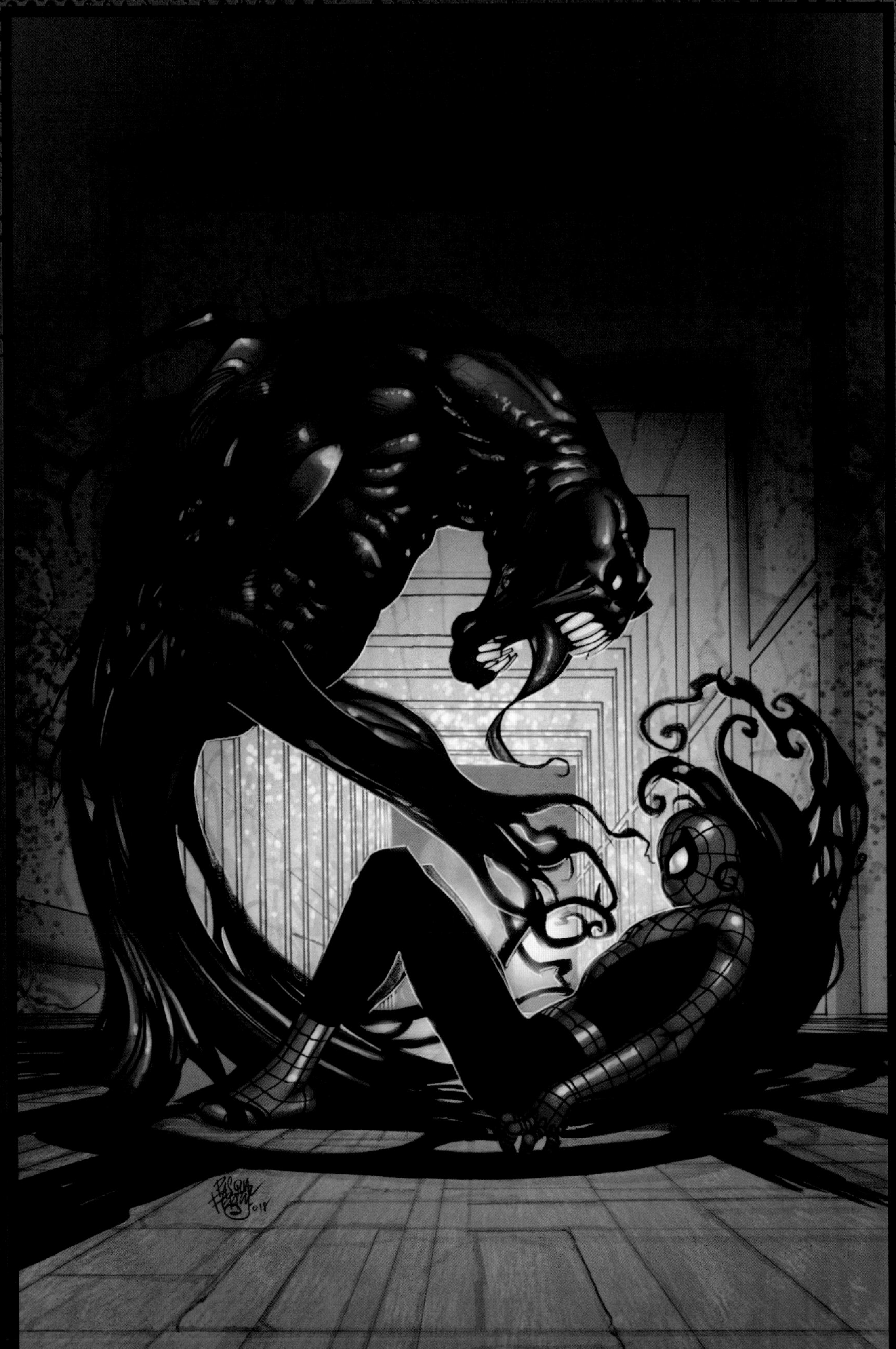

BLACK PANTHER #172 BY
PASQUAL FERRY & CHRIS SOTOMAYOR

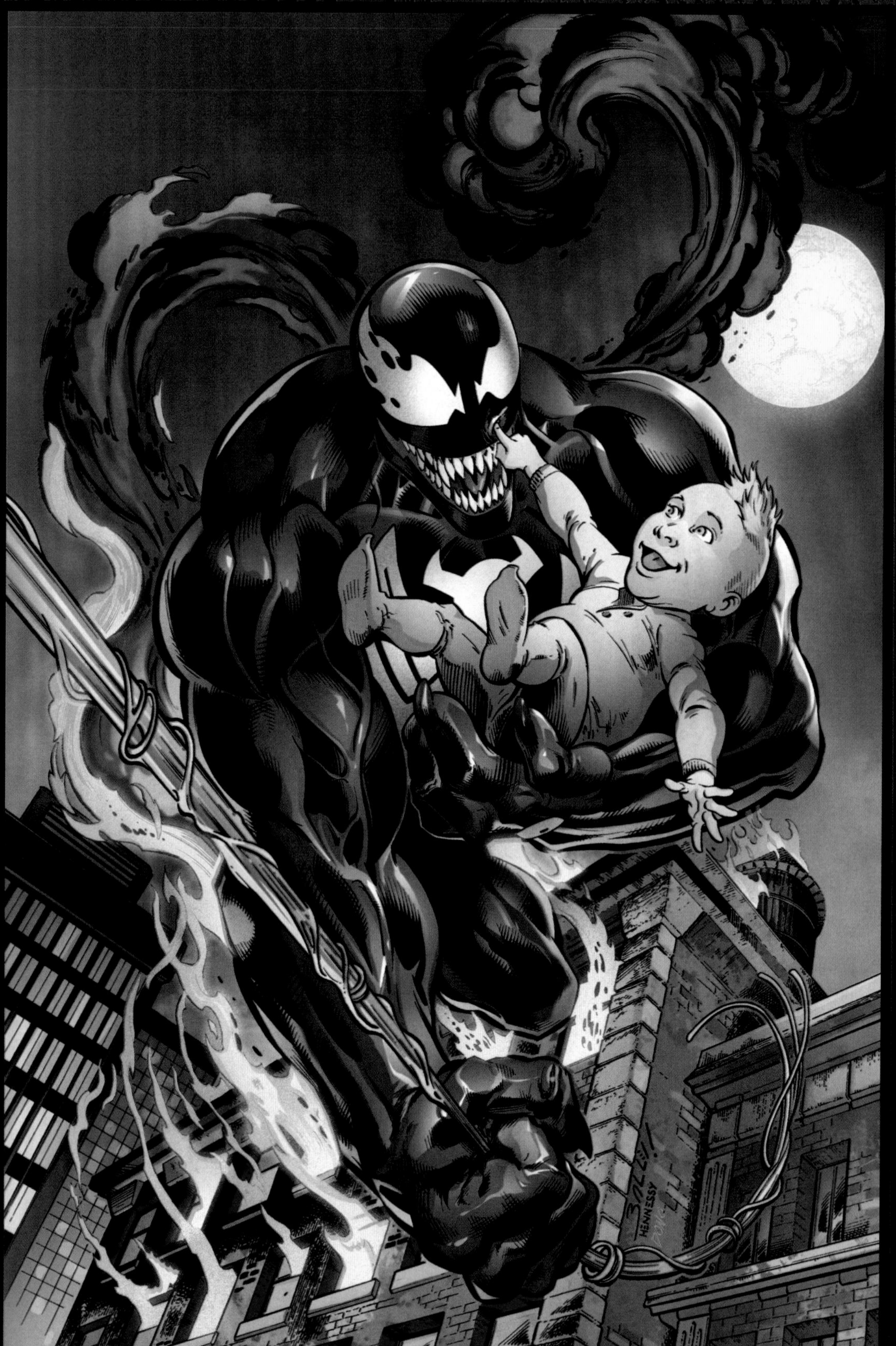
BAGLEY
HENNESSY

CAPTAIN AMERICA #700 BY
MARK BAGLEY, ANDREW HENNESSY & DONO SÁNCHEZ-ALMARA

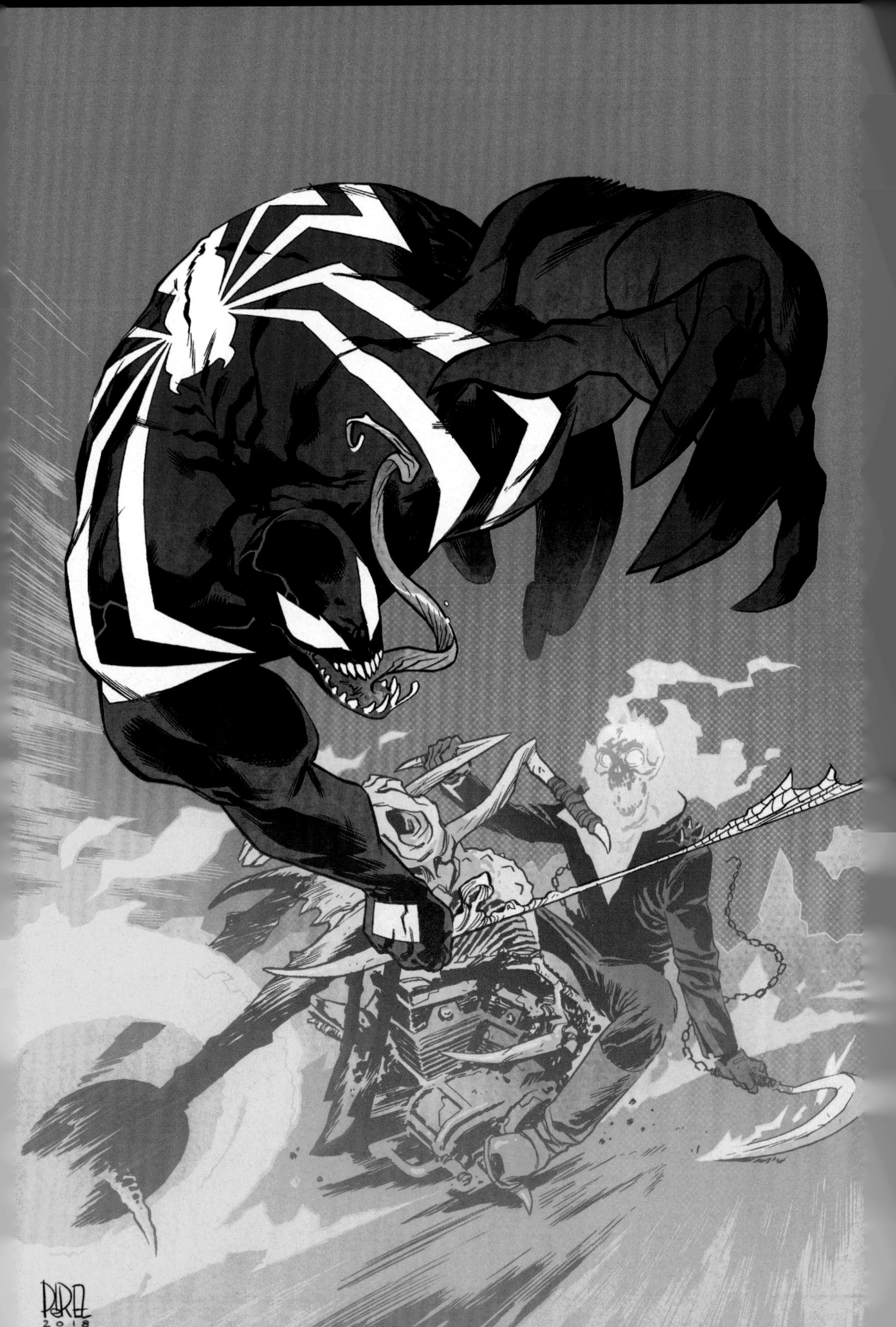

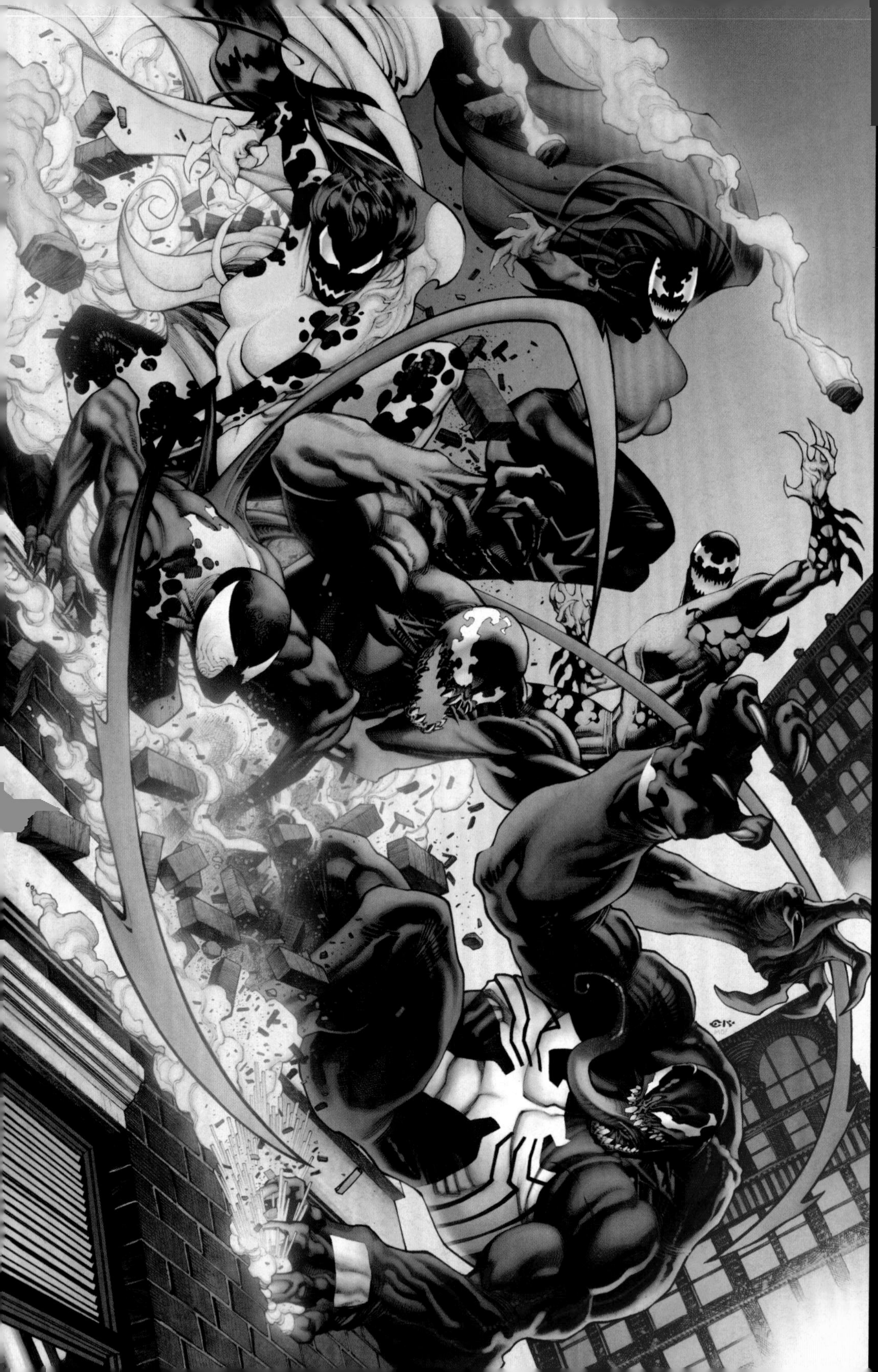

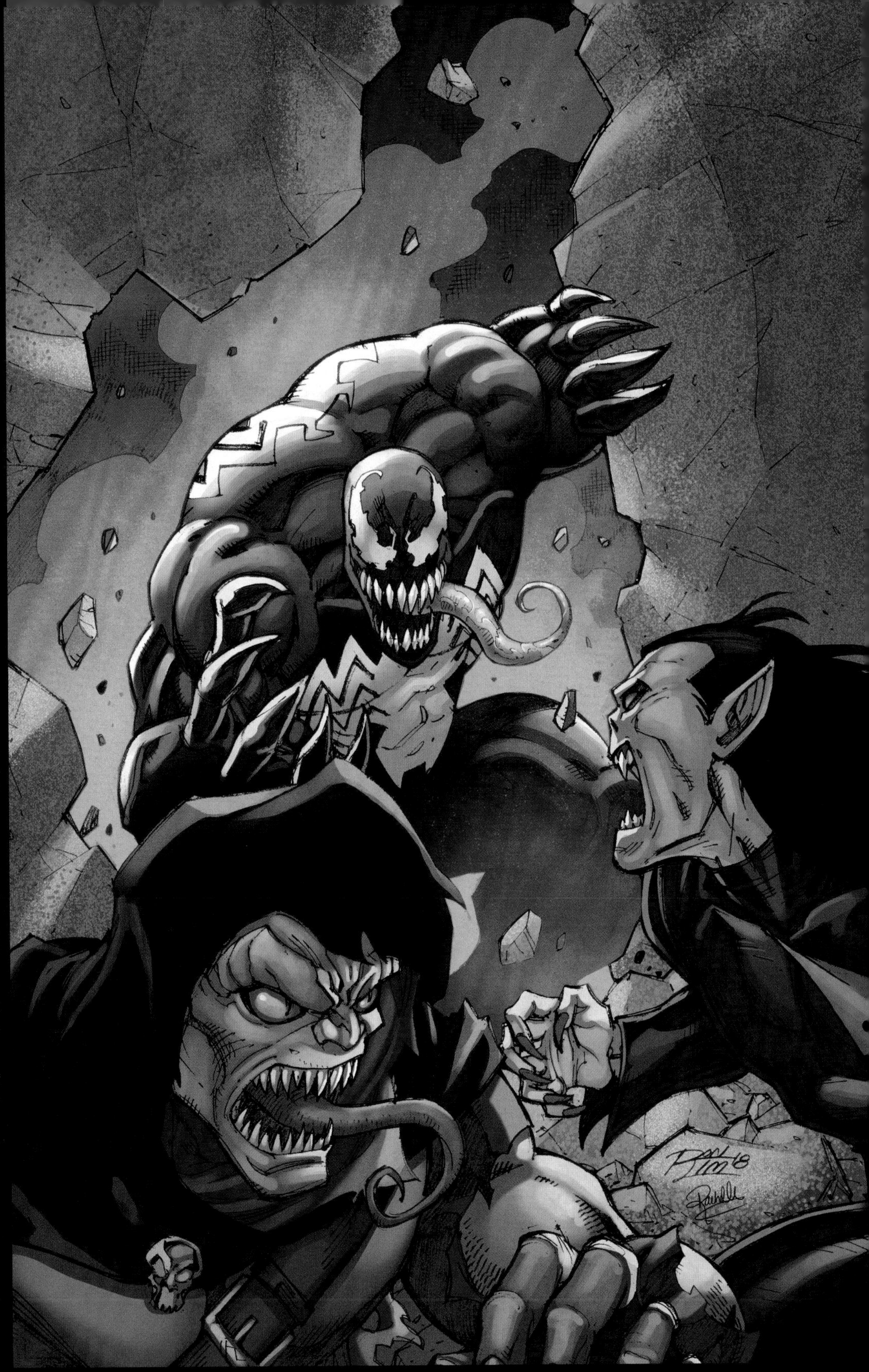

INFINITY COUNTDOWN #2 BY
RON LIM & RACHELLE ROSENBERG

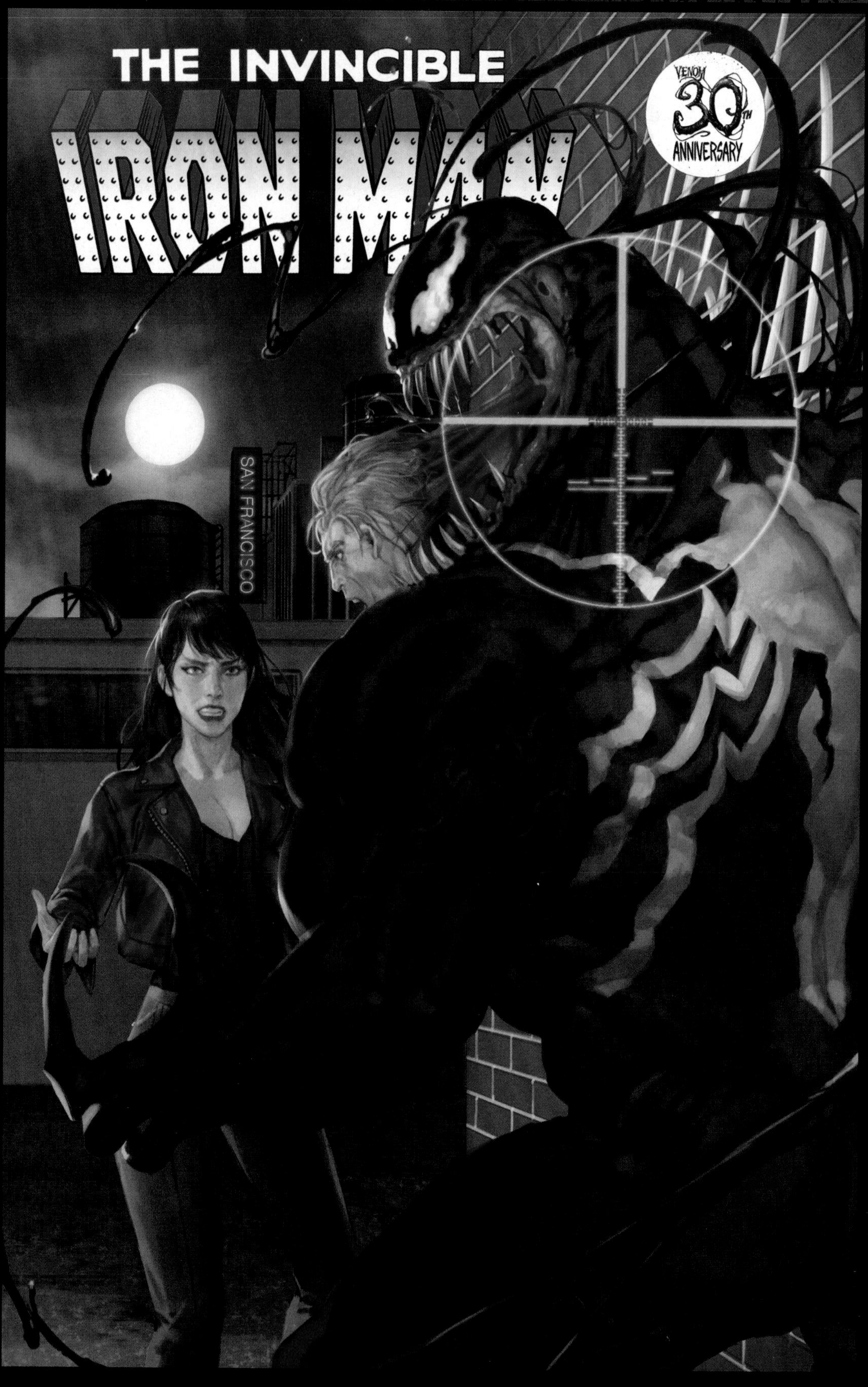
THE INVINCIBLE
IRON MAN
VENOM 30TH ANNIVERSARY
SAN FRANCISCO

INVINCIBLE IRON MAN #599 BY
AKCHO

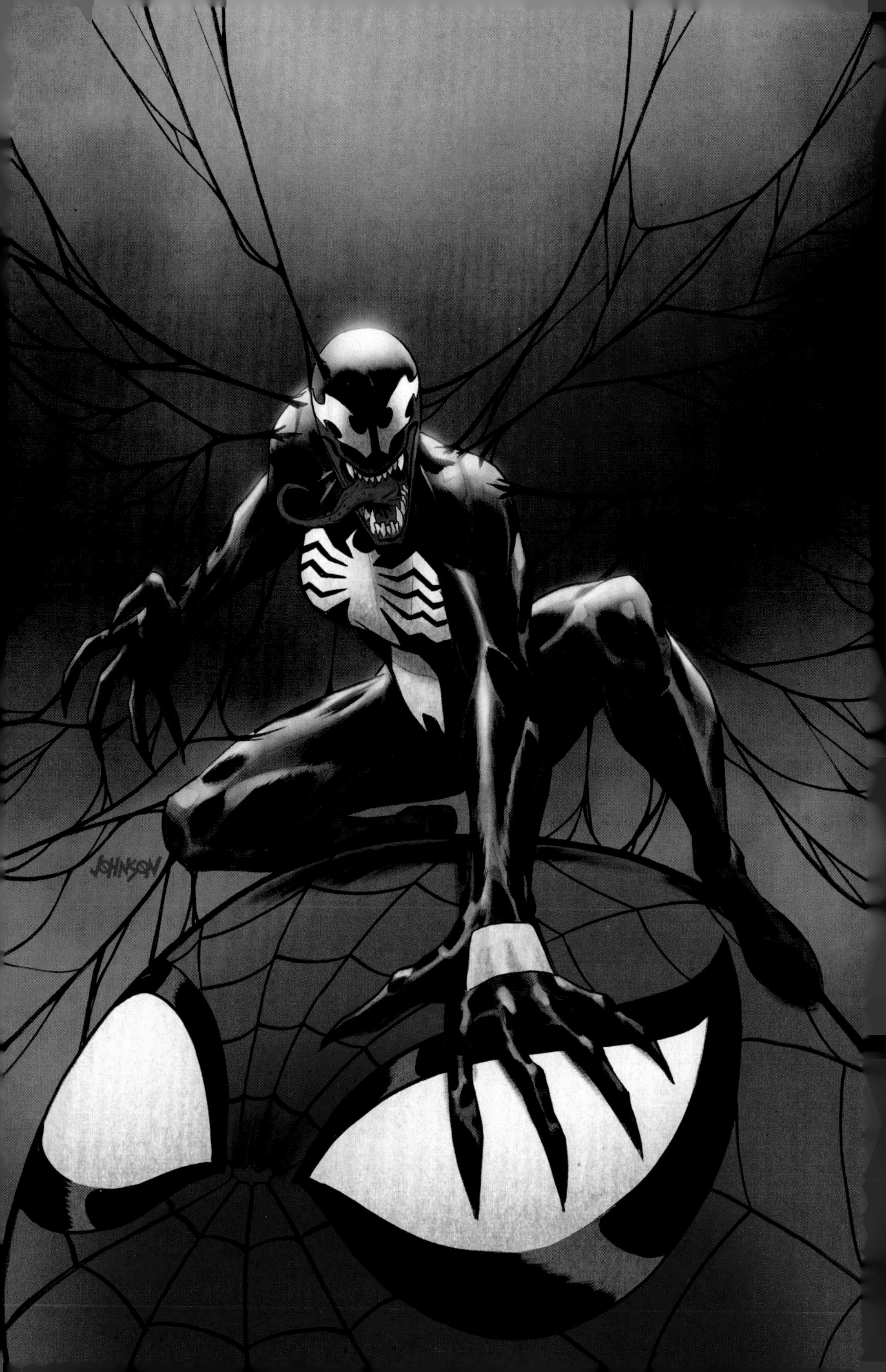
JOHNSON

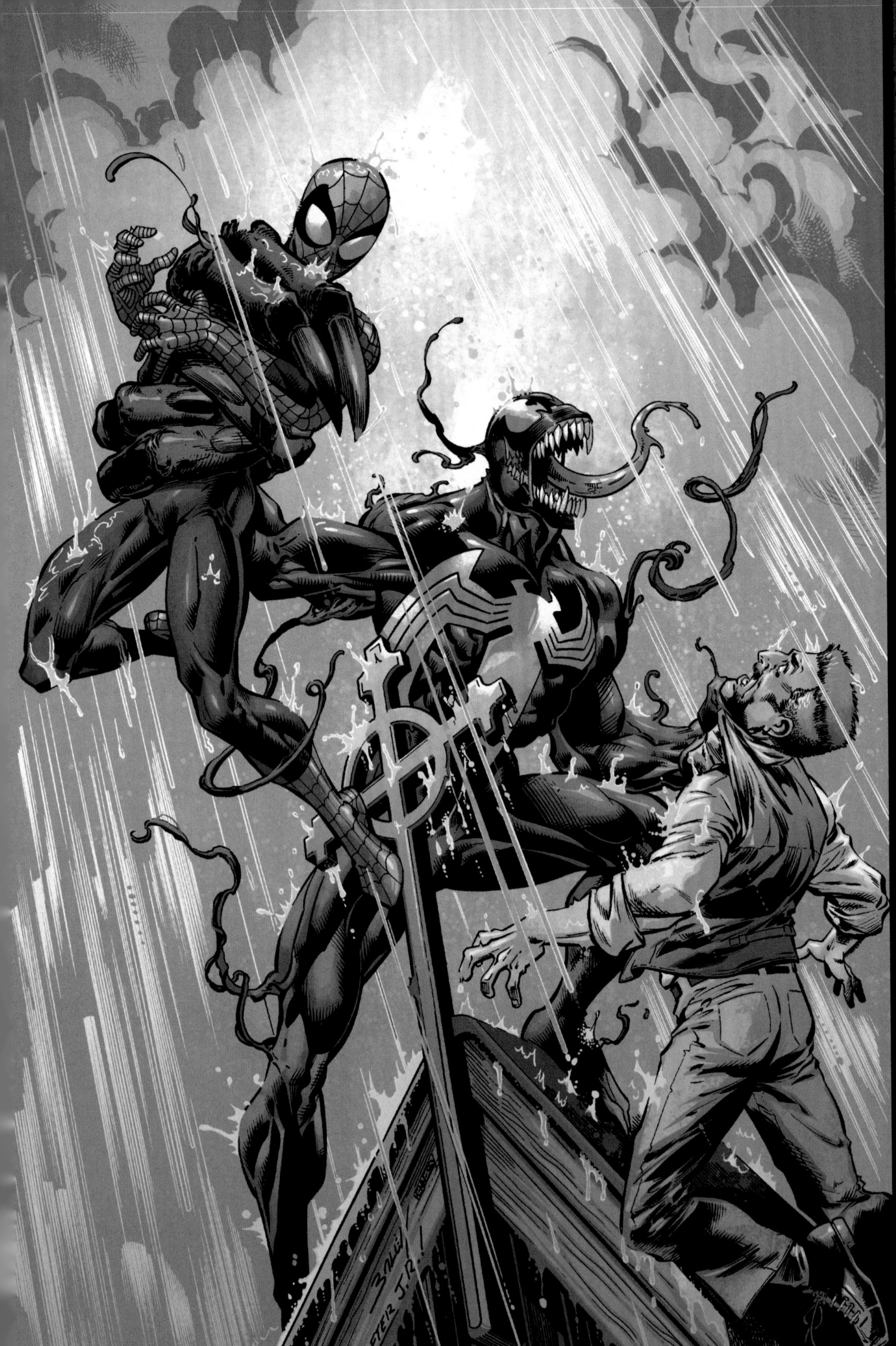

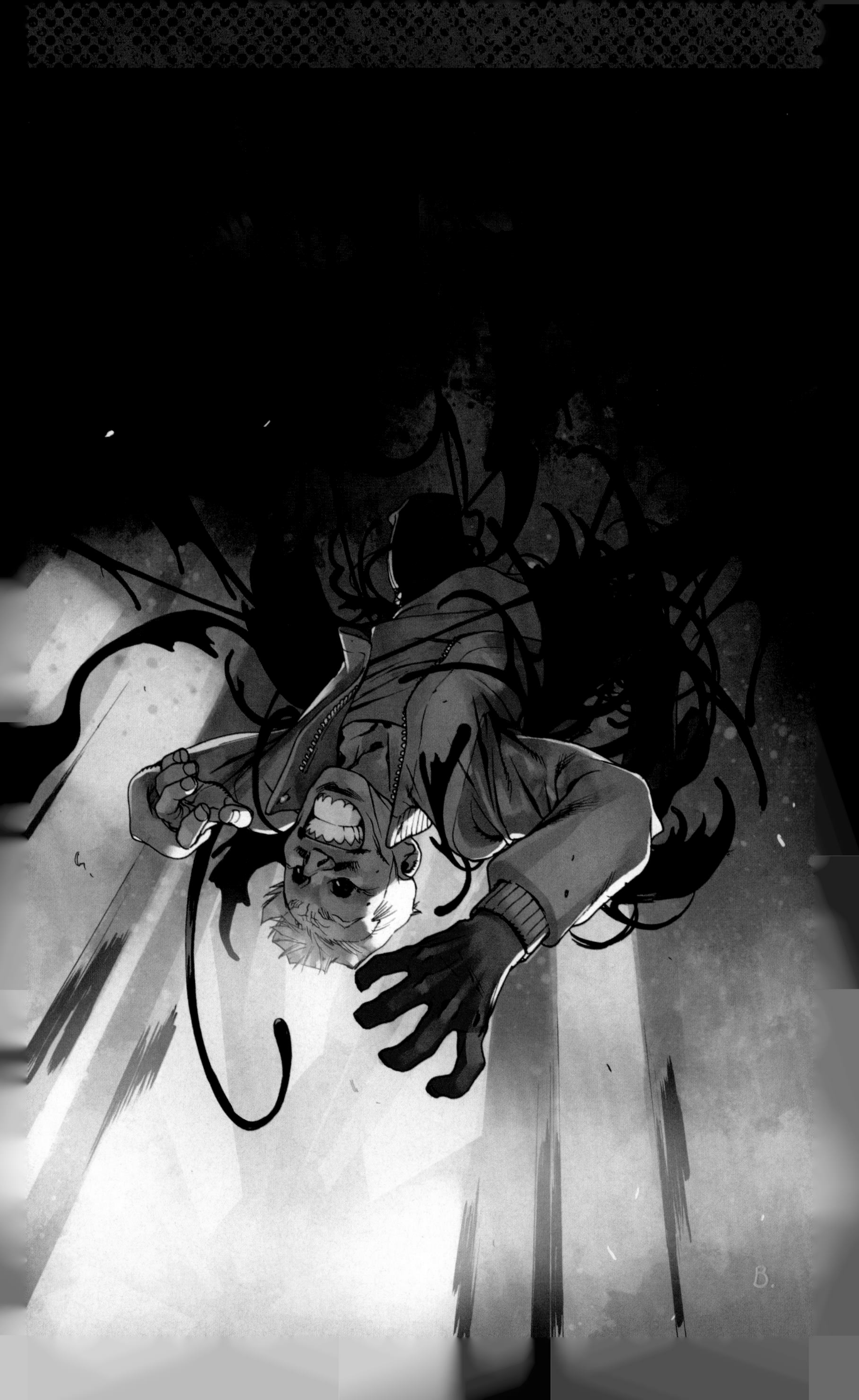

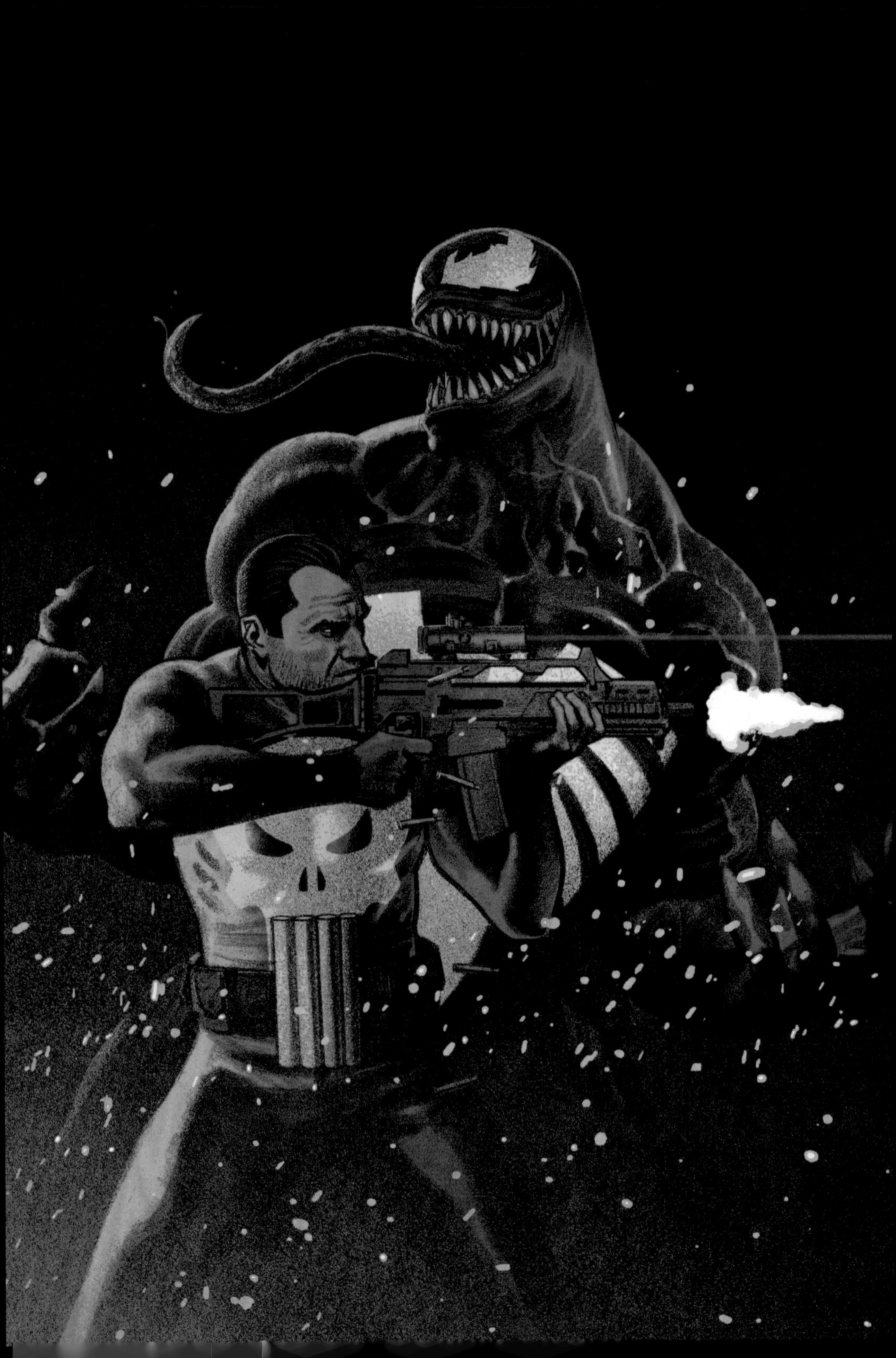

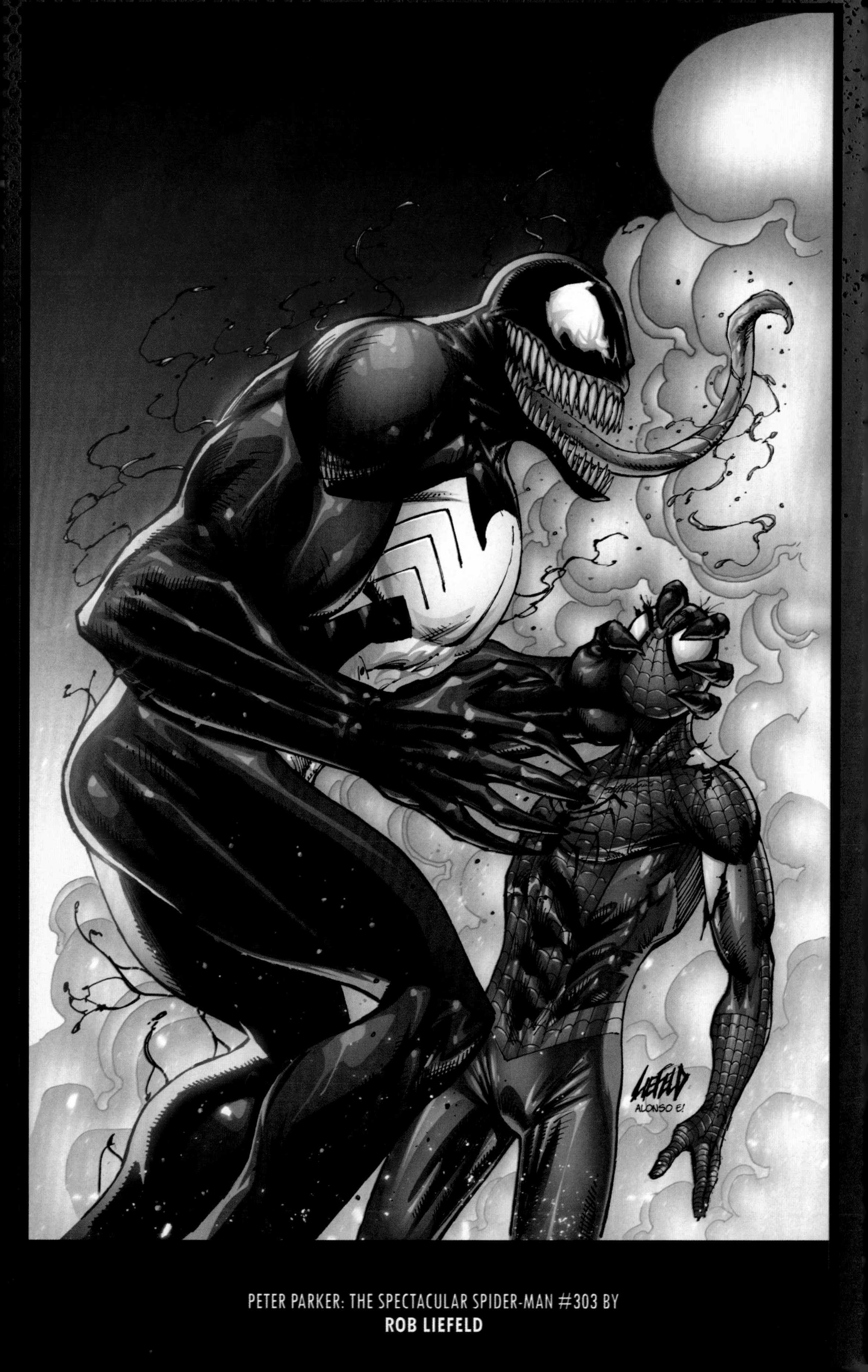
LIEFELD
ALONSO E!

PETER PARKER: THE SPECTACULAR SPIDER-MAN #303 BY
ROB LIEFELD

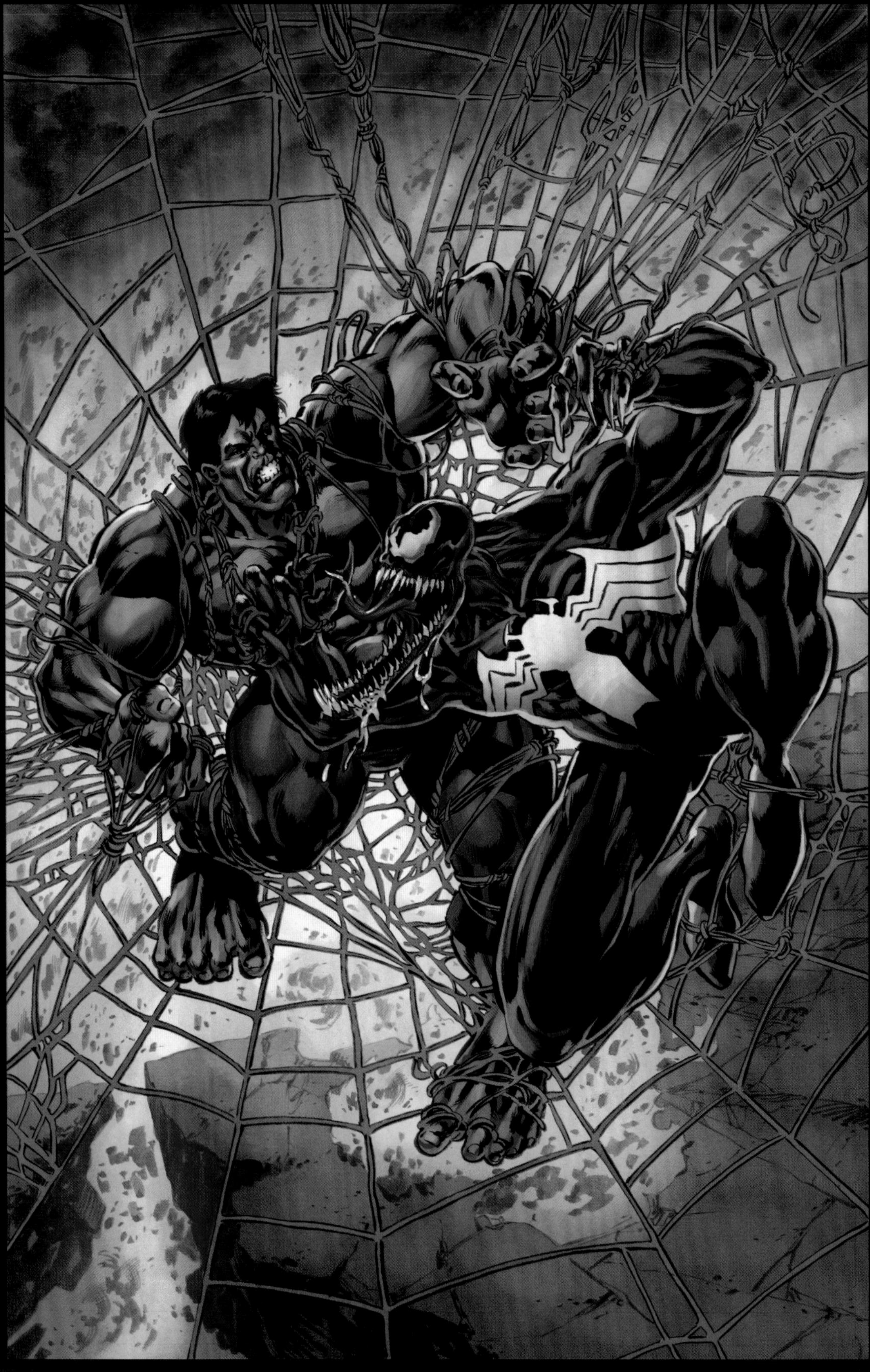

THANOS #18 BY
MIKE PERKINS

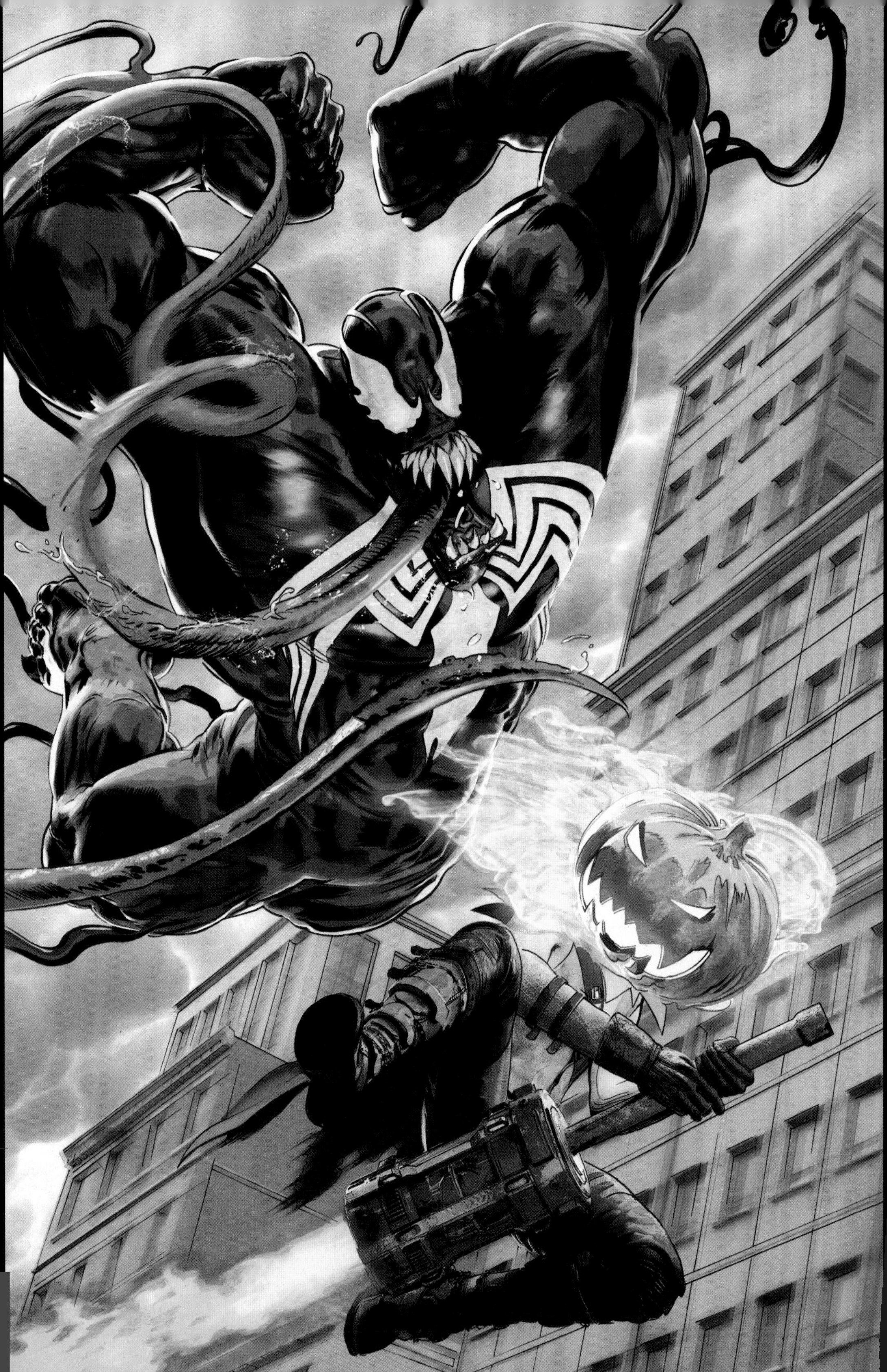

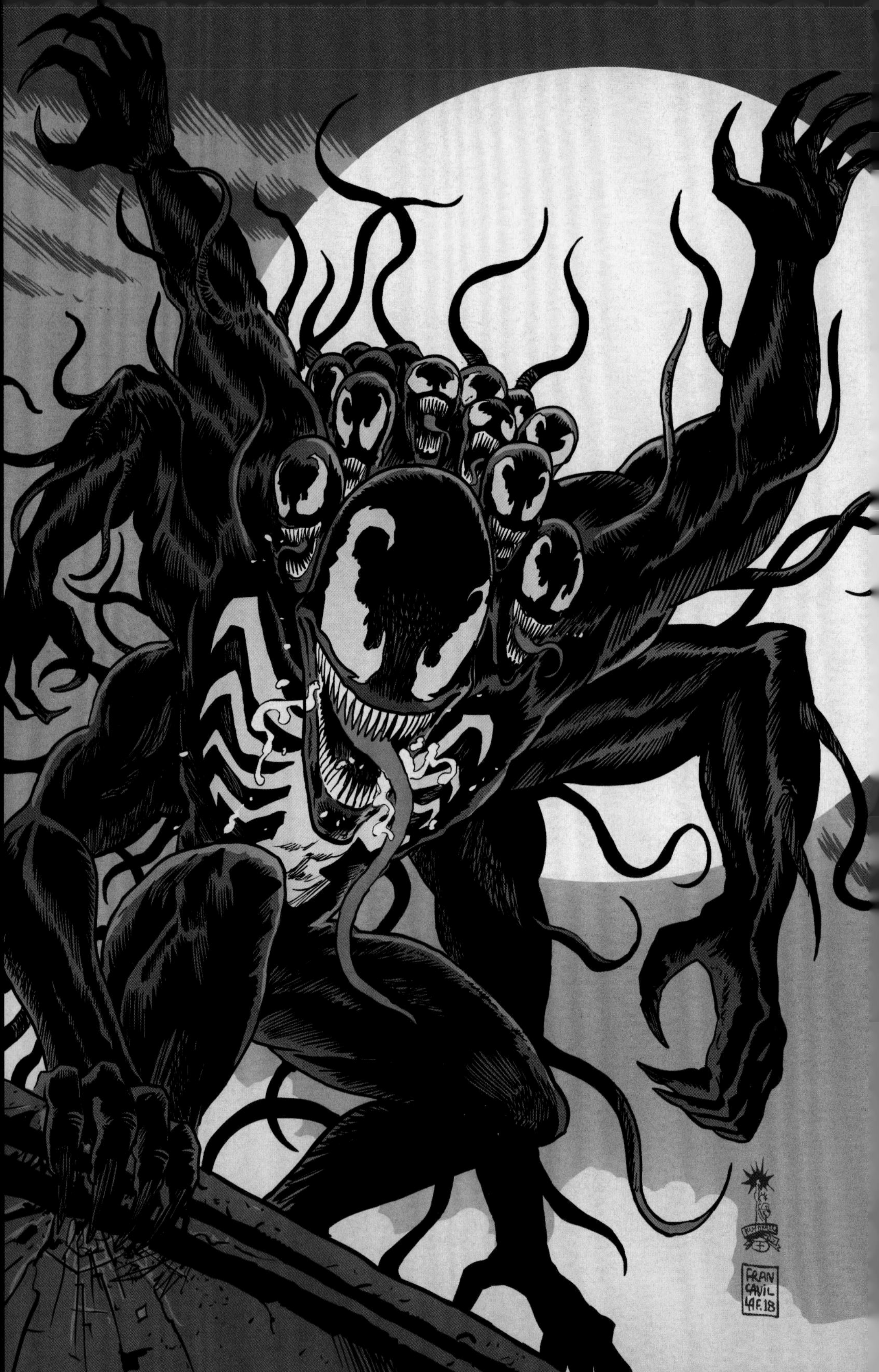
FRAN GAVIL 14F.18

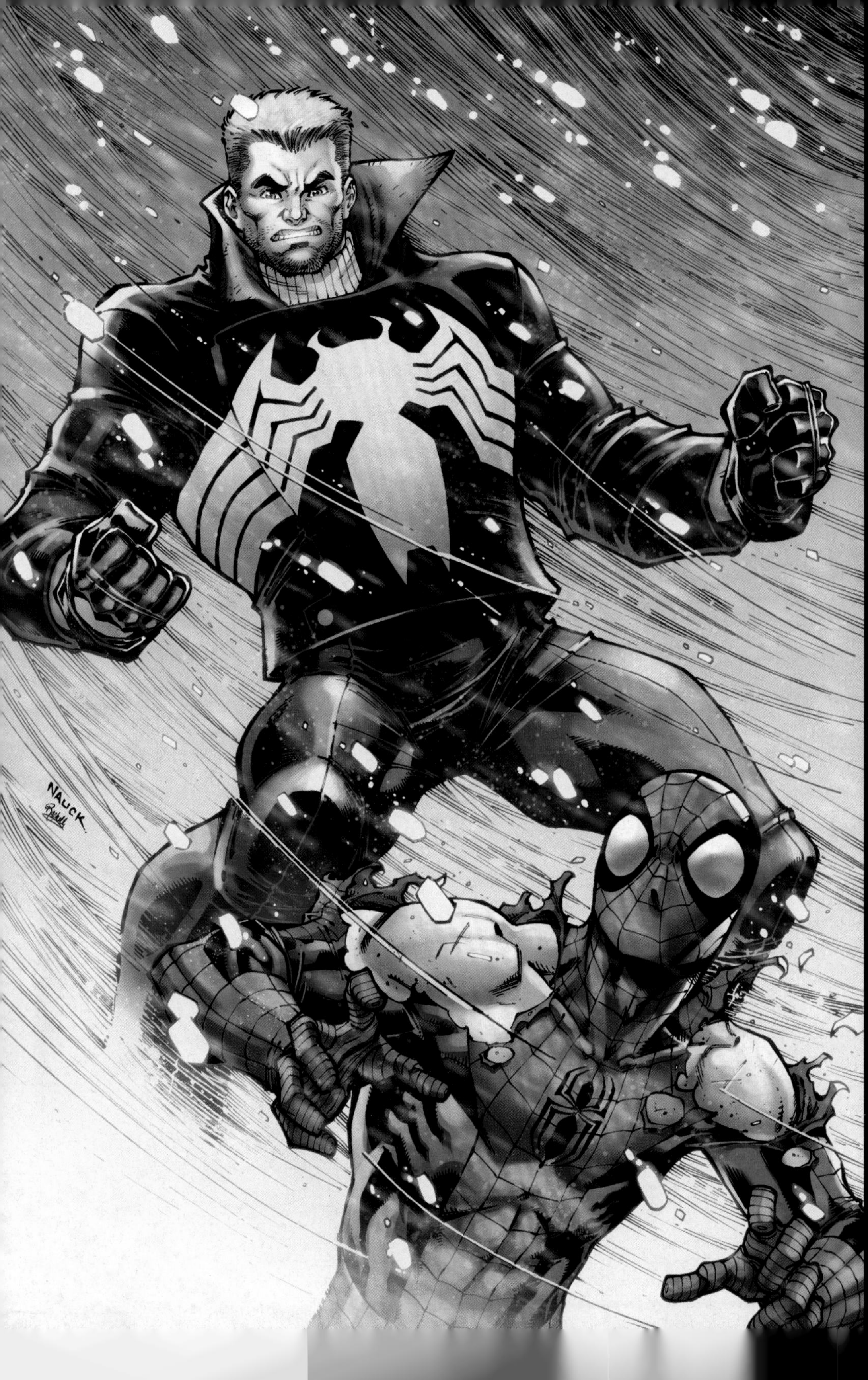
NAUCK

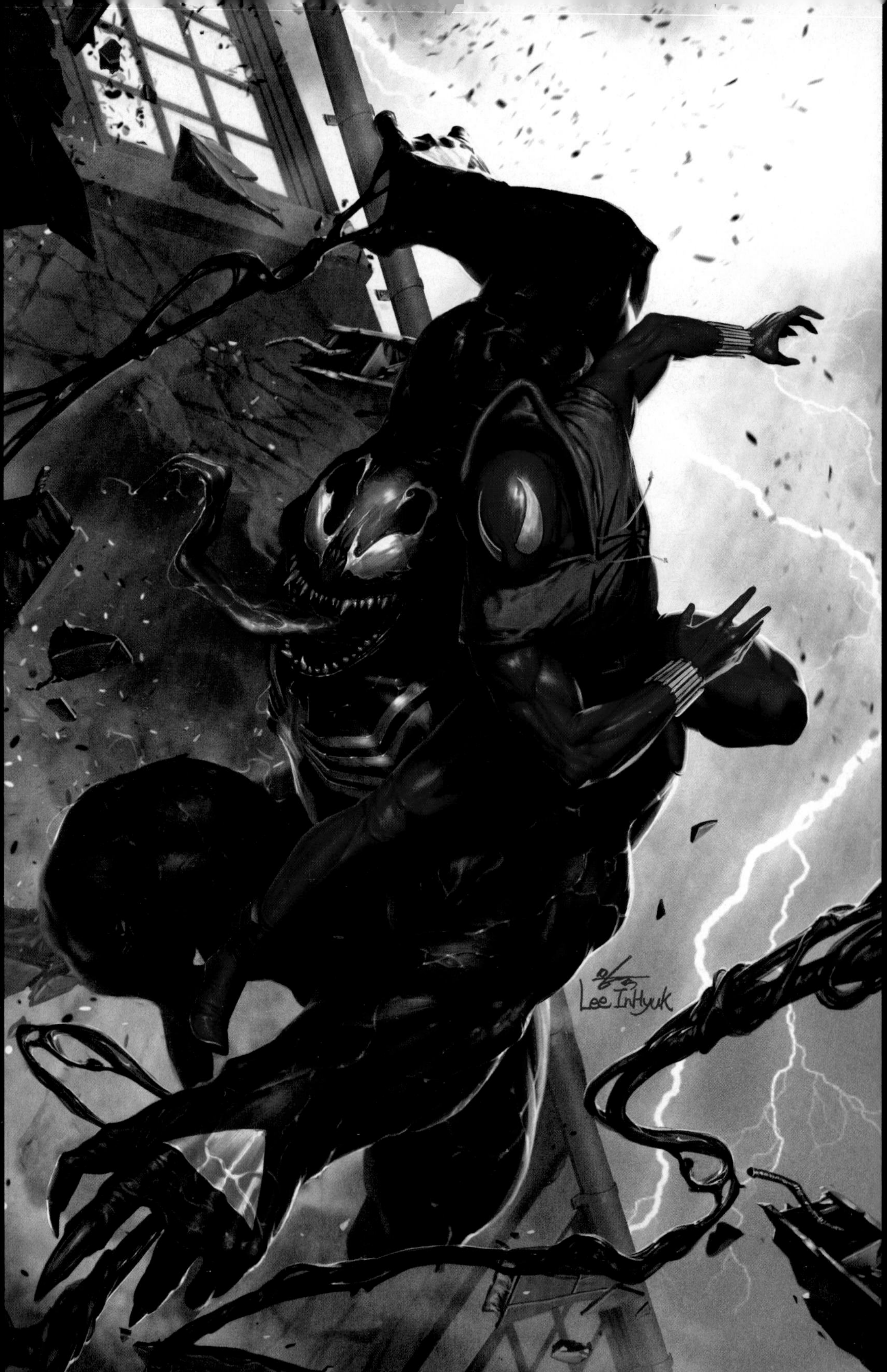
Lee InHyuk